Memoirs of the Comtesse de Boigne

The Comte de Boigne

AFTER A CONTEMPORARY PORTRAIT BY TARDIEU

Memoirs
of the
Comtesse de Boigne

VOLUME II

1816–1830

EDITED AND WITH AN INTRODUCTION BY

Anka Muhlstein

AFTERWORD BY

Olivier Bernier

HELEN MARX BOOKS
NEW YORK

This edition of the *Memoirs of the Comtesse de Boigne*
is an abridgment of a three-volume version
originally edited by M. Charles Nicoullaud and
published in 1907 by William Heinemann, London.

Copyright © 2003 Helen Marx Books,
an imprint of Turtle Point Press.

LCCN 2002106465
ISBN 1-885586-73-6

Printed in Canada

CONTENTS

DICTIONARY OF CHARACTERS

Adélaïde, Madame, daughter of Louis XV, 1732–1800. Of Louis XV's seven daughters, only the eldest, Elisabeth, married. Adélaïde and her sisters lived at Versailles and Bellevue, a château built for Mme. de Pompadour. At the onset of the Revolution, the two surviving Princesses, Adélaïde and Victoire, fled to Italy.

Adélaïde, Princesse d'Orléans, Mademoiselle, Madame, sister of Louis-Philippe, 1777–1847. She emigrated to England in 1792, and was not welcome in the circle of *émigrés* as her father, Philippe-Egalité, had voted for the execution of Louis XVI. She lived with her brother, Louis-Philippe, after he returned from his voyage to the United States in 1800, and always remained very close to him.

Alexander I, Emperor of Russia, son of Paul I and grandson of Catherine II, 1777–1825. Educated by a French tutor, he instigated a series of liberal reforms at the beginning of his reign in 1801, but by its end had become a reactionary. His alliance with Napoleon did not last long (1807–1812). In 1812, Napoleon invaded Russia and entered Moscow on September 14. The next day a huge fire destroyed the capital and Napoleon had to order the retreat of his troops. In 1815, Alexander and his allies triumphed over the French in the Battle of Waterloo.

Angoulême, Louis de Bourbon, Duc d', Monsieur le Dauphin, son of Charles X,
1775–1844. He emigrated to England where he married his first
cousin, Marie-Thérèse, the daughter of Louis XVI, and joined Wellington's army to fight against Napoleon. He renounced his rights to
the throne after the Revolution of 1830 in favour of his nephew, the
ten-year-old Comte de Chambord.

Angoulême, Marie-Thérèse de Bourbon, Madame Royale, Duchesse d', Ma-
dame la Dauphine, daughter of Louis XVI, 1778–1851. She was imprisoned with her parents and her brother in 1792 and liberated in 1795
in exchange for French prisoners held in Austria. The Orphan of the
Temple, as she came to be known, was then conducted to London
where she married her cousin. Quite unpopular in all circles of society,
despite her tragic past, she did not help the Bourbon cause during the
Restoration.

Arago, François, 1786–1853. Celebrated astronomer and secretary of
the Bureau of Longitudes. At the age of twenty-three, he was a member
of the Academy of Sciences, taught at the Polytechnic School. In 1830,
he was elected deputy and appointed director of the Observatory.

Artois, Comte d'. See Charles X.

Beauharnais, Hortense de, Queen of Holland, Duchesse de Saint-Leu, 1783–
1837. Daughter of Joséphine, stepdaughter of Napoleon, she was
married to Louis Bonaparte, King of Holland. Their son became Napoleon III.

Bernadotte, Jean-Baptiste, King of Sweden under the name of Charles XIV,
1764–1844. After a quick and glorious military career in Napoleon's
army, he became Ambassador to Vienna and Minister of War. He
backed Sweden against Napoleon in 1808. The grateful Swedes proceeded to elect him Prince Royal, and King Charles XIII adopted him.
He became King in 1818, thus founding the dynasty that still reigns
today.

Berry, Charles-Ferdinand, Duc de, son of Charles X, 1778–1820. Second son of the Comte d'Artois, future Charles X. Married Marie-Caroline de Bourbon-Sicile. He held extreme conservative views and was assassinated by Louvel in 1820. His posthumous son, the Duc de Bordeaux, was born seven months later.

Berry, Marie-Caroline de Bourbon-Sicile, Duchesse de, 1798–1870. Daughter of the King of Naples, she married the Duc de Berry and gave him two children, la petite Mademoiselle and the "miraculous" Duc de Bordeaux, the posthumous son. She followed Charles X into exile into Prague but soon made her way back to France and tried to inspire a Royalist insurrection. She failed miserably and ended in prison, where it was discovered that she was pregnant. She had to confess her secret marriage to an Italian count and was sent back to Palermo, humiliated, dishonoured, and deprived of the custody of her children.

Bertrand, Henri, General, Comte, 1773–1844. He remained faithful to Napoleon and followed him first to Elba, then to Saint Helena, where he returned in 1844 to bring back the Emperor's ashes. He is buried next to him in the Invalides in Paris. Bertrand married Fanny Dillon, a cousin of both Empress Joséphine and Mme. de Boigne.

Blacas, Pierre, Duc de, 1771–1839. This Ultra-Royalist politician was counsellor to Louis XVIII from the beginning of the Revolution. He was named Minister of the Royal Household in 1814. Always faithful to the Bourbons, he followed the royal family into exile in 1830.

Boigne, Benoît Leborgne, General, Comte de, 1751–1830. He was born in Chambéry, then a possession of the King of Sardinia, where his father was a furrier. He first entered an Irish regiment serving in France, then, finding that promotion was slow, switched to a Greek regiment in the service of Catherine of Russia. Having reached the rank of Major, he resigned and went to India, where he offered his expertise to several Hindu Princes. A Maharajah, Sindiah, accepted his services, and Leborgne, who had not yet changed his name to de Boigne, organised the Prince's army on European principles, won great victories over the neighbouring rulers, was appointed General of all the infantry and Governor of the conquered provinces, and was thus entitled to a share of the tribute—the origin of his enormous fortune. Sindiah died in 1794. Two years later, the General arrived in London, where he married Mlle. d'Osmond in 1798. The King of Sardinia made him a count, and Louis XVIII, a Knight of Saint Louis. The General became an important benefactor of his native town.

Borghese, Camillo, Prince, 1775–1832. Married Pauline Bonaparte, the beautiful sister of Napoleon, in 1803, and was Governor of the Piedmont from 1807 to 1814.

Bourbon, House of. From 1572 the Bourbon Princes were at different times Kings of Navarre, France, Spain, Naples, and Sicily. The senior line in France ran directly from Henri IV to Charles X. The names and titles of the different Princes are sometimes confusing because they change during their lifetimes. At the beginning of Mme. de Boigne's *Memoirs*, the King is Louis XVI. The Dauphin is his eldest son. His daughter is Madame Royale (a younger daughter would have been simply Madame). The King's immediate brother is always called Monsieur, the term preceding his actual title, which in this case is Comte de Provence. His youngest brother is the Comte d'Artois. Louis XVI is executed in 1793, and the Dauphin, though imprisoned, is King Louis XVII, at least for the Royalists. He dies in 1795 and his uncle, the Comte de Provence, becomes King in exile under the name of Louis XVIII. His brother, the Comte d'Artois, is then called Monsieur. Louis XVIII has no children and Monsieur, Comte d'Artois, has two sons. The eldest, the Duc d'Angoulême, is married to his cousin, Madame Royale, who is then known as Madame, Duchesse d'Angoulême. The second son is the Duc de Berry. When Louis XVIII dies, his brother becomes King Charles X. The Duc d'Angoulême, as eldest son of the reigning king, is then given the title of Dauphin and his wife that of Dauphine.

Calonne, Charles-Alexandre de, 1734–1802. He replaced Necker in 1783 and tried in vain to reform the financial administration of the kingdom. He was forced to resign in 1787 and fled France during the Revolution.

Cambacérès, Jean-Jacques, Duc de Parme, 1753–1824. A lawyer and a judge, he embraced the Revolution and worked on the new Civil Code. He was named Second Consul at Bonaparte's suggestion and during the Empire worked on the reform of the administration and the elaboration of the Imperial Civil Code. He rallied to the Bourbons in 1814 but abandoned their cause during the Hundred Days.

Carignan-Savoie. See Charles-Albert.

Caroline of Brunswick, 1768–1821. She married the Prince of Wales in 1795. The wedding night was an irreparable disaster and soon after the birth of their daughter, Charlotte, the Prince refused to have anything to do with his wife and did not allow her near her child. She travelled extensively in Europe and remained popular in England, where she was perceived as a victim. On her husband's accession as George IV, she returned to claim her rights as Queen but he initiated a bill to dissolve the marriage and refused her admittance to Westminster Abbey for the Coronation. She died shortly thereafter.

Castlereagh, Henry Robert Stewart, Viscount, 1769–1822. His role at the Foreign Office was crucial in consolidating the alliance against Napoleon in 1812. He committed suicide in 1822.

Caulaincourt, Armand, General, Marquis de, Duc de Vicence, 1772–1827. Though born to an aristocratic family, he adopted the new ideals and served in the Revolutionary Army. Napoleon noticed him and sent him as his Ambassador to Russia in 1801, then took him as his aide-de-camp. He returned to Russia from 1807 to 1811, where he gained the Tsar's respect. He traveled in Napoleon's carriage when the Emperor raced back from Moscow in 1811 and left an extraordinary account of their week-long conversation.

Cayla, Zoé Talon, Madame du, 1784–1850. She was the daughter of a secret agent of Louis XVIII before the Restoration. Admitted to court, she became the favourite of the old King, who left her a vast fortune.

Charles X, Comte d'Artois, Monsieur, 1757–1836. As a young man, the Comte d'Artois was a frivolous, fun-loving, unpopular Prince. The early stirrings of the Revolution scared him and he was the first to flee France on July 17, 1789. During exile, he became quite religious and more and more conservative. On his return, he became the head of the Ultra-Royalist party. He succeeded his brother Louis XVIII in 1824. His reactionary politics caused the 1830 Revolution. Once more, he fled his country and this time took refuge in Prague. He accepted the nomination of his cousin, Louis-Philippe d'Orléans, as the Lieutenant-General of the kingdom and as regent, while abdicating in favor of his grandson, the Comte de Chambord. His fall marked the end of the Bourbon reign in France.

Charles-Albert de Carignan-Savoie, King of Sardinia, 1798–1849. He was recognised by the Congress of Vienna as heir to the throne of Sardinia in the absence of male successors in the senior branch. He became King in 1831. His son, Victor-Emmanuel, would be the first King of Italy.

Chateaubriand, François-René, Vicomte de, 1768–1848. One of the most important figures in French literature, he would probably have preferred a great political career. He spent the first years of the Revolution in America, where he traveled extensively, and emigrated to England upon his return to Europe in 1793. Though he admired Napoleon and lived in France during his reign, he remained faithful to the Royalist cause. He was Ambassador to London and Foreign Minister from 1822 to 1824, and retired from politics during Louis-Philippe's reign. He married when quite young a friend of his sister's, Mademoiselle de Lavigne. She was loyal and intelligent, but they had nothing in common; she claimed she had never read a page written by her famous husband.

Clary, Desirée, Maréchale Bernadotte, Queen of Sweden, 1770–1860. The daughter of a rich merchant of Marseilles, she caught Bonaparte's eye on his way to Egypt, but he was already married to Joséphine. His brother Joseph was still single. He fell in love with her sister, Julie, and married her. When Désirée met Bernadotte, one of Bonaparte's officers, he proposed immediately and she accepted because he always stood his ground in front of Napoleon. She became Queen of Sweden in 1818 but hated her new country and succumbed to a mad passion for the Duc de Richelieu. After his death, she left France and rejoined her husband in Stockholm.

Condé, House of. A junior branch of the House of Bourbon. Louis I, first Prince of Condé, was the brother of Antoine de Bourbon, King of Navarre and father of Henri IV. The Condés were thus the first Princes of the blood. The junior branch of the Condé family took the name of Conti. Louis de Bourbon, eighth Prince of Condé, emigrated upon the fall of the Bastille in 1789 and set about raising the *émigré* "armée de Condé." He went to England in 1801 and returned to Paris in 1814. His son, the Duc de Bourbon, did not choose to assume the Condé title on the death of his father. His grandson was the Duc d'Enghien.

Constant, Benjamin, 1767–1830. A novelist and political writer, he was the epitome of the cosmopolitan European of the time. In 1794, he chose the side of the new regime under the influence of Mme. de Staël.

Cuvier, George, 1769–1832. A zoologist of genius, his work is at the origin of modern biology.

Damas, Baron, Duc de, 1758–1829. Followed Louis XVIII to Belgium during the Hundred Days. He was then nominated First Gentleman of the King's Household. Both his brother and his son also loyally served the Bourbon Princes.

Decazes, Elie, Duc de, 1780–1860. Decazes started his political career at the side of Louis Bonaparte, King of Holland. He switched allegiances in 1814 and was nominated Minister of the Police by Louis XVIII. The King took an immense liking to Decazes, who represented the moderate wing of the Royalist party, and entrusted the government to him. The Ultra-Royalists, led by Monsieur, detested him and forced his resignation after the murder of the Duc de Berry. In 1830, he went over to the side of Louis-Philippe.

Dillon, Edouard, Comte, uncle of Mme. de Boigne, 1751–1839. Fought in the War of Independence and went into exile to serve with the *émigré* army. Returned to France in 1814 and became Ambassador to Dresden and Florence and First Chamberlain of Charles X.

Elchingen, Duc d'. See Ney.

Elisée, Père, Marie, Vincent Talochon, 1753–1817. An excellent surgeon, Talochon, who was known as Père Elisée, emigrated to England. He cured Louis XVIII of an illness that had resisted all sorts of treatment and received a snuff-box filled with gold as a token of his gratitude. During the Restoration, he resided at the Tuileries and was one of the most influential men in the royal entourage.

Enghien, Louis de Bourbon, Duc d', 1772–1804. The last descendant of the Condé branch settled in Baden during the Empire. Napoleon, who suspected him of organising a plot, ordered him seized at Ettenheim. A military court hastily condemned the Prince. He was shot the next day. This execution roused the utmost indignation in France and throughout Europe.

First Consul. See Napoleon.

Fouché, Joseph, Duc d'Otrante, 1759–1820. One of the most amazing careers of the period. In 1789, Fouché, a teacher in a religious school, embraced the revolutionary cause and became one of the most efficient organisers of the Terror. He shifted in 1794 and contributed to the fall of Robespierre. His political skills and his incomparable network of spies led to the post of Minister of Police under Napoleon. Astoundingly, for the same reasons, he maintained his position during the Restoration.

Genlis, Félicité de Saint-Aubin, Comtesse de, 1746–1830. This interesting woman was given the responsibility of raising the children of the

Duc d'Orléans, including the future King Louis-Philippe. She was inspired by Rousseau's theories, and the enthusiasm of her charges for her was quite remarkable. Mme. de Gontaut said that she had seen them kiss the ground upon which she had walked. After the execution of her husband in 1793, she finally emigrated to England but returned to France during the Empire. Napoleon named her inspector of all the grade schools of the country.

Girardin, Emile, 1806–1881. He was the founder of the first moderately priced newspaper. He was extremely well-informed, and his salon was always full of people of different opinions. He was married to Delphine Gay, a writer and a poet.

Gontaut, Marie, Duchesse de, 1772–1857. She shared the responsibility for the education of the children of the Duc d'Orléans before the Revolution and became attached to the Duchesse de Berry in 1816. In 1819, she was named to the much-desired post of governess to her children.

Guizot, François, 1787–1874. A Protestant who opposed Napoleon and supported the Restoration and the July Monarchy. The Ultras hated his moderate policies, and he soon resigned from his ministerial post and resumed his academic career as a historian. He returned to politics under Louis-Philippe.

Jordan, Camille, 1771–1821. A constitutional Royalist, he emigrated to Switzerland in 1793. He returned to France in 1815 and was then elected to Parliament.

Joséphine Tascher de La Pagerie, Empress of the French, 1763–1814. She was first married to Alexandre de Beauharnais, who was executed during the Revolution. She met Napoleon Bonaparte in 1795. He fell violently in love with her, married her in March 1796, and was always kind and generous to her children, Eugène and Hortense. Unfortunately, she was unable to give him a child and he divorced her in 1809. She retired to Malmaison and stayed on very good terms with him.

Krüdener, Mme. von, 1764–1824. After the death of her husband, she became a disciple of Swedenborg, the Swedish founder of a mystical sect. For some years, she had a great influence on Tsar Alexander I.

La Fayette, Marie, Joseph, Marquis de, 1757–1834. The hero of the American War of Independence served in the French revolutionary army until August 1792. He was taken prisoner by the Austrians who surrendered him, as an American citizen, to the United States consul in Hamburg in 1797. He returned to political life under the Bourbons but his Liberal views put an end to his career. In 1830, he publicly espoused the Orléanist cause in a theatrical apparition on the balcony of the Hôtel de Ville. He died, disappointed by the new regime, four years later.

La Tour Du Pin, Henriette, née Dillon, Marquise de, 1770–1853. She left a very interesting account of her life as an exile in America during the Revolution, returning to France during the Empire. Her life ended sadly in Italy after she and her husband plotted against Louis-Philippe.

La Valette, Antoine, Comte de, 1769–1830. Aide-de-camp to Napoleon and Postmaster-General, he joined the Royalists in 1814 but wavered during the Hundred Days. He was condemned to death upon the return of the Bourbons but saved by the devoted intercession of his wife and friends.

Louis XVI, 1754–1793. He became King at twenty years of age. Immature and irresolute, he was torn between the influence of the court faction and the reform-minded Ministers. When the Revolution broke out in 1789, he was unable to respond to the challenge of the Liberal and democratic forces. After his failed attempt to escape the country on June 20, 1791, and his arrest in Varennes, he never regained any semblance of authority. Moreover, he was suspected of secret dealings with foreigners. In August 1792, he was imprisoned in the Temple with his wife and children, brought to trial for treason, and executed on January 21, 1793.

Louis XVIII, Comte de Provence, Monsieur, 1755–1824. He fled France at the time of Varennes but took a different route from his brother Louis XVI and managed to reach Brussels and Coblentz, where he put himself at the head of the *émigrés* and took the title of King after the death of his nephew on June 8, 1795. He settled in England in 1807, and returned to Paris on May 3, 1814, after issuing the declaration of Saint-Ouen, in which he promised to grant the nation a constitution. He did so by signing a Constitutional Charter. He had to flee once more during the Hundred Days and reentered his realm on July 8, 1815. By then he was sixty, suffered from gout and obesity, and though his personal policy tended towards prudence and common sense—except in questions of etiquette—he found it more and more difficult to oppose the ultra-reactionary bent of his brother and heir Charles X, his nephews, and their wives.

Louis-Philippe, Duc de Chartres, Duc d'Orléans, King of the French, 1773–1850. At the beginning of the upheaval, following his father's example, he joined the Jacobin club and fought in the revolutionary army. Later, Louis-Philippe deserted, although his father had changed his name to Philippe-Egalité and voted for the execution of Louis XVI. He did not choose, however, to fight on the side of the enemies of France, but settled in Switzerland and earned his living as a teacher of mathematics. After his father's execution, he sailed to America and lived in Philadelphia. He returned to Europe in 1800, made peace with his Bourbon cousins, married a distant cousin, Marie-Amélie of Naples, and stayed in England until the Restoration. During the reign of Charles X, Louis-Philippe became the center of the Liberal opposition. The July Revolution of 1830 gave him his opportunity. On August 9, 1830, he was proclaimed by the provisional Government "King of the French by the grace of God and the will of the people." He was to reign for eighteen years. A great revolutionary movement swept through Europe in 1848, and Louis-Philippe's growing conservatism and authoritarian attitude united many divergent interests against him. Faced with a revolution, he abdicated and escaped to England, where Queen Victoria placed the estate of Claremont at his disposal.

Madame. *See* Angoulême, Marie-Thérèse.

Marchand, Comte, General, 1765–1851. He commanded the department of Isère for Louis XVIII. Accused of surrendering Grenoble to Napoleon during the Hundred Days, he was tried and acquitted in 1816. He was appointed Peer of France during the July Monarchy.

Marie-Amélie, Princesse de Bourbon-Sicile, Duchesse d'Orléans, Queen of the French, 1782–1866. The daughter of Ferdinand IV, the King of Naples, and Marie-Caroline, elder sister of Marie-Antoinette, she married Louis-Philippe, with whom she had a very bourgeois and happy union. Their five sons, contrary to the royal tradition, were educated in public schools.

Marie-Antoinette, Archduchess of Austria, Queen of France, 1755–1793. The pretty, young, frivolous Queen was unpopular from the start. She was childless for eight years and took too energetic a part in the pleasures of the court. She changed when she became a mother, but it was too late to save her reputation. When the Revolution began, she was perceived as a reactionary influence on the King, and she did imprudently participate in secret intrigues. She was imprisoned with her family in August 1792, placed in solitary confinement in a tiny cell of the Conciergerie for the last three months of her life, and was guillotined in October 1793. She died with the utmost dignity and courage.

Marmont, Auguste Viesse de, Maréchal, Duc de Raguse, 1774–1852. Attached to Bonaparte since 1793, Marmont had a brilliant career in the *Grande Armée.* In 1814, he negotiated the surrender of Paris to the Tsar and withdrew his troops to Normandy without waiting for Napoleon's order. This action was considered treason by the Bonapartists. He then served the Bourbons and commanded the Royalist troops in 1830. His life ended in exile.

Martignac, Jean-Baptiste, Comte de, 1778–1832. His government lasted from 1828 to 1829 and marked the last effort of Charles X to work with the Parliament. He was replaced by the reactionary Polignac, whose politics led to the Revolution of 1830.

Metternich, Clemens, Count, then Prince, 1773–1859. Austrian statesman who stood as a resolute champion of conservative principles. He was Ambassador to Paris in 1806–1807. His triumph was the agreements reached at the Congress of Vienna, which reorganised Europe after Napoleon's defeat. As Foreign Minister and Chancellor, he remained in power until 1848, when he resigned as a result of the insurrectionary movements in Austria and in Italy.

Montmorency, Mathieu, Duc de, 1767–1826. He started out life as a Liberal, fought in the War of Independence, and adopted the first revolutionary reforms enthusiastically. He prudently emigrated in 1793 but came back under the Empire. During the Restoration, he turned into a rabid Ultra-Royalist.

Mortier, Edouard, Adolphe, Duc de Trévise, 1768–1835. A brave and talented young officer of the revolutionary army, he served Napoleon with distinction. He went over to the side of Louis XVIII, but refused to be a member of the court-martial that tried Marshal Ney. He was named Ambassador to Russia under Louis-Philippe and Minister of War.

Murat, Joachim, Marshal, then King of Naples, 1767–1815. The son of an innkeeper, Murat became Bonaparte's aide-de-camp in 1796 and participated in all the campaigns. His courage and his luck were legendary. In 1800, he married Caroline, Napoleon's sister, and became King of Naples in 1808. Though he intrigued against Napoleon in

1814, he lost his kingdom to the Bourbons after the Congress of Vienna. During the Hundred Days, he encouraged an Italian nationalistic movement, but he was caught in Calabria and shot.

Napoleon, 1769–1821. Born at Ajaccio in Corsica, he attended military school in France. He participated in the revolutionary campaigns. Seizing his opportunity during the troubled times of the Directory, he organised the coup of 18 Brumaire and set up a new Government, the Consulate. From then on, he was the master of France. He was First Consul from 1799 to 1804, Emperor of the French from 1804 to 1814, then, after he escaped from Elba, Emperor during the Hundred Days in 1815. Defeated at Waterloo, he was exiled to Saint Helena.

Necker, Jacques, 1732–1804. This Swiss financier established himself in Paris as a banker in 1763. Talented and unusually honest, he was called to the Government in 1776. He tried vainly to reform the system. The King demanded his resignation on July 11, 1789. His departure was an important element in the upheaval which ended three days later by the fall of the Bastille. His daughter was Mme. de Staël.

Ney, Michel, Maréchal, Duc d'Elchingen, Prince de la Moskova, 1769–1815. As "the bravest of the brave," he was an immense asset to Napoleon and participated in all his campaigns. In 1814, he was in favour of the Emperor's abdication, then switched to the side of the Bourbons. He was ordered to stop Napoleon's march on his return from Elba but instead joined him. Ney fought bravely at Waterloo and tried to hide after the defeat. But he was caught, accused of treason, and shot.

Orléans, Duc d'. *See* Louis-Philippe.

Orléans, House of. The title of Duc d'Orléans was traditionally given to the King's closest brother. The heir to the duchy was the Duc de Chartres. The house that survived as a major branch of the House of Bourbon issued from Philippe, the only brother of Louis XIV. His heir was regent from 1715 to 1723, during the childhood of Louis XV. King Louis-Philippe was his great-grandson. The pretender to the throne of France is a direct descendant.

Osmond, Rainulphe, Marquis d', 1788–1862. Adèle de Boigne's little brother, whom she always called "darling boy," was a charming, light-headed young man. He married an extremely rich girl, Aimée Destillières, who refused some of the greatest French aristocrats for him. His grandson inherited Mme. de Boigne's manuscript.

Osmond, René-Eustache, Marquis d', 1751–1838. Entered the diplomatic career in 1787 and emigrated first to Italy, then to England during the Revolution. A very intelligent, moderate man, he did not participate in the excesses of the emigration. Though he returned to France during the Napoleonic regime, he refused to serve the Emperor. Louis XVIII rewarded him by posting him first to Turin, then to London. He was extremely close to his daughter. His marriage with the daughter of Robert Dillon, a Catholic Irishman who had settled with his wife and their thirteen children in Bordeaux, was a love match. Needless to say, she was extremely beautiful and also quite penniless.

Otrante. *See* Fouché.

Oudinot, Nicolas, Duc de Reggio, 1767–1847. Had a brilliant career in the army, though Napoleon once said "it was impossible to have less brains than Oudinot." He welcomed the Bourbons in 1814 and became Governor of the Invalides in 1842.

Pasquier, Etienne-Denis, Baron, Duc, 1767–1862. A descendant of the great Renaissance humanist, Estienne Pasquier, he followed his father's example and became a counsellor in the Paris Parliament. During the Terror, his father was guillotined, and he was arrested. He resumed his career in 1795 and served the Empire, the Restoration, and the July Monarchy. Immensely respected, he was named Chancellor of France when this office was revived in May 1837. He may have been secretly married to Mme. de Boigne.

Philippe-Egalité, Louis-Philippe, Duc d'Orléans, 1747–1793. He was very hostile to Marie-Antoinette and rarely came to Versailles, either staying in the Palais Royal—he built the shops in the arcades to increase his income—or living abroad. Extremely popular, he was elected deputy of Paris to the assembly. He voted for the death sentence of Louis XVI but was arrested and executed one month after Marie-Antoinette.

Pichegru, Charles, General, 1761–1804. Fought the War of Independence and participated brilliantly in the revolutionary campaigns. During the Directory, his politics changed. He supported the right-wing opposition and made his way to England, where he became a Royalist agent. Sent secretly to France in 1804 to join Georges Cadoudal in a plot against Napoleon, he was arrested in Paris and found strangled in his cell.

Polastron, Louise, Comtesse de, 1764–1804. Sister-in-law of the Duchesse de Polignac, Marie-Antoinette's favourite, and aunt of Jules de Polignac, she had a long affair with the Comte d'Artois and was instrumental in bringing him back to the Church.

Polignac, Jules, Comte, Prince de, 1780–1847. This faithful companion of the Comte d'Artois was opposed to any concession to Liberal opinion. With little brains and no political acumen, he had a disastrous influence once Charles X gave him the highest government posts. He was judged after the Revolution of 1830, condemned to perpetual confinement and loss of civil rights, and locked up in the fortress of Ham until the amnesty of 1836.

Pozzo Di Borgo, Charles-André, Comte, Duc, 1764–1842. He was born in Corsica three years before Napoleon. Unlike the Bonaparte family, Pozzo was in favor of Corsica's independence and therefore refused to serve Napoleon. He entered the service of the Tsar, who sent him to Paris as his Ambassador during the Restoration. He was transferred to London in 1834.

Raguse. *See* Marmont.

Récamier, Jeanne, Mme. de, 1777–1849. One of the most enchanting women of her times, she was married at fifteen to the rich banker Jacques Récamier. From the early days of the Consulate until the end of the July Monarchy, her salon attracted fashionable, literary, and political society. She had many admirers but no lovers. Chateaubriand was a constant visitor and became the centre of her salon, where he read extracts from his works.

Regent, Prince of Wales, 1762–1830. Eldest son of George III, he became Regent during his father's illness and reigned as George IV from 1820 to 1830. He was married to Caroline of Brunswick (*see* Caroline), though his attachment to Mrs. Fitzherbert (see p. 9, Volume One) had been blessed by the Church.

Richelieu, Armand Emmanuel du Plessis, Duc de, 1766–1822. He joined the Russian army during the Revolution and was greatly appreciated by Tsar Alexander I. In 1803, he was appointed Governor of Odessa and, two years later, Governor General of the whole Odessa region. During his remarkable tenure, he established schools, reformed finances, and encouraged agriculture and exports. He returned to Paris in 1814, and was President of the Council twice. A moderate man, in constant opposition to the extreme Royalists, he resigned in 1821. His last years were clouded by the unwanted attentions of the Queen of Sweden, who pursued him wherever he went.

Sabran, Elzéar de, 1774–1842. A charming, witty poet with surprisingly strong conservative political views.

Salvandy, Achille, Comte de, 1795–1856. One of Napoleon's youngest officers, he energetically opposed the allied occupation of France in 1816. He became Minister of Education during the July Monarchy and founded the French School of Archeology in Athens.

Schlegel, August-Wilhelm von, 1767–1845. The great German proponent of Romanticism. His literary criticism and university lectures were crucial to the development of the movement.

Sièyes, Emmanuel, Abbé, 1748–1836. One of the chief theorists of the Revolution and an architect of the coup that replaced the Directory with the Consulate and marked the start of Napoleon Bonaparte's political career. He played an important, though discreet, role in political life until 1815. He spent the Restoration years in exile in Brussels and returned to Paris after 1830.

Staël-Holstein, Germaine Necker, Baronne de, 1766–1817. A brilliant woman of letters who wrote novels, plays, and political essays and was the main theorist of Romanticism. She was the daughter of Necker and married the Swedish Ambassador to Paris, whose diplomatic status allowed her to stay in France during the Revolution. Her salon flourished at the end of the Terror. She was too much of an aggressive female intellectual not to irritate Napoleon, who banished her from Paris. She spent the seven years of her exile either in Coppet in Switzerland or travelling extensively in Russia, Germany, Italy, and England. She returned to Paris in 1814.

Sweden, Queen of. See Clary, Désirée.

Talleyrand, Charles-Maurice de Talleyrand-Périgord, Prince and Duc de Bénévent, 1754–1838. A statesman and diplomat notable for his capacity for political survival. He held high office during the French Revolution—prudently spending the two years of the Terror in the United States—under Napoleon, during the Restoration, and under Louis-Philippe.

Talma, François-Joseph, 1763–1826. The most famous actor of the period. He imposed a more natural diction and a search for historical truth in both attitude and costume, and Napoleon regarded him highly.

Trevise. See Mortier.

Victor Emmanuel I, King of Sardinia from 1802 to 1821, 1759–1824. His possessions in Piedmont had been annexed by France during the Empire and returned to him in 1814. His reactionary politics provoked insurrections, and he was forced to abdicate in favor of his brother Charles Félix in 1821.

Villèle, Jean-Baptiste, 1773–1854. A naval officer whose Ultra-Royalist political career took off in 1815. He was named President of the Council during the last years of Louis XVIII's reign. He retired in Toulouse after the Revolution of 1830.

Wales, Prince of. See Regent.

Wellington, Arthur Wellesley, Duke of, 1769–1852. Born in Dublin, educated at Eton and at a military academy in France, he was the principal architect of Great Britain's victory over Napoleon.

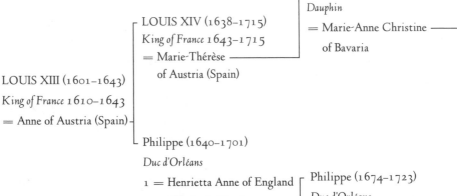

LOUIS XIII (1601–1643)
King of France 1610–1643
= Anne of Austria (Spain)

LOUIS XIV (1638–1715)
King of France 1643–1715
= Marie-Thérèse
of Austria (Spain)

Louis (1661–1711)
Dauphin
= Marie-Anne Christine
of Bavaria

Philippe (1640–1701)
Duc d'Orléans
1 = Henrietta Anne of England
2 = Elizabeth Charlotte
of the Palatinate

Philippe (1674–1723)
Duc d'Orléans
Regent of France 1715–1723
= Françoise Marie de Bourbon

*Bourbon Family Tree,
with the House of Orléans to 1830*

Louis (1682–1712)
Duc de Bourgogne
Dauphin 1711–1712
= Marie-Adélaïde of Savoy

LOUIS XV (1710–1774)
King of France 1715–1774
= Marie Leszczynska ———

Louis (1729–1765)
Dauphin
1 = Teresa of Spain (1726–1746) ———
2 = Maria Josepha of Saxony ———

Philippe (1683–1746)
Duc d'Anjou
King of Spain as Philip V
1700–1746
1 = Marie-Louise of Savoy
2 = Elisabeth Farnese

unnamed (1730–1733)
Duc d'Anjou

7 daughters:
1 Louise Elizabeth (1727–1759)
= Philip of Parma
2 Anne Henriette (1727–1752)
3 Marie-Louise (1728–1733)
4 Adélaïde (1732–1800)
5 Victoire (1733–1799)
6 Sophie (1734–1782)
7 Louise (1737–1787)

Charles (1686–1714)
Duc de Berry
= Marie, daughter of the
second Philippe Duc d'Orléans

Louis (1703–1752)
Duc d'Orléans
= Augusta Maria of Baden

7 daughters

Louis-Philippe (1725–1785)
Duc d'Orléans
= Louise Henriette ———
de Bourbon-Conti

Louis-Philippe (1747–1793)
Duc d'Orléans (Egalité)
= Adélaïde de Bourbon–Penthièvre ———

Louise (1750–1822)
= Louis Henri Joseph
de Bourbon-Condé

Marie-Thérèse (1746–1748)

LOUIS XVI (1754–1793)
King of France 1774–1793
= Marie-Antoinette of Austria

Thérèse (1778–1851)
= Louis Antoine duc
   d'Angoulême

Louis (1755–1824)
Comte de Provence
King of France as
LOUIS XVIII 1814–1824
= Louise of Savoy

Louis (1781–1789)
Dauphin

LOUIS XVII
(1785–1795?)
titular King 1793–1795

Charles (1757–1836)
Comte d'Artois
King of France as
CHARLES X 1824–1830
= Thérèse of Savoy

Louis Antoine (1775–1844)
Duc d'Angoulême
= Thérèse of France

Clotilde (1759–1802)
= Charles Emmanuel IV of Sardinia

Charles Ferdinand (1778–1820)
Duc de Berry
= Caroline of the Two Sicilies

Louise (1819–1864)
= Charles III of Parma

Elizabeth (1764–1794)

Henry (1820–1883)
Duc de Bordeaux
Comte de Chambord
= Thérèse of Modena

LOUIS-PHILIPPE (1773–1850)
Duc d'Orléans
King of the French 1830–1848
= Marie-Amélie of the Two Sicilies

Antoine (1775–1807)
Comte de Montpensier

Adélaïde (1777–1847)

Louis Charles (1779–1808)
Comte de Beaujolais

CHRONOLOGY

Events in the life of Mme. de Boigne are in italic.

February 21, 1781	*Birth of Adèle d'Osmond*
May 1783	End of the War of Independence
May 1789	The Estates General assemble in Versailles
July 14, 1789	Fall of the Bastille
October 6, 1789	The royal family is forced by the mob to leave Versailles
February 1791	*Adèle and her mother follow the King's aunts to Italy*
October 1791	Constitutional regime is installed in France
June 1791	Louis XVI tries to flee but is caught at Varennes
April 1792	France declares war on Austria
August 10, 1792	Louis XVI is deposed and imprisoned with his family
September 2, 1792	The First French Republic is proclaimed and the Terror begins
September 20, 1792	French victory at Valmy
December 1792	Trial of Louis XVI

January 21, 1793	Execution of Louis XVI
February 1793	Extension of the war: Great Britain, Russia, and Spain constitute a coalition with Austria against France
September 1793	The regime of Terror intensifies
October 16, 1793	Marie-Antoinette is executed
February 1794	*The d'Osmonds leave Italy to settle in England*
July 27, 1794	The Terror ends with the execution of Robespierre
June 11, 1798	*Marriage of Adèle d'Osmond and General de Boigne*
November 9, 1799	Napoleon Bonaparte seizes power (18 Brumaire)
May 18, 1804	Napoleon is proclaimed Emperor of the French
September 1804	*Mme. de Boigne returns to France*
January 1811	George III is declared insane. His son becomes Prince Regent
January 1812	*General and Mme. de Boigne separate*
April 4, 1814	Napoleon I abdicates and is exiled in Elba
June 4, 1814	Louis XVIII enters Paris. Beginning of the Restoration
September 1814	*Mme. de Boigne and her parents settle in Turin during her father's ambassadorship*
March 20 to June 22, 1815	The Hundred Days
August 1815	*Mme. de Boigne returns to Paris*
January 1816 to 1819	*Mme. de Boigne follows her father, who is named Ambassador to Great Britain*
January 1820	The Prince Regent becomes George IV

February 1, 1820	Assassination of the Duc de Berry
May 5, 1821	Death of Napoleon
September 16, 1824	Death of Louis XVIII. His brother, Charles X, becomes king
June 21, 1830	*Death of General de Boigne*
June 26, 1830	William IV succeeds his brother, George IV
July 26, 1830	A series of reactionary ordinances provoke an uprising
July 27, 28, 29, 1830	A three-day revolution puts an end to the Bourbon regime
August 9, 1830	Louis-Philippe is crowned King of the French
April 1835	*Mme. de Boigne starts writing her memoirs*
November 6, 1836	Death of Charles X
June 20, 1837	Victoria becomes Queen of England
February 1848	Louis-Philippe is dethroned and takes refuge in England
July 4, 1848	Death of Chateaubriand
December 1, 1848	Louis-Napoleon is elected President of the Republic
December 2, 1852	The Second Empire is proclaimed. Louis-Napoleon takes the title of Napoleon III
August 26, 1850	Death of Louis-Philippe
May 10, 1866	*Death of Mme. de Boigne*

Memoirs of the Comtesse de Boigne

CHAPTER ONE

England

1816–1820

After an absence of twelve years I was keenly interested in revisiting London. I recovered the charm of my early recollections, and reentered the country of my early youth: every detail was familiar to me, yet was sufficiently removed from my daily thoughts to have acquired the attraction of novelty. My sensations were those of meeting an old friend returned from afar, who is greeted with delight and brings agreeable recollections of past times, when life was less eventful, passed more quickly, and left more delightful thoughts, with perhaps more regrets, than memory can recall.

I was much struck with the great prosperity of the country. I do not think there had been any real increase in it, but former habit had blinded my eyes and made me incapable of appreciating it from an outside point of view, while absence had made me readier to notice these points. There were the admirable roads, upon which the post-horses trotted very agreeably; there was the multitude of public and private carriages, all delightful. The innumerable country houses of every kind gave a general impression of comfort at every rank of society, from the cottage of the peasant to the country seat of the lord. The windows of the smallest shop met the scanty rays of the sun with a glass never tarnished by the smallest stain; the neatly dressed country people passed from village to village on paths which we should be glad to have in our gardens; the children were clean and amused themselves with a freedom in contrast with the reserve of the rest of the family—all these things were familiar to me, and impressed me perhaps more deeply than if I had seen them for the first time.

I travelled from Dover to London one beautiful Sunday in May in a state of continual delight. From time to time some small jealousy for my own country came into my mind: Providence had been at least as kind to France, and why could not France have grown as prosperous as her island neighbour? Then the post-horses checked their rapid pace and fell into that mincing step which they assume in London, and the smoky atmosphere of the great town hung above my head. The silent inhabitants followed one another on their wide pavements like a funeral procession; doors, windows, and shops were closed, and seemed to betoken no less sadness within than without. By degrees my exaltation diminished, and when I reached the embassy my enthusiasm for England had received a blow.

Prodigious as is the commercial prosperity of London, and great as is the luxury displayed in every class of society, I believe that its aspect would appear less remarkable to a foreigner than any part of the rest of England. This great city, composed of identical little houses, and of broad streets laid out alike, is overwhelmed with monotony and sameness. No monument commands the attention of the weary traveller, and a five-minute walk will show everything that five days could reveal in districts which are always different and always the same.

The Thames, with its constant traffic, which would give some character to this capital of the Britannic world, is carefully hidden on every side. Special information is required to perceive its existence, even when setting out to look for it.

Cities anywhere might be seen resembling London, but I doubt if any other country could give an idea of the English countryside. I know of no country where it is in such strong contrast with the town. The visitor looks up to another sky, breathes another atmosphere; the trees have another aspect, and the plants different colours. The population, too, is different, though the dress of the inhabitants of Northumberland or Devonshire is similar to that of the passers-by in Piccadilly.

It must be understood, moreover, that the yellow cloud, striated with black, brown, and grey and permeated with soot, which seems like a vast extinguisher placed over the city, influences the morals and modifies the temperament of the population. Hence there is no language which sings the praises of the country in verse and prose with keener or more sincere passion than English literature. Anyone who has spent three months in London will understand the real benefit to be derived from a change of residence.

Notwithstanding the fits of vertigo which this gloomy atmosphere gives to newcomers, it is by no means unhealthy; the visitor soon grows so accustomed to it that he does not notice any unpleasant results. I have heard the health of London attributed to the changes of four tides a day in the Thames. This great displacement of water provides the only means of ventilation; it stirs and purifies the air, which seems thick even to the eye, and leaves positive proof upon the clothing that the eye is not deceived. A white dress, clean in the morning, will be soiled before the end of the day with more dirt than a week would bring in Paris. The extreme elegance of the inhabitants and their cleanliness, which such conditions make indispensable, are stimulated by these necessities to combat their bad influences; both houses and people appear perfectly neat and clean. Though my long absence had made me readier to appreciate the delights of the journey, I was even more struck by the inconveniences of London, which I had not hitherto observed. In early youth the outward world makes no great impression.

The day of my arrival the Prince Regent[1] gave a concert for the Queen, his mother. To secure an invitation, previous presentation at court was necessary. The Queen, knowing that I was in London, was good enough to remember that I had been previously presented, and

1. The future George IV.

sent me an invitation. My parents were dining at Carlton House. I arrived alone in the evening, hoping to mix unnoticed in the crowd. I was somewhat late, and the concert had already begun.

The hall with its gallery was divided by pillars into three almost equal parts. The central part was exclusively occupied by the court and the musicians, who were placed opposite the Queen, the Princesses and their ladies, the Ambassadresses, and some others of high rank; these persons were seated, while the rest of the company stood in the side parts separated by the pillars. In the other rooms people walked about, according to the general custom of the country, which regards a seated concert as terribly wearisome.

At the door I found Lady Macclesfield, one of the ladies of the Palace, who was waiting to take me to the Queen, and without giving me a moment to breathe led me through all these people, amid the music, the general silence, and the empty space, to her Majesty. I had not had time to grow timid. But when I approached the Queen rose, and the forty persons who surrounded her followed her example. This general rustle, which I had not expected, began to alarm me. The Queen was, I believe, most kind and gracious, but during the whole of her conversation I was preoccupied with the idea of securing my retreat. Lady Macclesfield had left me to resume her place among her friends. When the Queen made the slight bow which announced that the audience was concluded, I felt the floor heave beneath my feet. I was standing there, alone and abandoned, with the eyes of all England upon my person, and with a long journey before me to regain the groups behind the columns. I do not know even know how I achieved this object. I had been presented at many courts and to many potentates; I was no longer young enough to be shy and I was accustomed to high society, but to this day I preserve a dread remembrance of the evening and the presentation.

It was not that Queen Charlotte was in any way imposing to behold. Imagine a sugarloaf covered with gold brocade, and you will have a fairly accurate idea of her figure. She had never been tall, and already for some years she had become crooked and deformed. Her head, upon an extremely short neck, displayed a surly face, yellow and wrinkled, with grey hair dusted with powder. She used to wear a bonnet, turban, or toque, as occasion demanded, but I have always seen a little circlet of jewels forming part of her headdress, and have heard that she never appeared without this ornament. Notwithstanding her extraordinary face, she was not lacking in a certain dignity, conducted her court excellently, with extreme politeness and with a manner which could assume the most varied shades of expression. While strict in her views upon the behaviour of ladies at court, she prided herself upon complete impartiality, and even a cold look or a cross word from the Queen to one of her favourites sufficed to check a young person who was on the edge of a precipice. Towards divorced women she was inexorable, and no such woman, whatever excuse she might have, or however admirable her subsequent conduct, was ever able to cross the threshold of the Palace.

Lady Holland was striking proof of the fact. Her intelligence, her political influence, and the domination which she exerted over her husband had enabled her to recover her social preeminence. A refusal to go to Holland House would have been incredible prudery. Lady Holland's receptions were constantly attended by the most distinguished members of English and foreign aristocracy, but in spite of all her pains and trouble, and notwithstanding the many negociators whom she employed, including the Prince Regent, she was never able to gain admission to Saint James's Palace as long as the old Queen was alive.

I could not venture to say that the Queen was loved, but she was deeply respected. The Prince Regent was foremost in his consideration for her. In private life his care and tenderness were extreme, and he overwhelmed her with respect in public. I was much struck, on this evening, to see a footman bring a little tray, with a cup of tea, sugar basin, and cream jug, and hand it to the Prince Regent, who carried it himself to his mother. He remained standing before her while she helped herself to sugar and cream, without rising or hurrying or interrupting her conversation. She was accustomed to say to him in English, or whatever language she might be speaking at the time, "Thank you, George." She repeated the same thanks when the Prince Regent took the tray again from the footman to take her empty cup. This was a regular custom, and the ceremony was repeated two or three times during the evening. Though it took place when the Queen was at the house of the Prince Regent, in her own house it was usually one of the Princesses, sometimes one of the Princes, never the Prince Regent, but always one of her own children, who gave her her cup of tea.

All the other members of the royal family, including the Prince Regent, shared the refreshments prepared for the rest of the company without any distinction. Generally speaking, the formalities of etiquette were as much relaxed for them as they were strictly observed by the Queen. Princes and Princesses paid and returned calls like private individuals.

I remember that, the evening of my presentation to the Queen, I was standing at a short distance from a small, fair lady whose face the lapse of twelve years had blotted from my memory. She said to Lady Charlotte Greville, with whom I was talking: "Lady Charlotte, tell Mme. de Boigne my name." It was the Duchess of York. She remained talking with us for a long time on every subject, with great affability and without even the smallest trace of royal reserve. The next day my mother took me to call upon all the Princesses: we left cards where we were not admitted, and the ceremony of introduction was completed.

Princess Charlotte of Wales, the only daughter of the Prince Regent and heiress to the throne, had married the Prince of Saxe-Coburg and was still tasting the delights of her honeymoon. She had not yet left the country. My mother had been present at her marriage, which had been celebrated in a drawing-room at Carlton House. Afterwards, when I told the Princess how deeply I regretted that I had not shared this honour, she said to me:

"You are right: it is an unusual sight to see the heiress to a kingdom making a love match and giving her hand where her heart is already pledged. Perfect happiness is by no means common, and I shall be delighted if you will often come and observe it at Claremont."

Poor Princess! I did not make her acquaintance until the occasion of another journey. At that time I heard much of her. She was very popular, and affected the brusque manners attributed to Queen Elizabeth, which she carried so far as to adopt the said Queen's oaths. She was very decided in her political opinions. Greeting with the warmest clasp of her hand all men, young or old, whom she considered as belonging to her party, she never missed an opportunity of displaying her opposition to her father's Government and her personal hostility to her grandmother and her aunts. She professed a warm affection for her mother, Queen Caroline, whom she regarded as sacrificed to the desires of her family.

Princess Charlotte went out of her way to find opportunities for rudeness to the ladies who formed the intimate society of the Prince Regent. She had been persuaded that her father wished to obtain an annulment of his marriage and to deny the legitimacy of her birth. I do not know if there is any truth in this rumour; in any case her legal rights were written upon her face, for she resembled the Prince prodigiously. She was born nine months after the marriage, though cohabitation had not lasted many days. It is certain that at this time the Prince had been guilty of many frailties, only too justified by the conduct of his wife, but I do not know that he ever thought of attacking Princess Charlotte.

He accused Miss Mercer of having turned the head of the young Princess by telling her this fable; he had driven her from the Palace, and detested her accordingly. Miss Mercer kept up a clandestine correspondence with Princess Charlotte. She had aroused her objection to the Prince of Orange whom the English Cabinet wished her to marry, and had encouraged a taste for Prince Leopold of Saxe-Coburg, with which the Grand Duchess Catherine of Russia had also sought to inspire in her. These two women had carried their intrigue so far as to induce the Princess Charlotte to declare that she wished to marry Prince Leopold and had resolved to refuse any other match. The Opposition supported her demand.

Miss Mercer, daughter of Lord Keith, a rich heiress, but extremely ugly, desired on her side to marry the Duke of Devonshire and to bring him her influence with the future sovereign as her dowry. The Whig party in general approved of this alliance, and had combined to secure the Duke's agreement. I do not know whether this plot would have been successful, but when the marriage of the Princess seemed to have secured the success of this long intrigue, it failed completely before the good sense of Prince Leopold; he took advantage of his wife's affection to withdraw her from the clique by which she was beset, to renew relations with her family, and to change her political and social attitude. This was not the work of a day, but he took it in hand at once. During the first week Miss Mercer had called at Claremont, after writing several notes which had remained unanswered; she met with so cool a reception that she was obliged to cut short her visit, and return to the village for her carriage which she had sent there. Complaints led to explanations, which stated that the Princess would show disrespect to her father if she received a person whom he had forbidden her to see. Miss Mercer was furious, the Opposition party ceased to set any value on her marriage with the Duke of Devonshire, and everyone laughed at her for her ambition in this respect.

The Prince Regent lived the life of a man of the world. He went to dinner with private friends, and was present at evening parties. These habits of his obliged the Ambassadors to follow a special course of existence: they were continually invited to the same houses as the Prince, and he was almost exclusively surrounded by them. At every dinner he always sat between two Ambassadors' wives and at an evening party he was usually seated on a sofa with Lady Hertford on one side and an Ambassador's wife on the other. Lady Hertford, who was known as "the Marchioness" par excellence, was then the queen of his thoughts. She had been very beautiful, but was now past fifty, and looked it, in spite of all her dressing and efforts. She had a frigid bearing, a pompous mode of speech, and was pedantically accurate in her choice of words, with a manner both calm and cold. She exerted great influence upon the Prince, and was a great lady in every sense of the word; she also considered that she granted high favours to the sovereign by permitting him to bore her every day. Princess Charlotte had attempted to be rude to her, but she had met her match. The old Queen received her with a consideration which proved her good opinion, and Lady Hertford carried her Tory views into every drawing-room with the pride of a sultana.

The Prince rose in the morning extremely late, and his toilet was neverending. He was in his dressing-gown two full hours; into his dressing-room he would admit some few friends, his Ministers, and the foreign Ambassadors when they requested the permission to enter, which he was always glad to give. If anyone wrote to secure an audience, or asked for one in advance, he would receive the visitor in full dress in his drawing-room, but this disturbed his habits and annoyed him. Anyone who called at his door without a previous engagement was usually admitted. He would begin the conversation by some excuse for his untidy condition, but was in the best possible humour, and as a result more ready to talk.

His dressing was never finished until the last moment, when his horses were announced. He rode, followed by a single groom, and went to the Park, where he was ready to speak to anyone. Unless he said, "Let us ride together," people simply contented themselves with a passing word, without attempting to follow. When he stopped it was an act of great politeness, but did not imply familiarity or a desire to be accompanied. During the first year he used to stop for my father, but when he became more friendly he either made a previous engagement to ride with him or beckoned with his hand without stopping.

From the Park he went off to Lady Hertford's, where he spent the rest of the morning. Generally his carriage came for him, but sometimes he would come back on horseback. Only his special favourites were ever asked to Lady Hertford's house at the hour when the Prince was generally there, and even then visitors were often not admitted. The Ministers were constantly present at that time.

Though Lady Hertford was not especially intellectual, she had excellent good sense, never attempted to intrigue, and never desired anything either for herself or her family: on the whole, the Prince, for whom female society was a necessity, could have chosen no better friend. The Ministers had realised this more distinctly when the Prince Regent, after his accession, replaced this decorous friend by a whim for Lady Conyngham, the ridiculous part of this connection being by no means its sole drawback.

The Prince Regent had three styles of sending out invitations to dinner. The High Chamberlain informed the visitor by order upon an enormous card that he was invited to meet the Queen. Full dress was then necessary.

His private secretary, Sir Benjamin Bloomfield, would send out a private note in his own writing that the Prince desired one's company for such-and-such a day. Ordinary dress clothes and the usual formalities of society were then prescribed. These notes were sent to ladies as well as to men. The dinners were never attended by more than twenty; usually by twelve or fifteen people.

The third manner of invitation was reserved for intimate friends. The Prince would send a footman in the morning with a verbal message to the effect that if Mr. So-and-so was not engaged and had nothing better to do, the Prince would be glad if he would come and dine at Carlton House, but begged him not to inconvenience himself. At the same time it was understood that people never did have anything else to do, and I think the Prince would have been much surprised if anyone had refused this invitation. My father was ultimately frequently invited in this manner; this form of invitation was never addressed to ladies. The dinners were never for more than five or six people, and the list of those invited was very restricted.

My examination of social customs was the more interesting to me upon my return, because in my youth I had no standard of comparison, and my conclusion was that though England was far superior in material life, social life was much better understood in France.

No one can have a stronger appreciation than myself of the noble character and public spirit by which the English nation is distinguished. With that admirable common sense which is the backbone of the country, the Englishman, in spite of his personal independence, is ready to recognise class distinctions. In passing through a village one may often hear a man on his cottage doorstep say to his little daughter, "Curtsey to your betters, Betsy." But this man would never admit any superior to himself upon a point where his legal rights were in question. He can apply to the law for protection against the county lord by whom he may think himself injured, or for a summons against a neighbour with whom he has quarrelled in a public-house. This confidence that the law will protect him in every aspect of life forms the basis of that feeling of independence, whence is born that self-respect which marks the free man.

On the other hand, this independence, which is the enemy of social intercourse and implies a certain roughness of character, is modified by the desire among the lower classes to do nothing which is not "genteel," and among the upper classes to do nothing which is not "gentlemanlike." Such is the tie which unites English society. The whim for being fashionable is the ideal of comparatively few, and is often pushed to ridiculous extremes.

In observing the two countries closely, one may note how people who fundamentally are equally sympathetic can nonetheless wound one another by their way of expressing themselves, I may almost say of conceiving, their thoughts. I am reminded of this by my recollection of a dinner at the house of my old friend Lady Dunmore, a very quiet affair. The sensation of the moment was being discussed: the verdict given against Lord Bective by the ecclesiastical court of Doctors' Commons. The circumstances were as follows:

Lady George Beresford, the preceding year, had been one of the most charming, distinguished, and fortunate women in London. After a confinement, complications set in, and she went mad. Her husband was in despair. The necessity of finding certain business papers obliged him to open a strong-box belonging to his wife, which contained a highly compromising correspondence of hers with Lord Bective. The husband was furious. Although his wife continued insane and was under restraint, he began legal proceedings against her. Witnesses who dragged her name in the mire were heard, and a verdict was given against Lord Bective with twelve thousand pounds damages. It was the amount of this sum which was under discussion at a table where I was seated. Some thought the amount was disproportionate to the merits of Lady George, others thought that it was an accurate estimate. One urged that she was so fair, so graceful, had such a beautiful figure, and so many talents. Not so many, said another, and then she was not so young as she once was. But she had such beautiful children. Oh, but her health was growing worse, and her complexion was spoilt. Still, she was a clever woman. But she had been very depressed and rather sulky for some months.

The discussion continued with arguments almost equally balanced, when the mistress of the house concluded the matter by saying:

"I admit that twelve thousand pounds is a great sum, but then poor Lord George was so fond of her."

The force of this argument seemed irresistible, and satisfied all disputants. I listened with amazement. I felt hurt to hear women of the highest rank enumerating and discussing the merits of one of their equals as one might go over the points of a horse. Equally astonishing was the cash valuation of the grief which her loss must have caused to the husband, whose conduct seemed to me disgusting for his persecution of the mother of his children, whom the hand of God had stricken with the worst calamity to which a human being can be condemned.

Are we hence to conclude that the upper classes in England are wanting in good feeling? It would be as unjust as to assert that Frenchwomen are without modesty because they use certain phrases proscribed upon the other side of the Channel. The fact is that different customs show conditions from a different point of view, and that one should hesitate to pass judgement upon foreigners before making a profound investigation of their social customs.

What society does not present staggering anomalies to the unaccustomed observer? Theoretically, I had every respect for the English system of social gradation, and yet as a Frenchwoman my social instincts were irritated when I saw that system in operation in the drawing-room.

The great ladies open their doors once or twice a year to everyone who can venture to call upon them on arriving in London, either by virtue of some slight connection, or, and especially, in view of services performed at election times. Such calls are returned by the sending of a large card upon which is printed: The Duchess of ———— at home, at some date several weeks hence. The name of the person invited is written below by hand. Heaven knows what energy is employed to get one of these cards, or what toilsome manoeuvres are expended to secure the right to an invitation.

The day arrives. The mistress of the house stands at the door of her drawing-room, and bows to everyone who comes in but, what a bow! It is as though she said to them, "Though you are in my house, please understand that I do not know you, and do not want to know you." This mode of reception is rendered the more striking by the very different greeting given to members of fashionable society. However, in this sensible country no one is shocked, but everyone has what he wanted. Intimate friends have a warm reception, and others the delights of an invitation. The invitation card has been stuck in the looking-glass for a month, and has been seen by every visitor to the house. In second-class society it is now possible to discuss the furniture of the Duchess of ————'s drawing-room, the dress of the Marchioness of ————, and to make other observations of this kind. The object which these guests had in view is secured, and probably they would be less proud of their invitation by the Duchess if she were more polite.

In France such treatment would not be endured for a moment. I have sometimes thought that the superiority of French society to all others is due to the understood fact that the mistress who issues invitations for a dinner or evening party is under an obligation to those who come, whereas the contrary is the case in other countries. A little reflection will, I believe, show how great a difference this can produce in the course of social interplay and in politeness of manner.

The immense English routs are so utterly disproportionate to the size of the house that sometimes the overflow from the drawing-rooms extends to the staircase and occasionally to the street, where the block of carriages increases the hardships of these meetings. The principles of English liberty, though in this point I do not recognise the sound legal sense of the country, do not permit any order of precedence among the arrivals. It is at full speed, by driving the horses one against another, that the guest reaches the door, or rather fails to reach it. There are few evening parties with any pretence to fashion where two or three shattered carriages are not left on the pavement, a fact more astonishing in London, where carriages are so fine and so carefully kept.

The routs increased my admiration for our good and useful police, and invariably put to flight my love of liberty. I remember one case where I cast them to perdition with all my heart, when we spent an hour and three-quarters in misery, with the prospect of being smashed to matchwood every moment, in the effort to reach the house of Lady Hertford. We started from Portland Place, and she lived in Manchester Square, a distance that might be walked in a minute. In order to spare the Prince Regent the annoyance of this block of carriages, it was arranged that he should reach the drawing-room of the Marchioness by crossing a little garden and going through the window. It was doubtless an extremely simple device, but when the window flew up with a crash to admit him an involuntary smile was seen upon every face.

Apart from the physical fatigue of these meetings, the foreigner is also disgusted by the hour at which they begin. On one occasion I had forgotten what this hour was. We were engaged to attend a ball the evening following Lady Hertford's rout, and midnight had struck, while my mother had not thought of starting. I urged her to set out.

"Well, certainly, if you wish; but we shall cause some annoyance."

On this occasion we found no row of carriages: we were the first to arrive, and the drawing-rooms were not entirely lighted. The mistress of the house came in pulling on her gloves, her daughter only finished dressing half an hour later, and the crowd did not begin to arrive until nearly one o'clock in the morning. I have heard that many women used to go to bed between dinnertime and the hour when social amusements began, in order that they might appear the fresher. This may be a fiction, but many certainly went to sleep at these functions from sheer weariness.

While I am on the subject of balls, I must say a word upon a ball that was very beautiful and very extraordinary, owing to the position of the people who gave it. The Marquis of Anglesey, after he had been married for twenty-one years to a Lady Villiers, by whom he had a multitude of children, had been divorced by her in Scotland, where the law admits marital infidelity as adequate cause. He had just married Lady Emily Wellesley, who had also been divorced in England, and who had also left a number of children in the care of her first husband.

The Marchioness of Anglesey on her side had married the Duke of Argyll. She did not come under the category of divorced women, and was therefore received at court and in society. At the same time, this second marriage had been so precipitate that she was supposed at least to have agreed with Lord Anglesey to accelerate their divorce. Several daughters, the Ladies Paget, of ages from eighteen to twenty-two, continued to live at their father's house, and went into society under the care of the Duchess. Lord Anglesey had lost a leg at the battle of Waterloo. For some time his situation had been critical, and he had received many proofs of the general interest which society took in his recovery. To show his gratitude he conceived the idea of giving a grand entertainment to his numerous friends upon the occasion of his recovery. A ballroom was immediately arranged in the beautiful apartments of Uxbridge House.

All preparations were made by the Marquis and the new Lady Anglesey with the utmost state and magnificence. Invitations, contrary to general custom, were in the first person. Lord Anglesey thanked Mr. and Mrs. So-and-So for their kind inquiries, and hoped that they would be able to spend the evening of ———— at Uxbridge House.

A moment before the arrival of the company Lady Anglesey, the divorced wife who was not seen in society, gave a last look at all the arrangements and started for the country. Lord Anglesey, who was too gallant and affectionate to leave his wife in solitude, accompanied her.

Hence there was no master or mistress in this house where so great an entertainment was given. The daughters of the first wife did the honours, assisted by courtesy of the Misses Wellesley, daughters of the second wife by the first husband, with whom they were staying. It must be admitted that a stranger idea could hardly be conceived than that of inviting people to one's house under such circumstances.

This ball was remarkable for another incident. Lady Caroline Lamb had published her novel *Glenarvon* a few days before. This was the story of her adventures with the famous Lord Byron, pushed to its most extravagant. She had brought into her novel every personage known in society, including members of her own family and her husband, William Lamb, who afterwards became Lord Melbourne. She had given him an excellent character, and attributed noble actions to him, but she had been less benevolent to many others. As the names were fictitious, there was much discussion as to the persons whom she had proposed to describe. At this ball at Uxbridge House I saw her hanging lovingly on her husband's arm and distributing the key to her characters, to use her own phrase, with great liberality. She had been careful to have a number of copies printed in which the fictitious and the real names stood face to face, and these were names belonging to visitors present, or to their relations and friends. This scene completed the extraordinary nature of this remarkable entertainment.

I very soon abandoned London life: apart from its wearisome nature, I was very ill. I had brought back from Genoa a kind of rheumatism in the head, which was only cured four years later by the waters of Aix, and which made me unable to take any part in fatiguing amusements.

Hence I felt no regret at my inability to be present at the festivities in France upon the occasion of the marriage of the Duc de Berry. The accounts which reached us described these festivities as magnificent, as far as the distress prevailing throughout the country would allow. They had been more animated than might have been expected under such painful circumstances. The majority of those called to partake in them belonged to a class of people who regard the court as necessary to complete their existence. Should some circumstance of disfavour or politics withdraw them from its atmosphere, they feel that something has gone from their lives. The events of the Revolution had prevented many of them from participating in court festivals; they thus displayed the animation of newcomers and the zeal of neophytes, pretending gaiety even if it was not entirely heartfelt.

I do not know how much the public shared these joys; I was absent, and reports were contradictory. The only story that has remained in my memory is a saying of the Prince de Poix on the day of the meeting at Fontainebleau: The Duc de Maillé, addressing a group of courtiers who were coming out of the apartments with him, observed, "Do you know, gentlemen, that our new Princess has one eye smaller than the other?"

"I did not notice anything of the kind," said the Prince de Poix rapidly, but after a few seconds' reflection he added, "Possibly the left eye of the Duchesse de Berry is a little larger than the right." This reply is too classical of its kind to be omitted.

To return to London. I hardly ever left the interior of the embassy, to which we had eventually attracted some intimate friends, except to visit some colleagues in the diplomatic body, or to go to the house of Ministers and to the court when my presence was indispensable.

I had paid my respects at court when I arrived for a visit in Paris, but I had not seen the Duchesse de Berry, whose condition had obliged her to remain at home. I saw her for the first time at a ball given by the Duke of Wellington, and she looked far better than I had expected. Though small, her figure was pleasing; her arms, hands, neck, and shoulders were of dazzling whiteness and graceful form; her complexion was beautiful, and her head was adorned with a mass of fair hair of lovely shades. The whole rested upon two of the smallest feet that could be seen. When she was amused or when she grew animated in conversation the defect of her eyes was hardly visible, and I should not have noticed it if I had not known it beforehand. Her condition prevented her from dancing, but she walked about the room several times on her husband's arm. She had neither grace nor dignity. She walked badly, with her feet turned inwards, but the feet were so pretty that their mistakes might be pardoned, and her excessive youth atoned for her awkwardness. Upon the whole, I thought her admirable. Her husband seemed greatly attached to her, as also were the Comte d'Artois and the Duchesse d'Angoulême.

As for the Duc d'Angoulême, he was so uncomfortable in a drawing-room that as soon as he had entered his one desire was to get out. He never stayed more than a quarter of an hour, and only put in an appearance when his presence was required.

The Duchesse de Berry had arrived in France in a state of complete and total ignorance. She could hardly read. Masters were provided for her, and she might have profited by their instruction, as she had plenty of ability and a taste for the fine arts. But no one treated her reasonably. While they attempted to teach her to murder pieces on the piano or to spoil sheets of paper, they never thought of teaching her her duty as a Princess. Her husband looked upon her as a child, and took pleasure in spoiling her. The King showed her no serious attention, and Monsieur was merely affable, as usual. The Duchesse d'Angoulême was the only person who tried to guide her, and this she did with the acerbity of a governess.

At first the Duchesse de Berry was afraid of her, and speedily detested her. The Duchesse d'Angoulême was soon aware of these feelings, which the Duc de Berry hardly attempted to check. While doing justice to the virtues of his sister-in-law, he cared nothing for her. Moreover, as he was leading a somewhat immoral life, he did not wish to vex his wife, and attempted by his kindness to atone for the wrongs he had committed elsewhere. It was a bad arrangement for both parties, for the little Princess eventually became sulky and tyrannical. Her husband continually told her that she need do only what pleased and amused her, that she need not put herself out for anybody, and that she might laugh at what people said. Of all the lessons that were showered upon her, this was the one which she learnt the most readily and which she hardly ever forgot.

It was curious to see her holding her court, giggling with her ladies and speaking to no one. Any boarding-school girl would have performed the ceremony with greater dignity, yet I insist that there was
good material in the Duchesse de Berry, and a clever hand might have
brought it out. Nothing about her was suitable, except perhaps the
Duchesse de Reggio, her lady of honour. She, however, had no influence. This nomination did credit to the good judgement of the Duc de
Berry and to the wisdom of the King.

She was the wife of Marshal Oudinot,* and represented the Imperial Régime at the new court with such propriety and dignity that
no one ventured to regret her appointment, though court nominations
aroused the special envy of the Royalist party, who regarded them as
their exclusive property. The Duchesse must have had great dignity
and good sense to establish her position in an environment which was
quite new and entirely hostile. She had succeeded without any help,
for Marshal Oudinot, a brave soldier if ever there was one, could do
nothing but smoke and gamble, romp with the children, and run into
debt. His wife, therefore, had to think for both of them, and she did
this with success. It should be added that the Marshal had grown-up
children by a first wife, whose affection the second wife had entirely
gained.

He would have been very glad to see his wife secure some influence
over the Duchesse de Berry, but this did not happen. The Duchesse de
Reggio inspired her with respect, and she had recourse to her to repair
her stupidities, but they bored one another. The Duchesse de Berry
had no confidence in her, and as the conduct of the former became more
dubious, the latter held more aloof.

I had proposed to remain only a few weeks in Paris, but a family
event detained me longer than I had intended to stay. I had found my
brother deeply attracted by Mlle. Destillières. We had known her
from her early childhood; she was a charming girl, and my mother
doted on her. It seems that from her earliest years she had said she
would marry only M. d'Osmond.

The death of her parents had left her heiress to a great fortune and mistress of her own future. The best matches in France became suitors for her hand, and my brother had not thought of entering the lists. But she made such advances that he fell genuinely in love with her and joined the battalions of suitors, though with some shyness. She did not leave him unnoticed for long and authorised him in a short time to request my father to formally ask for her hand in marriage from an uncle, M. de Bongard, who was her guardian, but from whom she was independent. This uncle had cherished the idea that she would remain single so that he could continue to manage her fortune. This situation was so agreeable to him that he desired it to continue for an indefinite period. Consequently, far from trying to oppose the objections which Mlle. Destillières had raised to matches previously proposed, he tried to increase them by hinting to her, through persons attached to his interests, that her health was very delicate, and that marriage would be consequently impossible for her.

Hence, when the official letter from my father was handed to him by a common friend, M. de Bongard very politely returned an absolute refusal, and informed his niece of the request and of his answer, which had been based, as usual, upon the belief that she did not wish to marry.

"You are wrong, Uncle. I did not want to marry the others, but I do want to marry M. d'Osmond."

M. de Bongard was greatly staggered. He was obliged to withdraw his refusal, but did his best to delay the marriage. Either he flattered himself that some circumstance might arise to break off the engagement, or he required a long interval to make up the accounts of his stewardship, which had been kept with incredible carelessness; in any case, he exhausted every pretext to gain time. The young people, on the other hand, were in a great hurry, and begged me to stay on from day to day, asserting that my departure would provide M. de Bongard with an additional argument for delaying the marriage. He succeeded, however, in his designs, for though the marriage was arranged for the month of February, and rearranged for the 1st, the 10th, and the 20th of each succeeding month, it did not take place until December.

Though the marriage of Mlle. Destillières was the most interesting event of this period for me, I still continued to pay attention to public affairs, and was astounded one morning to learn that King Louis XVIII was very ill. For the moment his health gave rise to keen anxiety.

The Chamber of Deputies was discussing the election law.[2] The Princes were directly opposed to the Government, as the Cabinet was then composed of reasonable people. The Duc de Berry was fomenting opposition to the law, and at one of his evening parties openly canvassed for supporters. The King was informed of the fact, sent for him, and soundly berated him. The Duc de Berry complained to his sister-in-law. They discussed their common grievances and whipped themselves into a fury in the process; at length, in the evening after dinner, Monsieur proceeded to expound their views to the King in no uncertain terms. The King replied with vigour. Madame and the Duc de Berry intervened, and the quarrel rose to such a pitch that Monsieur declared he would leave the court with his children. The King replied that there were fortresses for rebellious Princes. Monsieur answered that the Charter did not provide for state prisons—the unfortunate Charter being constantly invoked by those who hated it most bitterly—and on these friendly terms they parted.

The Duc d' Angoulême had been the only member of the family to keep silence. His respect for his father balanced his respect for the King, so that he would not have felt justified in pronouncing in favour of either party. Once their anger had subsided, they all regretted the violence of their language. The poor King wept when he told his Ministers of the scene in the evening. He had, however, been so shaken that he was unable to digest his dinner. An attack of gout in the stomach occurred; his breathing almost failed entirely in the night, and he was ill for several days afterwards. His family seized the opportunity for a display of affection which he pretended to believe in order to gain a little

2. The result of the discussion was that the electors had to be thirty years old and pay three hundred francs in direct taxation in order to vote. To be a candidate, one had to pay one thousand francs in direct taxation.

peace, but for which he really cared very little. The public was just as aware as the King of the opposition which the Princes had offered, and the jest of the moment was to call the black balls in the ballot box the prunes of Monsieur.

My relations with Princess Charlotte of Wales began in 1817. Under pretext that her house was not ready, she had determined to stay away from London. Though this was the time when social functions were at their height, she remained under the cool shade of the trees at Clare-mont, which she said was a better place for her in view of her condi-tion. My parents were invited to come and dine with her, and I was included in the invitation. My curiosity concerning the young future sovereign of a great country had been stimulated by numerous disap-pointments, as hitherto I had always missed seeing her.

We were met at Claremont by Lady Glenbervie, the Princess's lady, and by a German baron, the Prince's aide-de-camp, who was the only other inmate of the house. A number of guests had preceded us, and others were following. Prince Leopold appeared in our midst and then retired. After waiting a very long time we heard a loud and echo-ing step in the neighbouring rooms, which I can only compare with the tramp of a drum-major. People around me said, "Here is the Princess."

I then saw her come in on her husband's arm. She was in full dress and looked well, but was evidently anxious to imitate the Great Eliza-beth with the intentionally heavy step and the haughty carriage of her head. As she entered the drawing-room on one side, a butler appeared on the other to announce dinner. She merely walked across the room without speaking to anybody. When she reached the dining-room, she called two Ambassadors to her side, and the Prince sat down op-posite between the Ambassadors' wives. After vainly attempting to see him by leaning to the right and left of a centrepiece, the Princess summoned up her courage and had the ornament carried away from the middle of the table.

The clouds which had gathered upon her brow lifted to some de-gree. She smiled graciously at her husband, but was little more than courteous to the others. Her neighbours were able to extract but few words from her. I had full leisure to examine her during the progress of a somewhat bad dinner. Of her figure I can say nothing. All that could be seen was that she was tall and strongly built. Her hair was fair almost to the point of whiteness, and her eyes were porcelain blue; her eyelashes and eyebrows were invisible, and her complexion was uniformly white, without colour. The reader may cry, "What insipidity! It must have been a very inexpressive face." Nothing of the kind. I have rarely observed a face of greater alertness and mobility; her look was most expressive. Her red lips, showing teeth white as pearls, formed a mouth which was the most delightful that I have ever seen, while the extreme youth of her features compensated for the want of colour in her complexion, and gave her an appearance of remarkable freshness.

When dinner was over, she made a slight signal to the ladies, and we followed her into the drawing-room. She sat in a corner with one of her friends whom she had known from youth, and who was also newly married and *enceinte*; I have forgotten her name. They whispered together until the Prince and the gentlemen came in.

He found all the ladies at one end of the drawing-room, and the Princess absorbed in her boarding-school conversation. He made vain efforts to bring her into contact with her guests, placing armchairs for the Ambassadors' wives, and attempting to begin a general conversation, but his efforts were fruitless. At length the Countess Lièven, wearied by this exclusiveness, took a seat without invitation on the same sofa and began a conversation in a low tone, which was apparently not without interest, as it seemed to absorb her entire attention.

The efforts of the Prince to induce his wife to distribute her favours somewhat more impartially remained entirely useless. Everybody was impatiently awaiting the moment for departure. At length the carriages were announced and we took our leave, being dismissed as carelessly as we had been received. As for myself, I did not even receive the smallest bow when my mother introduced me to the Princess. As I got into the carriage I said:

"I wished to see her; I have seen her, and have had more than enough of it."

My mother assured me that the Princess was usually more polite, and I was bound to admit that the anxiety of the Prince supported her statement. Probably he reproached her for her bad manners, for a few days afterwards, when we were regretfully anticipating the necessary call to express our thanks for the obliging reception which we had received, a fresh invitation arrived. Upon this occasion the Princess went to great trouble to show an equal amount of attention to her guests, but her special favour was reserved for us. She kept us with her until midnight, talking familiarly of everybody and everything, of France and England, of the reception of the Orléans family in Paris, of their connection with the Tuileries, of her own relations with Windsor, of the manners of the old Queen, of the etiquette which she could not endure, and of the weariness which awaited her when it would be necessary to open her London house and spend some months in the capital.

My mother pointed out to her that she would be much more comfortable than in the residence she had occupied at the time of her marriage.

"That is true," she said, "but when one is so entirely happy as myself, one fears a change even for the better." With such confidence did the poor Princess look forward to continued happiness. The same evening she said she was certain she would have a boy, since her every wish had always been realised.

The conversation turned upon Claremont and its gardens. I knew them of old, for M. de Boigne had been on the verge of buying this residence. Princess Charlotte assured us that it had been greatly altered in the last twelve years, and begged us to come one morning in order to look around. A day was arranged, subject to the weather; should that day prove inconvenient, we were to come as soon as the weather and my father's business would allow. She no longer went out except for a walk in the Park, and from two to four o'clock we should always find her delighted to see us.

We separated after reiterated handshakes, delivered with a violence that nearly dislocated the arm, and accompanied by protestations of affection uttered in a voice that was naturally sweet and would have been pleasant if the memoirs of the sixteenth century had not informed us that Queen Elizabeth's conversation was loud and curt. I will not deny that Princess Charlotte appeared infinitely more amiable and more beautiful than at the preceding dinner. Prince Leopold was more at his ease, and seemed to be enjoying the success of his admonitions.

On the morning fixed for our visit to the park of Claremont it was raining in torrents. We were obliged to put off our visit for a few days, and when we arrived the temper of Princess Charlotte had undergone yet another change. She received us more than coldly, excused herself by saying that her condition only allowed her to walk a few steps, and called a German aide-de-camp to show us around the gardens which she was to have displayed to us with so much pleasure; in short, she was obviously most anxious to be rid of our company. When we had reached the far end of the park we saw her in the distance giving her arm to Prince Leopold and running like a greyhound. She made a wide circuit and then came up to us. This studied and almost audacious rudeness had shocked us so much that we were ready to treat her with equal coldness.

But the wind had changed. She told us that Leopold had forced her to come out, that the exercise had done her good and made her better able to enjoy the company of her friends. She was as gracious and as kind as anyone could be. She particularly attached herself to me, as I was a better walker than my mother, took my arm, dragging me after her with long strides, and began to speak confidentially of the happiness of her household and of the great gratitude which she owed to Prince Leopold for his willingness to marry the heiress to a kingdom. She drew with much gaiety, archness, and wit a picture of the position of the "Queen's husband," but she added with emphasis, "My Leopold shall not be exposed to that humiliation, or my name is not Charlotte," and here she stamped on the ground with a foot which was far from small. "Should they wish to cross my will, I would rather renounce the throne and find a cottage, where I can live according to the laws of nature, in submission to my husband. I will not and cannot reign over

England except upon the condition that he shall reign over England and myself. He shall be King, recognized as such and independent of my caprices. You see, Mme. de Boigne, I know my faults: you have seen some of them, and they used to be much worse. You smile as though you thought it impossible, but upon my honour it was far worse before Leopold undertook the difficult task of making me a good girl, quiet and reasonable," she said with an enchanting smile. "Yes, he shall be King or I will never be Queen. Do not forget what I am now telling you, and you shall see that Charlotte can keep her word."

She was fond of referring to herself as Charlotte, and pronounced the name with a kind of emphasis, as though it had already acquired the celebrity which she intended for it. Our conversation was concluded beneath the portico of the house, which we had reached before the rest of the company; it was then that she uttered the phrase which I have previously quoted concerning the perfect happiness which reigned at Claremont, begging me to come often and see her. I never saw her again, and my acquaintance with the brilliant and witty heiress to the three kingdoms ended at that moment.

I had already left England, when a few weeks later death carried off in one hour two generations of sovereigns, the young mother and the son whom she had just brought into the world. Both were victims to the caprices of the Princess. Prince Leopold had been able to secure her reconciliation with her father, the Prince Regent, but all his influence could never overcome the animosity which she felt for her grandmother and her aunts. Fearing that they would be present at her confinement, she attempted to hide her condition as long as possible. Her labour, however, was so difficult that it was necessary to inform her relations. The old Queen, who had purposely been deceived by the calculations of the Princess, was at Bath, while the Prince Regent was with the Marchioness of Hertford, a hundred miles away from London. The only person with the Princess was her husband, and the physician Croft had persuaded him that there was nothing to fear from a labour which had lasted sixty hours.

The doctors who were waiting in the neighbouring rooms desired to be admitted to the chamber of the Princess. She absolutely refused, and the Prince, who was inexperienced and misled by Croft, did not venture to insist. Eventually she brought a child into the world which was perfectly healthy and had died merely from exhaustion; the exhaustion of the mother was also extreme. They put her into her bed. Croft insisted that she only needed rest, and ordered everyone out of the room. An hour afterwards her nurse heard her calling weakly:

"Fetch my husband," she said, and expired.

The Prince, who was lying on a sofa in the next room, could not be sure that he had received her last breath. His grief was such as can only be imagined, for he had lost everything in the world.

I do not know whether the character of Princess Charlotte would have promised an equally happy future for him. At that moment she was under the influence of an affection which made her passionately devoted to him, and showered kindness upon him with a love that was increased by the innate reserve of her character. He was taming her, if the expression may be used. The care which he took to soften this rough nature, now dominated by love, must have been very striking, as long as it was followed by success. At the same time, it was obvious that he was obliged to be careful lest he frighten her, and he certainly felt that the young tigress might remember that she possessed claws.

I may be allowed to doubt whether the young Princess would always have appealed to the law of natural rights, which subjects a wife to the authority of her husband. However, at the time when she assured me of this she entirely believed it, and possibly the Prince believed it also. Probably after he lost her he remembered nothing but the fine qualities of his noble wife. It is certain that when she wished to please she was extremely attractive. Notwithstanding all her caprices, her popularity in England was indescribable; she was the daughter of her country. From her earliest childhood she had been brought up as the heiress to the throne, and she knew so instinctively the means by which to win the national favour that she was almost an incarnation of the national prejudices.

The zeal with which she carried on her opposition to her father had made her most careful in her expenditure and exactly punctual in her payments. When she went into a London shop and the salesman tried to tempt her by some expensive novelty, she would reply:

"Do not show me that; it is too expensive for me."

A hundred newspapers repeated the phrase, and praised the sentiment the more loudly as it was a criticism directed at the extravagance of the Prince Regent. Claremont was itself proof of that simplicity of life of which the Princess was careful to set the example. Nothing could be less elaborate than the furniture. In the whole house the only mirrors were that of her dressing-table and a small oval mirror two feet by three hung across a corner of the drawing-room. The furniture was in harmony with the decorations. Even now I can see the large four-poster bed of the Princess. The curtains hung straight down without loops, fringes, or ornamentation; they were of flowered chintz lined with pink cambric. There was no superfluous luxury in this room, where the duplicate furniture, intended more for use than for ornament, displayed the intimacy of marriage according to the custom of the country. This extreme simplicity in the house of a young and charming woman contrasted strongly with the exquisite magnificence and almost exaggerated luxury which surrounded the Prince Regent at Carlton House and Brighton; the contrast inevitably aroused his dissatisfaction. This was not diminished by the fact that the Princess was known to be generous, and ready to give to the deserving poor what she refused to her own caprices. She had assuredly admirable qualities and a love of glory very rare at her age and in her position. Her death spread consternation throughout England, and when I came back in December the entire population from the post-boys to the street sweepers were in mourning, and continued to wear it for six months. Dr. Croft became the object of public execration, was eventually driven out of his mind, and blew out his brains.

I found the Orléans family greatly irritated by the nature of their position at court. The King never lost an opportunity of showing them some discourtesy. He attempted to adopt a different mode of behaviour towards the Duchesse d'Orléans, her husband, and her sister-in-law, apparently based upon the title of "royal highness" which she bore. But he really intended to provoke the two latter personages whom he did not like. As long as the emigration had lasted he had defended the Duc d'Orléans against the hatred of the Royalist party, but after his return to France he had himself adopted the exaggerations of the party. In particular after the events at Lille in 1815[3] he persecuted the Prince with untiring animosity. The d'Orléans family had been excluded from the royal pew in the chapel of the palace, from the royal box at the theatre, and in short from every mark of royal distinction. Eventually, at a public ceremony in Notre-Dame, Louis XVIII had ordered the cushions upon which the Duc d'Orléans and Mademoiselle were kneeling to be moved and put outside the carpet, upon which they had no right to place themselves.

Only a Prince can appreciate how these little insults may wound the feelings of others. The Duc d'Orléans himself told me what had happened upon the occasion of the birth of the Duc de Berry's child, which only lived a few hours. The birth certificate was drawn up and brought by the Chancellor to the King's study, where the whole family and part of the court were gathered. The Chancellor gave the pen to the King to sign, then to Monsieur and Madame, the Duc d'Angoulême, and the Duc de Berry. When the turn of the Duc d'Orléans came, the King cried loudly, in the shrill voice which he assumed when he wished to be rude.

"Not the Chancellor, not the Chancellor; the Master of the Ceremonies."

M. de Brézé, Grand Master of the Ceremonies, who was present, came forward.

"Not M. de Brézé; the Master of the Ceremonies." The Master of the Ceremonies presented himself.

"No, no," cried the King with greater acerbity, "the Assistant Master, the Assistant Master."

3. During the Hundred Days, Louis-Philippe refused to follow the King to Ghent and took refuge in England.

Meanwhile the Duc d'Orléans stood before the table with the pen in front of him which he did not dare take, as this would have been a misdemeanour, and waited for the end of this outburst of ill-temper. There was no Assistant Master of the Ceremonies at hand, and it was necessary to send for one from the adjoining rooms. The waiting time seemed extremely long to everyone, and the other Princes were themselves much embarrassed. At length the Assistant Master arrived, and the ceremony of signature, thus tactlessly interrupted, was concluded, though the Duc d'Orléans was smarting with irritation. As he went out he said to the Duc de Berry:

"Sir, I hope you will be good enough not to expose me a second time to any similar unpleasantness."

"Upon my word, cousin, I understand you so well that I should say the same in your place."

Thereupon they shook hands cordially.

The Duc d'Orléans justly observed that if etiquette demanded this change, and if the King was anxious to secure a rigourous adherence to conventional forms, he should have arranged the matter beforehand. It mattered little to him whether the cushions were on the carpet or whether the pen was given to him by one officer or another, but the whole business looked like an attempt to humiliate him in public. These continual petty persecutions alienated and aroused the hostility of the Orléans family.

I am certain that they never began any serious conspiracy. But when they returned home wounded by this treatment, which is, I repeat, doubly wounding to Princes, and when they found themselves surrounded by the respect and the good wishes of every malcontent, they certainly did not reject these tokens of homage as vigourously as they would have if the King and the royal family had received them as relatives and friends. On the other hand, the members of the Opposition made a show of surrounding the Duc d'Orléans and proclaiming him their leader, and in my opinion he did not refuse this dangerous honour with sufficient emphasis. The part seemed to please him, and one may ask whether he regarded it as a road to the Crown. Possibly it seemed a distant prospect for his children, and was only entertained with the idea of accommodating the Legitimist principle[4] to the necessities of the age.

The ephemeral existence of the little Princesse de Berry gave rise to another vexatious occurrence. I cannot remember whether in these disjointed passages the name of M. de La Ferronnays has already occurred: it is very probable, for I was intimate with him for years.

He had always accompanied the Duc de Berry, was tenderly and sincerely devoted to him, and able to tell him the truth; he sometimes told it with undue excitement, but always with a friendly frankness which the Prince was able to appreciate. Relations between them were on a footing of the most perfect intimacy. M. de La Ferronnays, after reproaching the Duc de Berry for his foolish actions, did his best to avert as many of them as he could, and spent his life in palliating the rest and hushing them up whenever possible. He had vainly hoped that the Prince would settle down after his marriage, but he seemed rather to redouble the scandalous nature of his private intimacies. M. de La Ferronnays had never given the smallest assistance in satisfying the transitory desires of the Duc de Berry. At this time he loudly proclaimed his dissatisfaction with the actions of the Duc while watching over his safety day and night, but relations between the two men became somewhat strained.

M. de La Ferronnays was First Gentleman of the Chamber in theory, and in fact absolute master of the house, where he gave orders rather than the Prince. His wife was Lady of the Bedchamber to the Duchesse de Berry and they lived in a magnificent suite of rooms in the Elysée, where they seemed to be permanently settled.

When the Duchesse de Berry was expecting her child, the choice of a governess was made. The Duc de Berry requested and secured the appointment of Mme. de Montsoreau, the mother of Mme. de La Ferronnays. It was usual for the King to give the layette to the children of the sons of France and one of great magnificence was sent. As the little

4. The *légitimistes* was the name given after the Revolution of 1830 to the supporters of Charles X and his descendants who refused to recognize Louis-Philippe.

Princess had only lived a few hours, the layette was claimed by the civil list. Mme. de Montsoreau asserted the rights of her position, which guaranteed her the "profits of the layette." She was informed that it only belonged to the governess if she had actually performed the duty, and several letters on the subject were exchanged. Eventually the disputants wrote directly to the Duc de Berry, and I believe that the King spoke to him upon the subject. He was transported with rage, sent for Mme. de Montsoreau, and scolded her so violently that she went to her room again in tears. There she found her son-in-law, and was so imprudent as to excite his anger by her complaints. He went down to the Prince. The Duc de Berry called out:

"I will not have that woman sleeping in my house."

"You forget that 'that woman' is my mother-in-law."

Nothing more was heard, for the door was shut upon them. Three minutes afterwards M. de La Ferronnays came out of the room, ran into his own apartments, ordered his wife to pack up and immediately left the Elysée, to which he never returned. I have never been able to learn precisely what transpired during that short conversation, but the breach was complete, and every member of the royal family retained a dislike for M. de La Ferronnays, who survived the Duc de Berry and even the overthrow of the throne.

I was never able to extract from either M. de La Ferronnays or the Duc de Berry any answer other than that they must not speak of it. If M. de La Ferronnays lost an excellent position, the Duc de Berry lost a real friend, a much more difficult loss to repair. The conduct of M. de La Ferronnays was irreproachable, since he was both modest and dignified. He was without means, and obliged to support a numerous family. M. de Richelieu, who was always ready to listen to any demand that seemed honourable, considered his case, and appointed him Minister in Denmark.

When he informed the Duc de Berry of his choice, the latter merely replied, "I offer no objection." The other Princes were much displeased, and this nomination added to their dislike of M. de Richelieu, the more so as shortly afterwards M. de La Ferronnays was appointed

Ambassador to Saint Petersburg. Delight at his retirement from court counterbalanced to some degree the vexation that was felt at his good fortune. We shall meet him again as Minister of Foreign Affairs, when he continued to enjoy the displeasure of the Tuileries.

The Duchesse de Berry was expecting another child, and was therefore obliged to fill the place of Mme. de Montsoreau. The Duc de Berry demanded Mme. de Gontaut* as governess for his children. This choice surprised everybody, and scandalised those who had been wit-nesses of Mme. de Gontaut's early years, but we must hasten to add that she fully justified her appointment.

The education of Mademoiselle was as perfect as she could make it, and it would have been very fortunate for the Duc de Bordeaux if she had been solely responsible for his education. Mme. de Gontaut lived for a long time with Monsieur and his son, but her political opinions never became high-flown or intolerant. The customs acquired by liv-ing almost exclusively in English society, together with her wise and enlightened intellect, had enabled her to avoid the prejudices of the *émigré* party. Her special favour at the moment with the Duc de Berry came from the fact that she helped to conceal from his young wife the indiscreet rumours which disturbed their household.

The Duchesse de Berry was extremely jealous, and although the Prince would not give up his habits, he was too kindhearted at bottom not to be most anxious to make his wife happy and to keep the peace in his own house. He was infinitely grateful to Mme. de Gontaut, who replaced Mme. de La Ferronnays, for the moment as Lady of the Bed-chamber, for her efforts to maintain domestic peace.

Prince Castelcicala had blunted the early jealousies of the Du-chesse de Berry. He used to repeat, with his Italian gestures, in the most ridiculous manner, a conversation when in answer to her lamen-tations and her fury he had assured her that all men had mistresses, that their wives knew it and were perfectly satisfied; this was pronounced so decisively that she did not venture to rebel against conditions which he asserted to be universal, the only exception being the Duc d'Angoulême.

The Duchesse was too much of a Neapolitan to have cared by any means for such a husband. She had made particular inquiries concerning the Duc d'Orléans, and Prince Castelcicala did not hesitate to reply:

"Most certainly, Madame; for whom do you take him?"

"And my aunt knows it?"

"Undoubtedly, Madame; the Duchesse d'Orléans is too clever to take offence at this point."

Notwithstanding this good advice from her Ambassador, the little Princess was constantly seized with fits of jealousy, and Mme. de Gontaut was useful to both calm her and keep from her ears such revelations as indiscretion or malice might have disclosed. She continued to play this part as long as the Duc de Berry was alive.

The Comtesse Juste de Noailles was personally appointed Lady of the Bedchamber by the Duc de Berry, who asked her to accept the post. This nomination was generally approved, and no one seemed more likely to fill such a position with dignity and propriety.

The eminently perfect tact of Mme. de Noailles compensated for her want of intellectual power, while her politeness always made her very popular, though she had been in succession Lady to the Empresses Joséphine and Marie-Louise and Lady of the Bedchamber to the Duchesse de Berry; the latter never regarded her as a favourite, though she always treated her with much respect.

I omitted at the proper time to mention the death of Mme. de Staël; this took place during one of my absences in England, after a long illness, during which she went out as long as possible into that Parisian society which she so keenly appreciated. It was painful to see her at the beginning of an evening party. She would arrive exhausted by her sufferings, but in a short time intellect would entirely overpower instinct, and she was as brilliant as ever, as if she had wished to show to the end that inimitable superiority in which she was unrivalled. The last time that I saw her was in the morning, and I was going away the next day. For several days she had been unable to leave her sofa, and livid spots covered her face, her arms, and her hands, clear symptoms of blood decomposition. I was painfully aware of the thought of an ever-lasting farewell, yet she spoke only about her future projects. She was busy looking for a house where her daughter, the Duchesse de Broglie, who was expecting her confinement, would be better lodged. She was making plans for the following winter, and saying that she wished to be at home more often and to give dinners more frequently. She even mentioned by name the guests who would be regular. Possibly she was attempting to deceive herself; in any case, the contrast between this dying figure and these words of hope was heartrending, and I left her greatly saddened.

There was too big an age difference and certainly one of intellectual power between us to enable me to boast of a friendship with Mme. de Staël in the true sense of the word; but she had been extremely kind to me, and I was greatly flattered. Her manner of enlivening a party was precisely that which especially pleased me, because it was in perfect conformity with my own idle inclinations. Mme. de Staël could enliven a circle of guests without ever rising from her sofa. Intellectual vigour is as agreeable to me as physical exercise is burdensome. When I am obliged to look for pleasure out-of-doors, I risk losing it in the course of the search. Though my grief at the death of Mme. de Staël was not heartrending, it was nonetheless sincere. The sorrow of her children was overwhelming. They loved her passionately, and the revelation which she made during her last hours, of which I have already spoken, in no way diminished their affection or their regret.

Auguste de Staël undertook the publication of the book on which she was working,[5] which appeared in the spring of 1818. It produced an effect which was not without important results. Under the Empire, the Revolution of 1793 and its major players were in disgrace. The Restoration did not restore their credit, and no one would claim the dangerous honour of having worked to overthrow the throne of Louis XVI. It would have been vain to look in France for a man willing to admit any participation in this work. The regicides themselves made

5. *Considérations sur les principaux évènements de la Révolution Française.*

excuses for their action, saying that a purely fortuitous circumstance had driven them to the precipice, and that upon the whole the only guilty party was the *Little Cat*[6]—possibly because he was not in a position to explain his conduct.

Mme. de Staël's book entirely changed current opinion upon this subject by boldly speaking in honourable terms of the Revolution and of the revolutionaries. She began by distinguishing principles from actions, and differentiating between the thwarted hopes of honourable people and the atrocious crimes which stained these fatal days and obliterated in blood all the reforms with which they had thought to endow their country. She thus rehabilitated the title of "revolutionary": formerly it had been a deep insult, now it became almost an honour. The Opposition did not reject it. The Liberals recognised themselves as the successors of the revolutionaries, and retraced their parentage to 1779. MM. de La Fayette,* d'Argenson, de Thiard, de Chauvelin, de Girardin, et cetera, et cetera, formed connecting links. The Lameth family, though they claimed the title of patriots of '89, and were disowned by the *émigrés* and the Restoration, did not join the anti-Royalist opposition. They remained moderate Liberals, after serving the Emperor with much less zeal than those whose names I have just quoted.

In my opinion, this posthumous work of Mme. de Staël was an ominous gift to the country, which contributed in reviving that revolutionary spirit which afterwards took hold of the young generation, with the fatal results that we have seen. As soon as Mme. de Staël's book had set the example, panegyrics upon 1789 poured forth continually. Very few minds retained sufficient balance to extract the good grain from amid these bloodstained tares, and thus the figures of the Revolution, even including that of Robespierre, were sanctified.

The third volume was almost entirely written by Benjamin Constant; the difference in style and especially in thought is obvious. It is more bitterly republican, and the aristocratic leanings which were al-

6. Nickname given to Robespierre.

ways visible beneath Mme. de Staël's democratic tendencies have disappeared.

A malignant fever from which I nearly died kept me confined to my
room for several weeks. I left it to nurse my sister-in-law, who had had
a miscarriage and was causing us considerable anxiety, apart from our
disappointment. As soon as she had recovered her health I returned to
London.

It might be thought that after the triumph of Aix-la-Chapelle[7] the
President of the Council would return to Paris with supreme power.
It was not so: the two oppositions from the Right and Left drew together for the purpose of minimising this success, while the Ministerial party under the influence of M. Decazes took little trouble to give
that success the importance it deserved. M. de Richelieu was the least
competent of men to fully use his triumph, while M. Decazes was an
expert in the art of using it. As it stood, he did not wish to do so, an
attitude due to intrigues within the Ministry. M. Decazes had joined
the semi-Liberal party, which has since produced the wing of the
party known as the doctrinaires.[8] This party had long been inveighing
against the Ministry of Police, and persuaded M. Decazes that if he reformed this Ministry after the withdrawal of the foreigners, it would
seem as though he had only been appointed to act at a critical moment,
and that the King would position himself to secure all the popularity
from this action. M. Decazes was ready to consider the idea, though
under normal circumstances he would remain an influential Minister.
He spoke of it to M. de Richelieu, who adopted the idea. M. Lainé,

7. The Allies organised the congress of Aix-la-Chapelle, from September 29 to Novem-
ber 21, 1818, to discuss the French proposal of putting an early end to their military occupation of France. The evacuation started promptly and the Duc de Richelieu, representing the French government, was then asked to join the Alliance.
8. The doctrinaires founded a political party opposed to both the extreme Royalists, or
Ultras, and the Liberals. They refused to accept the principle of royalty by divine right
but affirmed that the King had the right to govern effectively. "The throne is not an
empty armchair" summed up their convictions.

Minister of the Interior, was constantly proclaiming his disinterestedness, his want of ambition, and his weariness of public business.

M. de Richelieu, who had perfect confidence in M. Lainé and in his words at this time, went to him with his usual straightforwardness and asked him to hand over his portfolio to M. Decazes, who wanted it. M. Lainé was furious at the proposal, and the Duc de Richelieu, with the usual clumsiness of his loyal candour, informed M. Decazes that his idea must be abandoned because M. Lainé would not hear of it. He fully recognised the advisability of abolishing a special Ministry of Police, and admitted the difficulty of maintaining the ministry as explained by M. Decazes, but he said that some other means of suppressing it must be found. After this extraordinary manner of satisfying M. Decazes and M. Lainé, he went off to Aix-la-Chapelle with full confidence in the loyalty of his colleagues. The empty nature of this trust became clear to him on his return.

I have no clear knowledge of the intrigues which were carried on, or of the affronts by which he was surrounded, but at the end of a year he resigned, as also did MM. Pasquier, Molé, Lainé, and Corvetto. General Dessolle became the ostensible leader of the new Government, which was in reality guided by M. Decazes. I could never understand why M. Decazes failed to recognise that the veil of purity with which the presidency of M. de Richelieu covered his favouritism was necessary to maintain his credibility. Only under the protection of this noble and transparent aegis could he make headway against the hatred of which he was the object. M. de Richelieu never envied his favoured position, and allowed him all the power which he enjoyed, all the importance, all the profits, and also all the weariness; for it was not a matter of mere amusement to keep an old valetudinarian monarch good-humoured when the domestic peace of his household was disturbed.

The news of M. de Richelieu's retirement was not expected by my father, and was a serious blow to him. The important business of the embassy was conducted between them by means of confidential letters which did not go through the office. My father had no personal connection with M. Dessolle, and could not continue a similar corre-

spondence with him. He received from the new Minister a letter intended for general circulation in the politest of terms, which informed
him with many compliments that the policy of the Government had
changed. My father was already anxious to follow his chief into retirement, and this letter decided him. He replied that his task had been
accomplished. Like the Duc de Richelieu, he had thought it his duty
to remain at the post until the complete withdrawal of the foreign
troops, since negociations in progress should be conducted by the
same people as much as possible; however, as a new era with new
views seemed about to open, he would take advantage of the opportunity to request that relief to which his age entitled him.

My mother and I were delighted by this decision. I hated diplomatic life, and my mother could not bear to be separated from my
brother. Moreover, we observed that my father was growing unable to
deal with the work which he had so conscientiously performed. His
powers of judgement remained unimpaired, but we noticed that his
memory was failing. When a man has been out of business between
ages thirty and sixty, and then returns to work, he either mismanages
his duties or is crushed by them. My father's was the latter case.

M. Dessolle replied, begging him to reconsider his decision, but
he insisted. He said he had no intention of refusing his support to the
King's Government, but he believed that a new appointment would
be able to deal better with the English Government than a man who
seemed bound to contradict himself. Negociations, for instance, had
been opened to induce the King of the Netherlands to expel from Belgium the nest of conspirators who sent out pamphlets, and the agitators who disturbed the kingdom. M. Decazes attached the greatest
importance to the success of these negociations, and spoke of them
daily to the Duc de Richelieu, whom he persuaded to enlist the good
offices of the English Government. On the other hand, one of the
first duties of Dessolle's Ministry was to send a letter of thanks to the
Dutch King for the noble hospitality he had extended to those refugees, who would soon, it was hoped, reestablish their powers and
their talents for the service of their country. A copy of this letter was

shown to my father by Lord Castlereagh* in answer to a note written in the spirit of the earlier policy. This action was perhaps prudent, but a new negociator was required to conduct a new policy.

Another letter then arrived from M. Dessolle, who now seemed more inclined than before to follow in the footsteps of his predecessor. My father had announced his intended retirement in London, and would not change his mind, notwithstanding the kindly protests of the Regent and his Ministers. The Marquis de La Tour Maubourg was appointed to take his place. With his invariable straightforwardness, my father immediately did his best to smooth the path of the new Ambassador and to make his diplomatic and social position as easy as possible. M. de La Tour Maubourg, who was also a keen Loyalist, was deeply touched by this action, and has always remained profoundly grateful.

My father added another service to these kindnesses. When he had returned to Paris and had no personal interest in the matter, he explained clearly that the London embassy was insufficiently funded, and secured the addition of sixty thousand francs to the salary of his successor. If M. de La Tour Maubourg was touched by my father's action, M. Dessolle, on the other hand, was irritated by his return; M. Decazes was also wounded because he thought that my father's action had perturbed the King's favour towards him. The favourite was not entirely wrong. The retirement of a man as respected as my father, who had hitherto pursued the same policy, might be interpreted as a breach of friendly relations. Notwithstanding the extreme moderation of my father's language and that of his family, the enemies of M. Decazes immediately seized upon this pretext and turned it to account against him.

Some weeks had elapsed during which the discussions between my father and the Ministry were in progress. Although his resignation had immediately followed that of M. de Richelieu, it was not accepted until the end of January 1819. I immediately set off for Paris to prepare a house for the family.

I found the King highly exasperated, and asserting that hitherto he had believed himself to be represented by Ambassadors who acted in his name, but that the Marquis d'Osmond preferred to represent only M. de Richelieu. It will be observed that the author of the Charter had not entirely thrown off the temper of his ancestor, Louis XIV, and Louis XVIII was speaking in the language of Versailles. He would probably have appreciated my father's action better if it had been agreeable to his favourite.

The latter in any case received me with a kindness the sincerity of which I have reason to doubt. Though my father had been overwhelmed with compliments throughout the conduct of his embassy, he not only received no mark of satisfaction upon his retirement, but had much trouble in securing the retirement pension which was indisputably his right, the pretext being that no funds were available. In any case, he was not the only man to endure the *ben servire e non gradire*: the retiring Ministers, and especially M. de Richelieu, reaped a rich harvest of ingratitude at court, in the Chambers, and in public opinion.

Monsieur and Madame treated me with more than usual kindness when I went to pay my respects upon my arrival from London. The Duc de Berry attempted to force an admission from me that my father was abandoning the party because he saw it in the hands of the Jacobins. I declined to be forced, and emphasised his age which required rest, the advisability of retiring when the task of liberating France had been accomplished, and my mother's health. The Prince persisted in vain and displayed some small vexation, though he was no less friendly than usual. As for the rest, when they saw that our attitude was not one of opposition, and that my father voted with the Ministry in the Chamber of Peers, they ceased their affability and resumed their habitual coldness of demeanour.

My mother had fallen dangerously ill at Dover, and caused us much anxiety. At length she was able to make the crossing, and we were united at Paris, to our great satisfaction. My father began to feel that want of occupation which always affects men when they retire from an active life. His sound sense and admirable character speedily triumphed over these feelings. No one is more likely to feel regrets of this nature than an Ambassador when he retires to private life. His social connections are broken, he is a stranger to the influential personages of his country, he no longer has that intimate knowledge of petty details which occupies the attention of men in power—for they gossip as much as we do; he is accustomed to lay stress upon social distinctions, and these are suddenly withdrawn. In my opinion, there is no situation more disagreeable, and none in which the chief actor can so entirely play the part of the donkey loaded with relics, none in which every mark of distinction is so dissociated from all esteem and from all considerations of personal merit.

I am aware that there is a general theory that a diplomatic career is the most pleasant of all, especially when the rank of Ambassador is reached. My acquaintance with the career is confined to its ambassadorial stage, and I pronounce it detestable. A man may work all night to report his accomplishments of the day, may succeed in a difficult and complicated negociation, often hampered by clumsy instructions from him, but the credit of the success goes to the Minister. Ambiguous despatches have allowed his Ambassador to guess his intentions, expressed with sufficient obscurity to enable him to disavow the negociations if they should fail. On the other hand, if failure is the result, the Minister shrugs his shoulders and the Ambassador is pronounced to be wanting in tact, and as secrecy is the first law of the trade, self-justification is impossible.

I have seen a diplomatic career under the most pleasant conditions—when my father occupied an embassy of first importance, enjoyed the complete confidence of his own Government, and was in high favour with the London authorities. Nevertheless I emphatically repeat that it is one of the least agreeable professions that a man can pursue.

I can understand that a politician who might find a temporary absence suitable to his purpose might like to spend a few months at a foreign court in a diplomatic position. Nothing, however, is worse for the business of a country than the appointment of such Ambassadors, who do not have their hearts in their work. I admit that this kind of exile is not without its attractions. Still, it is inadvisable for a man to attach himself too permanently to these pleasures, for no other kind of absence breaks his connection with his friends and adherents more rapidly or more definitely.

We have seen M. de Serre, the first orator in the Chamber, unable to secure his reelection after an ambassadorship of two years at Naples: he died of vexation as a result. It is certain that if he had spent those two years at his country seat in absolute retirement, his election would not have been contested, and his political career would have continued unbroken.

I am only speaking here of men with political ambitions; those who merely want positions and salaries will obviously prefer an embassy to retirement. But they also, if their absence is prolonged, will return at the close of their career to end a life devoid of interest in their native land. They will be strangers to their own families, deprived of all friendship, and possessing none of those habits which can replace the tastes of youth when old age arrives. The more intimate the social life of the country to which an Ambassador belongs, the more striking are these disadvantages. The fact is especially true of Frenchmen, who live in cliques which are formed more by community of taste than by connections of rank or family. No tie can be stronger, and yet none can be more fragile; it is a tie that can last forever or be broken by a trifle, and one that is hardly ever proof against a long absence. Affection may remain, but mutual understanding has disappeared. Great delights are anticipated from the first meeting, and yet there is often coldness, for there is no unity of language or of interests. Common sympathies are nonexistent, for the tie has been broken.

Frenchmen are so well aware of this social tendency that our diplomats are always anxious to revisit their native society at frequent intervals, and thus keep in touch with it. Hence, of all Europeans the French diplomats are those who reside least regularly at the courts to which they are accredited. These were reflections which came home to me as clearly then as they do now, and I took great satisfaction in finding that my own position was unchanged.

Our resolution not to adopt a hostile attitude towards the new Ministry was checked by the decision of M. Decazes to appoint a group of sixty peers on March 6, 1819. It was not likely that I could regard this measure calmly after three years spent amid the fogs of London reviving my British education. My father insisted upon my silence, but he shared my view that this was a mortal blow to the peerage. The measure bore its fruit, and it would not be difficult to connect the destruction of the hereditary principle to the creation of enormous batches of peers, the first example being set by Decazes. The list of 1815, although numerous, possesses an entirely different character. The object then was to found an institution, not to secure a majority.

The nominations of 1819 were based on a proposal advanced by M. de Barthélémy for the revision of the electoral law. M. Decazes had himself demanded the repeal of this law a few months later. I have never been able to understand how they induced M. de Barthélémy to bell the cat.[9]

He was greatly staggered when he eventually understood the uproar which he had caused. The same thing had happened to him as Director of the Republic, and that almost without his knowledge. The shock had been more severe on that occasion, since it ended in his transportation to the inhospitable shores of Guiana. I knew him well, and I have never been able to understand these two incidents in his life. He was the most honest and upright of men, talented, a man of many acquaintances, an easy and often stimulating conversationalist. However, he was timid, cautious, and overscrupulous; he was always afraid of displeasing someone and was anxious to follow others and to seek cover behind them. No one could be more unsuited to play a leading role, and no one was less anxious to do so. Far from attaching im-

9. To do a daring or dangerous thing.

portance to the fact that he had been the fifth part of a king,[10] he was vexed by the memory.

When M. de Barthélémy's motion, as it was called, caused such a terrible explosion in the Chamber and among the public, M. Decazes was panic-stricken. He was so horrified at the uproar he had caused that he fell seriously ill. However, these are events which make a stir for the moment, but leave a more transitory impression upon the memory than perhaps they should; they often bear within themselves the germ of a catastrophe which other forgotten events nurture until some final circumstance brings the growth to blossom.

The Ministry was reorganised before the end of the year. Pasquier became Minister of Foreign Affairs. This was a return to the methods of Richelieu's Government, and my father consequently was less disposed to join the Ultra colours. M. Roy took over the finances, and M. de La Tour Maubourg the Ministry of War. In this position he displayed the same uprightness, the same honesty, and the same incapacity as he had shown in London.

My frequent journeys to England had prevented me from visiting Savoy; in the summer of 1819 I seized the opportunity to pay a visit to M. de Boigne and to take the waters at Aix. At the beginning of the winter I settled with my parents in a house which I had taken in the Rue de Bourbon.[11] There I spent the ten years which prepared and completed the fall of that Restoration for which I had so earnestly prayed and which I had seen begun with such joyous hopes.

10. Barthélémy had been one of the five Directors in 1797 who headed the government that marked the transition between the revolutionary government and that of Bonaparte.
11. Currently, rue de Lille.

CHAPTER TWO

Last Years of Louis XVIII

1820-1824

My habits and my friends ~ The Queen of Sweden's mad passion for the Duc de Richelieu ~ Mme. de La Rochejaquelein ~ The Princesse de Poix ~ Family connections of the Duc de Richelieu ~ Assassination of the Duc de Berry ~ Second Ministry of the Duc de Richelieu ~ Intrigues against him ~ His death ~ Mathieu de Montmorency ~ Last illness of Louis XVIII ~ Adroitness of Mme. du Cayla ~ The King's death ~ His funeral ~ Entry of Charles X into Paris

*H*enceforward I shall have less occasion to speak of Governments and their policies; my father's retirement diminished my interest in these matters. My desire to keep him informed had encouraged me to pay close attention to public affairs for some years. This stimulus was now wanting; my interest had been damped by the course of events, and I no longer followed their progress with the same enthusiasm. From time to time I received some special information or some secret piece of news. But I no longer took the trouble to inquire into the authenticity of the information or to trace its consequences and results. Except for the fact that I was more willing to talk of these matters than people who took no interest in them, and that I did not believe in news without examining it, I was not much more informed than the vast majority of society at large.

I was extremely pleased with the way I had arranged my life. I went out very little, but when I was away my mother received visitors, so that our salon was open every evening. Some long-standing friends came in daily, and when the hour for visitors had passed, that of conversation began and was often prolonged till late at night.

From time to time I invited people to these evening parties which had become fashionable. My invitations were verbal, and were supposed to be given to people whom I met by chance. I was, however, careful to see that chance should bring in my way those persons whom I wished to have meet one another and whom I knew would harmonise. In this way I avoided an excessive crowd and the necessity of opening my house to the bores whom courtesy obliges one to invite, and who invariably rush forward at the first sign. In the course of the winter I invited all my acquaintances to small parties, that my drawing-room might not be overcrowded. The uncertainty of an invitation made these parties more valued and gave them a special distinction.

I saw people of every shade of political opinion. The Ultras made up the majority of my invited guests, because my family and social relations brought us together. But the regulars on other days included people of every political clique. We were the Royalists of the King and not the Royalists of Monsieur, of the Restoration and not of the emigration—in short, Royalists who would, I believe, have saved the throne if the throne had been willing to listen to them. I admit, however, that we ourselves considered at that time that the Decazes Ministry had fallen too far to the Left, and was lending too kind an ear to those whose arguments chiefly served their own interests. Many people would have wished to rally around the Duc de Richelieu to counterbalance this alarming tendency. He, however, positively refused, and withdrew.

M. Decazes, who perhaps somewhat regretted his conduct towards the Duc, was working energetically to secure a decree awarding him a national recompense. But the seeds of ingratitude which had been carefully sown for several months now began to bear fruit. When attempts were made to extol those services which had been depreciated with so much trouble, sufficient energy could not be mustered to resist the ill will from both the extreme Left and the extreme Right. Instead of a unanimous vote, the national reward was disputed and discussed, and the proposal was only carried by a small majority. M. de Richelieu, who was the most disinterested of men, was deeply wounded by this. He used the sum voted by the Chambers to found a charitable institution in the town of Bordeaux. Since he was accustomed to frugality and simplicity in life, his personal income sufficed his needs.

He had entered the Foreign Office with a portmanteau as his only luggage, and he left it the same way. However, notwithstanding his modesty, he had a Frenchman's pride. He cared little that his services should be ill rewarded, but was cruelly hurt that they were not better appreciated. Hence he was profoundly disgusted with affairs, and declined to return either as leader of an Opposition or still less as head of a Government. He felt like a convict who had been freed from his chains, and was firmly resolved never to resume them. The desire to enjoy the freedom which he had secured induced him to make a tour in the south. He did not suspect the fresh persecution which he was about to encounter there.

The wife of Bernadotte had spent the winter of 1815 in Sweden. The rigour of the climate had brought out a skin disease on her face, and this kind of leprosy, together with her longing for Paris, had inspired her with such a dislike of Stockholm that she refused to stay there any longer. She had settled at Paris in her residence in the Rue d'Anjou, where she led a somewhat ambiguous existence. Her servants and her husband's Ambassador addressed her as "Your Majesty," while the rest of mankind called her Mme. Bernadotte. Louis XVIII would receive her in the mornings in his study "on business." She never visited the other Princes or the court. However, she used to visit her old friends on an equal footing, and frequented a small clique. I have often met her at Mme. Récamier's house, and her bearing was by no means that of royalty. Although she had herself announced as the Queen of Sweden,* she neither demanded nor received any social distinction.

Towards the close of M. de Richelieu's Ministry she had business to transact on behalf of a relative. She wrote to the Minister and asked for an audience. M. de Richelieu called at her house, as Ministers were formerly wont to do in order to oblige ladies of society. M. de Richelieu was the only Minister who continued this tradition in my time. He was politeness itself. The wishes of Mme. Bernadotte were granted, and he called in person to inform her of the fact. She invited him to dinner, and he accepted. He did not suspect that he was thus inspiring a madness which pursued him to the tomb. Mme. Bernadotte was seized with such a passion for the poor Duc that she followed him like a bloodhound throughout his tour. At first he thought it extraordinary, and could not understand why she should always arrive three hours after himself in every place that he visited. Soon he began to realise the fact that he himself was the attraction. Then he became angry. He concealed his route and his plans, laid false scents, chose the gloomiest towns and the dirtiest inns. His schemes were fruitless, for the accursed coach invariably arrived three hours later than his own postchaise. The thing became an obsession.

He was, moreover, aware that this pursuit would end in ridicule. He therefore found a means of informing this royal heroine of the high road that he had decided to return to Paris at once if she persisted in following him. On her side she inquired of a doctor whether the waters which the Duc was to take were necessary for his health. When an affirmative answer was given, she decided to call a truce, and spent the season at Geneva. However, as soon as it was ended she reopened the campaign. It was this persecution rather than the opening of the session that brought the Duc back to Paris, as he thought he could defend himself better in the capital.

The house of Mme. de Duras was always the pleasantest in Paris. Her husband's position at court brought her into connection with every personage of note, from the foreign sovereign who was passing through France to the artist who wished his work to be brought to the King's notice. She had the tact necessary to choose the persons with whom she wished to be intimate from amid this crowd and had thus surrounded herself with a charming circle, in the midst of which she was overwhelmed with sadness. The marriage of her eldest daughter to M. de La Rochejaquelein[1] had been a real calamity for her. She had constantly refused her consent, and would not be present at the ceremony when Mme. de Talmont, having attained her twenty-first birth-

1. Auguste de La Rochejaquelein came from a family of Vendée heroes. Both his brothers were killed during the insurrection.

day, resolved to remarry. The Duc de Duras reluctantly accompanied his daughter to the altar. It seemed remarkable that she was twice married on her birthday. At the earliest date allowed by the law, on her fifteenth birthday, she married the Prince de Talmont amid the enthusiasm of her family; on her twenty-first birthday she married M. de La Rochejaquelein, notwithstanding the disapproval of her relatives. The great merit of M. de La Rochejaquelein in the eyes of his wife was his Vendean name and the hope that she would be called upon to play some part in the civil disturbances of the west.

Félicie de Duras was hardly out of her childhood when the manuscript of Mme. de Barante, known as the *Mémoires de Mme. de La Rochejaquelein*, went the round of our salons. The story took hold of her youthful imagination. From then on, to become part of a civil war was the height of her aspirations. In order to prepare herself, as soon as she became mistress of her own actions, she went out shooting, learnt the use of weapons, shot pistols, broke in horses, rode them barebacked, and practised all the accomplishments of a dragoon subaltern, to the great despair of her mother and the ruin of her own beauty, which had disappeared with this way of life before she was twenty years of age.

From 1830 on, Mme. de La Rochejaquelein enjoyed the pleasures of traversing the country—pistol in hand, fomenting trouble, attracting ruin and misfortune. I do not know whether these things were in reality as wonderful as her imagination had painted them, but her rash desire to participate in a civil war is more understandable given that she had dreamed of nothing else since she was twelve years old. Her mother-in-law, the Dowager Princesse de Talmont, was pleased by her marriage with M. de La Rochejaquelein, chiefly, I think, because the Duchesse de Duras was in despair at this event; she kept house for the newly married couple. She left the whole of her fortune to Félicie, whom she seemed to love passionately, and who was adored to the point of insipidity within this little household. I have heard these words addressed to her by one of her mother-in-law's friends:

"Princess, permit me to take the liberty of informing you that you are always perfectly right."

I have never forgotten this charming circumlocution. Mme. de Duras attempted, though with some show of diffidence, to assume the position which Mme. de Staël had vacated. She was frightened by her own audacity, and desired that her position should be recognised, although she did not wish to claim it aloud. For instance, she would not display the sprig of green which Mme. de Staël invariably caused to be brought in after lunch and dinner, and which she constantly twiddled in her fingers both at home and on visits. Mme. de Duras had taken up strips of paper, which a footman brought in on a tray after coffee, and with which she made knots during the evening, tearing them up one after another. She then began to write novels which have since been printed, and which certainly displayed gracefulness, talent, and a thorough knowledge of our salons and their customs. Possibly only those who frequent these spots can fully appreciate her works. *Ourika* is an analysis of the inner life of Mme. de Duras. In the person of this blackamoor she has depicted the torments which she suffered from an ugliness which she was inclined to exaggerate, and which had even disappeared at this period of her life.

These literary occupations did not calm her grief at the growing attachment of M. de Chateaubriand for Mme. Récamier. Her grief again was not sufficiently poignant to distract her mundane ambitions. She had no son. The second marriage of her eldest daughter had made her so angry that she lost interest in her existence. All her hopes were set upon her second daughter, Clara, whom she was anxious to settle happily in order to demonstrate to Félicie what she had lost by her rebellion.

Mme. de Duras chose Henri de Chastellux and secured his promise that he would change his name to that of Duras, knowing that if he married Clara he would inherit the duchy and all the prospects which the Duras family could have offered to a son. Thus we were present at the marriage of the Marquis and Marquise de Duras; when we returned in the evening the Duchesse de Duras, after paying a visit to M. Decazes, proceeded to introduce us to the Duc and Duchesse de Rauzan. This was an ancient title of the family of Duras, which the King had revived for the benefit of the newly married pair. He wanted this wedding present to arrive through the favourite, to whom the Duchesse de Duras had appealed, notwithstanding party objections and drawing-room coolnesses, in order to secure the hereditary title and peerage of the Duc de Duras for Henri de Chastellux.

Many blamed M. de Chastellux for abandoning a name which was quite as good as that of Duras. In my opinion, he did nothing more than bring two duchies and a fine fortune into the Chastellux family, for his children will be Chastellux, whatever promises to the contrary he may have made.

Mme. de Duras made it her business to surround Clara with all the attractions and amusements which could charm a young lady, with the object of making Mme. de La Rochejaquelein feel the weight of her displeasure. Her vengeance was that of a betrayed lover, for Félicie had been her favourite, and even while she strove to annoy her she still adored her. In any case, she never succeeded in separating the two sisters, who remained genuinely attached to one another, to the honour of them both, although the eldest was treated as a stranger in her father's house while her sister was placed upon an altar and worshipped. Contemporaries of Mme. de Rauzan have asserted that her intelligence was very limited, but that is not my opinion. She had excellent good sense, much tact, was well educated, and knew several languages and their literatures. Possibly she had not much natural wit, but she had seen so much of society during her early youth that she remained sufficiently sociable to please me entirely. I do not know whether I am blinded by my affection for her, but she seemed to me far superior to the majority of her critics.

Though I habitually remained at home, I was, nonetheless, often to be found in two salons in addition to that of Mme. de Duras. These were held by the Princesse de Poix and by the Marquise de Montcalm. Mme. de Poix used to receive me with the utmost kindness, and I was delighted with her social circle. It was a society absolutely different from that of the ordinary salon; it took a keen interest in all the events of the day, and might be thought of as representing the last century standing at the window to watch the passage of the present age. A young lady who could talk at once became a general favourite and was the object of warm compliments which, though inopportune, were nonetheless welcome. Such at any rate was my impression of them.

The Princesse de Poix was the most delightful old lady that I have ever met. Her intellectual accomplishments and her perfect social tact were united to a strong and dignified character which fitted her to be both the head of a family and a leader of society. The exemplary conduct of her youth permitted her to be indulgent in her old age, and she used her privilege so discreetly that her favour was both an honour and a support. She died, full of years, dignity, and respect, after surviving all her contemporaries and even her son, the Duc de Mouchy, whose loss was a heavy blow which hastened her own death. For several years she had been entirely deaf, an affliction which she bore with admirable patience, employing every reasonable means to alleviate her burden, and bearing the inevitable discomforts of it with that courageous and cheerful resignation which alone can mitigate such a calamity.

As Mme. de Poix had never gone into exile, her salon had been little influenced by the Revolution, and some of the guests who met there every evening had been accustomed to visit her daily for forty years. Others, after an absence of greater or lesser duration, had gathered round this centre, reasserting the social tone and conventions of which, until recently, the old wife of the Marshal de Beauvau had been the example and the oracle. Thus this circle was a direct connection to society as constituted under Louis XV.

The social tone of this company was sensitive and enthusiastic about matters which seemed very trifling to our generation and had been recalled to simplicity by the importance of events, although these seeming exaggerations did not exclude courtesy and kindness. A remark which showed any trace of wit in conversation was received with an approval marked by hand-clapping. Such exclamations as "How charming she is!" "What wit!" et cetera, were lavishly scattered on the subject. Mme. de Staël has retained something of these traditions, though at an earlier age she was also able to incorporate them into the changed habits of a new century (the changes which she had been forced to feel). In the salon of Mme. de Poix, any story in the least degree touching would evoke floods of tears. This too was a cus-tom that survived from the youth of these ladies, when soft-hearted-ness was fashionable.

A story is told of the Princesse d'Hénin, who professed a passionate friendship for Mme. de Poix. One evening, when the latter was very far from well, Mme. d'Hénin was obliged to leave her, being on duty as Lady of the Palace at Versailles. The next morning Mme. de Poix re-ceived a letter from her young friend. She said that she was writing as she had not been able to sleep all night, that she had counted every hour, and that when the hour which should mark the crisis of an illness had struck, she had herself been seized with a kind of shuddering. This had terrified her. She feared it was a presentiment, was unable to bear her anxiety, and was sending a man upon the spot. Until the messen-ger's return she would be in mortal dread, and begged that a reassuring word might be sent, et cetera. Mme. de Poix was greatly touched by Mme. d'Hénin's account of her condition, and hastily wrote a note say-ing that she had spent a fairly good night; she then summoned the foot-man to hand him the note.

"Take this answer to Mme. d'Hénin at once. She has had a very bad night, has she not?"

"I do not know, Princesse."

"Was she very poorly this morning?"

"No one had gone into her room when I started."

"She did not, then, give you the letter herself?"

"Oh yes, Princesse; she gave it to me yesterday evening."

Mme. de Poix was much amused at the apprehensions of her friend, but this incident in no way shook their intimacy, which continued un-til death. It must be added that Mme. d'Hénin was the most affected of all these ladies, whereas Mme. de Poix was the most natural, the most amiable, and reasonable of them.

Among her contemporaries, the Comtesse Charles de Damas was

always considered very clever. I have never seen any trace of her pow-ers, but I will not venture to oppose my views to the general opinion. She was always in tears and lamentations, and was for me the personi-fication of "doleful Elegy in long habiliments of woe," and her senti-ments were too affected to arouse my interest.

A few days before her confinement, her husband found her in tears. He asked:

"What is the matter, my dear?"

"Alas! I am grieving for my child."

"But what a foolish idea; why should you lose it?"

"Lose it! Such a frightful thought would be the death of me; but alas! I am to be separated from it."

"Separated from it? But you propose to nurse it?"

"It will no longer be within my womb."

The salon of Mme. de Montcalm was composed of our contempo-raries, and until the death of her brother, the Duc de Richelieu, this society was marked by a strong political bent. The Duc de Richelieu, when seventeen years of age, had married Mlle. de Rochechouart, who was twelve. According to the custom of the time, he had been sent forth on his travels. During the three years of his absence, he received constant letters from his child-wife, who wrote with much grace and wittiness. At his urgent request, she sent him her portrait, which re-vealed to him the features of the little childish countenance engraved upon his memory, though somewhat more developed. When the Com-tesse de Chinon, this being the title of the young couple, had com-pleted her fifteenth year, the husband was recalled. Full of hope, he reached the Hôtel de Richelieu, and his relatives came forward to meet him upon the staircase. The old marshal, his grandfather, and the Duc de Fronsac, his father, had placed between them a little, stooping, humpbacked monster, whom they presented to the Comte de Chinon as his companion for life. He staggered back three steps and fell down senseless upon the staircase. Then he was carried to his room and said that he felt too ill to appear in the salon. He wrote to his parents stating his firm resolve never to consummate a marriage which was so wholly repulsive to him, ordered post-horses the same night, and went away in despair to Germany, afterwards joining in the campaigns of Souvarov against the Turks. The Duchesse de Fronsac, his father's second wife, had visited him during his short stay in Paris, and presented two charming little sisters to him, of whom he carried away pleasant memories.

In 1803, while Bonaparte was Consul and when the revolutionary uproar had somewhat subsided, the Duc de Richelieu obtained permission through the Emperor Paul, whose service he had entered, to journey in France. Revisiting his sisters with memories of the past, he found two little hunchbacks no less ugly than his wife. On this occasion, however, being more hardened to such sights, he did not run away. He sold his property, paid the debts attached to the estate, and divided his share of his father's inheritance among his sisters. He then returned to the Crimea, where he occupied himself in founding the town of Odessa. The difficulty of communications during the Revolution had kept the Duc de Richelieu as ignorant of the physical development of his sisters as the ill-advised silence of his family had concealed the appearance of his wife. He retained a kind of instinctive repugnance to hunchbacks. Long afterwards, when he was appointed guardian to his niece, Mlle. d'Hautefort, who became Baronne de Damas, he found her similarly misshapen, and could not help exclaiming, as he shook hands with a friend:

"Good Heavens, this is too much! I seem to have been born to be pursued and beset by hunchbacks."

Though the little monster of fifteen years had inspired the Duc de Richelieu with an invincible repugnance, the sight of him had produced a very opposite effect upon his wife. His noble appearance and attractive face had confirmed the impressions produced by the tender correspondence which the young couple had maintained. Beneath her ugliness, Mme. de Richelieu possessed a noble mind and generous heart.

Although she was very young when the Revolution broke out, her virtues had already secured her considerable influence, which she used to preserve the peace in her own circle. She was the good genius of the whole Richelieu family; far from showing any resentment towards the Duc, she constantly manifested her disinterested friendship by the most delicate attentions, and gave no sign that she was ever animated by any stronger sentiment than friendship. The Duc de Richelieu was overcome by this generosity, while his own loftiness of character obliged him to pardon one whom he had so grievously insulted. After the Restoration, he occasionally went to visit her at Courteilles, her beautiful estate, where he was received with extreme joy. Their respective ages would have eventually made this mode of life both simple and easy, and I am persuaded that at the moment of his death M. de Richelieu had almost resolved to take up his residence at Courteilles. As for his wife, nothing would have induced her to confront Parisian society, from which she had withdrawn before she had entered it.

Mme. de Montcalm was the eldest of the two sisters of the Duc de Richelieu. Exceedingly bad health forbade her to leave her couch, and the hope of hiding her figure gave her patience to bear this affliction. Her face was handsome, and the rest of her person was so wrapped up in shawls and coverings that her deformity was almost entirely hidden. It is to this circumstance that I have always attributed the marked preference which M. de Richelieu showed her as compared with her sister, Mme. de Jumilhac, who paraded her appalling figure without the smallest embarrassment at every social gathering or festivity. Yet her mordant wit, her imperturbable gaiety, and a wholly natural animation, which I have never seen surpassed, made her the favourite of the most fashionable members in the best of society. No festivity was complete without Mme. de Jumilhac. She was very fashionable, and, strange to say, to be fashionable was the aim and object of her life, notwithstanding her figure.

Mme. de Montcalm was a more cultivated woman, but in my opinion far less agreeable than her sister. She was very exacting and anxious to be admired by people who could appreciate her merits, which she thought were transcendent, whereas her sister's only object was to pass the time pleasantly with anyone at hand. Possibly my judgement of the two sisters is not wholly impartial. I was very friendly with the younger, and it has been very difficult for me to hold the balance between them. In all important circumstances nothing could exceed the nobility and delicacy of their consideration for one another; but upon the details of daily life they teased and harassed one another so constantly that their mutual detestation became most cordial. Their intimate friends were necessarily influenced and were induced to take sides. In any case, M. de Richelieu showed a marked preference for Mme. de Montcalm. He would spend the greater part of his evenings at her side, and thus she was able to gather all the French and foreign notable personages around her couch.

The carnival of 1820 was extremely gay and brilliant, for the wounds inflicted upon the country were beginning to heal. Meager as had been the gratitude for the Government whose efforts had succeeded in liberating the country, the very people who feared this result and tried to prevent it nonetheless felt enormous relief when they no longer saw foreign uniforms strutting in our streets as though they were their own.

The Duc de Berry gave a great ball at the Elysée. Invitations were numerous and distributed with great liberality. The Duc de Berry considered that court society was far too exclusive. Members of this society had profited from the sedentary and retired tastes of the Princes to monopolise them entirely; to have access to the Princes it was necessary to be a member of their household or closely connected with it. The Duc de Berry disliked this exclusiveness, and announced his intention of breaking with it. He had already given some dinners to which he had invited peers and deputies who were famous in the political world, and he proposed to extend further the circle of his guests. He himself would have had everything to gain, for he was sufficiently intellectual to benefit from the conversation and to attempt to stimulate it. He was encouraged in this project by the attitude of the Palais-Royal.[2]

2. The Palais-Royal was the residence of the Duc d'Orléans.

The Duc d'Orléans had more than anyone shown his relief at the departure of the Allies, and had changed his mode of life in consequence; he liked people to notice the greater freedom with which he now could breathe. The first Wednesday of every month he was at home as a Prince, though not in court dress. Court dress was only worn at the Palais-Royal by ladies who were presented for the first time, and they, again, were often excused. There was no separation between gentlemen and ladies, as at the Tuileries, nor were the guests herded in batches and marshalled by an usher to receive the word or the nod, which was given with as much boredom as it was received.

The drawing-rooms of the Palais-Royal were brilliantly lighted, filled with ladies in magnificent dresses and with men sparkling with orders and gold braid, who moved about as they pleased. People could meet one another and join their own circles; thus they were very ready to wait for the progress of the Princes, who bestowed their favours with the utmost graciousness. Receptions at the Palais-Royal were thus excellent parties, where people could be amused and from which they came away pleased with their entertainment and with their hosts. Hence these receptions were very fashionable. I do not know for what reason they were afterwards abandoned in favour of one sole reception on the first Wednesday of the year, when the crowd was so great that attendance was an unendurable infliction.

Apart from the social gatherings of which I have spoken, there were numerous and excellent concerts, as well as large dinner parties by no means dull; care was taken to ensure that the invitations were sufficiently mixed for every shade of opinion to be represented, to the exclusion of no particular party.

I went constantly to the Palais-Royal. On ordinary days the Princesses and their ladies worked at a round table placed at the end of the gallery, and the children played at the other end. The Duc d'Orléans divided his time between these two groups and the billiard table. As soon as the children were in bed he came up to the table, and conversation went on in a wholly informal and often very amusing manner. The Duc d'Orléans was abreast of every novelty in art or science. Scientific men communicated their discoveries to him, and those which were likely to interest the Princesses were exhibited and demonstrated in the salon. Artists who came in met with appreciation and introduced an element of variety much prized by habitual guests. The list of guests was so wide that some thirty people were always to be found in the course of an evening composed of those to whom the doors were always open, and of those who came by appointment to pay their respects. The Duc de Berry came sometimes with his wife, and seemed to be entertained. It was only on rare occasions that I ever saw him. After the second Restoration he had ceased to pay calls, and after his marriage he only went out to the great balls to which he accompanied his wife. When, however, we happened to meet, we easily resumed the long-standing familiarity which dated from our youth. I remember that one evening at the Palais-Royal I was seated beside him upon a bench in the billiard-room. He then expressed his approval of the social habits of the master of the house, and said how much better it was than to be always "by ourselves like Jews, as we always are."

I pointed out to him that it would be very easy for him to put the receptions at the Elysée on the same footing, and that he would have everything to gain by becoming better known.

"Not so easy as you seem to think. My father would like it and would even be ready to turn it to advantage, for he likes society notwithstanding all his religious scruples; but I do not think that it would suit the King, and I am sure that it would displease my brother, and my sister-in-law still more. She does not like people to be entertained except in her way, 'very sadly'; you know what I mean." And he began to laugh. This "very sadly" is a phrase which Froissart, the medieval chronicler, used in speaking of English amusements. After some long dinner in London the Duc de Berry often used to exclaim, "Ah! we have indeed been 'very sadly' entertained, according to the custom of their country."

Apart from the strictness of the Duchesse d'Angoulême, there was another obstacle which he did not state, but of which he was well aware: this was the differences that existed between the Duchesse de

Berry and the Duchesse d'Orléans. However, the Prince's approval could not entirely conceal his great jealousy of the Palais-Royal. I had fresh proof of this on the day of that ball at the Elysée, to which I now revert after this long digression. The illness of the Duke of Kent[3] induced him to consider the advisability of postponing the ball, but a slight improvement encouraged him to give it. A telegram brought the news of his death upon the very day when the entertainment was to take place. I learnt the news from the Duc de Berry. A long row of carriages had delayed me, and I found the Duc when I arrived, looking as he usually did when he was displeased. The ball was so beautiful, so brilliant, and so animated that I could not understand his dissatisfaction. He approached me.

"Well, I suppose you know that the Palais-Royal is not coming, and has sent excuses?"

"Really, Sire?"

"It is most inopportune. The King had decided that the news of the death of the Duke of Kent should not be made known until the morrow, and now they are spreading the news by their absence, which will require an explanation. It is to put me in the wrong."

I tried to calm him by reminding him of the fact that the Duc d'Orléans was an intimate, personal friend of the Duke of Kent, that he must be much grieved, and that his position was wholly different from that of the Duc de Berry.

"Oh, nonsense," he replied impatiently; "it is always their aim to keep themselves to themselves." There was indeed some small shard of truth in this ill-tempered exclamation.

The ball was magnificent and perfectly arranged. The Prince did the honours of it with full courtesy and condescension, and the success of this entertainment, which was dear to his heart, brought back his good temper before the end of the evening. He told everyone about him that he was delighted to see their pleasure, and that these balls would often be given upon future occasions. None of us blind mortals could have foreseen that it was the last!

3. A son of George III whose daughter was to become Queen Victoria.

Etiquette did not allow us to leave the ball before the Princes. I was utterly exhausted when I met the Duc de Berry after supper. He seemed in excellent good humour, and delighted with the success of his ball.

"You are tired," he said; "you had better go home."

I offered some objections.

"Nonsense, it is I who tell you to go. Good evening to you, my dear old Adèle."

This was his friendly mode of address for me, and they were the last words that I ever heard him speak, while the grasp of the hand which accompanied them was also the last which he ever gave me. I cannot re-call these moments without emotion. With all his faults, he had most attractive qualities, and within his princely breast there beat the heart of a generous man.

The following Saturday, preceding Shrove Sunday, February 13, 1820, there was a fancy dress ball given by M. Greffulhe, a rich banker who had married Mlle. Duluc de Vintimille, and had been made a peer of France. It was a magnificent entertainment, and the most fashionable members of Parisian society were there. The Duc and Duchesse de Berry honoured the ball with their presence. The Princess did not dance, but as she was dressed in the costume of a queen of the Middle Ages, with a floating veil and velvet covered with gold brocade, the reason was not detected.

M. Greffulhe never left the Prince for a moment while he was at the ball. He seemed anxious and preoccupied, and as soon as he had placed his illustrious guests in their carriage and the vehicle had left his courtyard, he seemed to be relieved of a heavy burden. I heard that he had received numerous warnings that some assassin might use the occasion of a masked ball to attack the Duc de Berry, but, apart from the master of the house, no one attached any importance to these anon-ymous threats. Everyone was happy and cheerful, and every kind of amusement was in progress.

The coterie to which I belonged met the next day, which was Sun-day, at the house of Mme. de La Briche. A masquerade had been pre-pared representing a village baptism. A certain M. de Poreth, a man six feet high, was the baby, and he carried his nurse in his arms. The whole affair proceeded in a similar vein, and the absurdity was quite amusing. Everyone was highly cheerful, although one of the characters of the farce, M. Greffulhe, the host of the previous evening, was kept at home by an indisposition, which, by the way, ended in his death five days later.

Bursts of laughter were at their height when Alexandre de Boisgelin came in. He sat down by the side of Mme. de Mortefontaine near the door and spoke to her in a low voice. I was upon the point of going out, but they called me back. Alexandre had just come from the Opera and knew that the Duc de Berry had been struck down. He had seen the assassin and the bloodstained dagger, but he was unaware of the danger of the wound. He thought that the wounded man could be moved, had been to give orders at the Elysée, and was on his way back there to wait for him. He insisted upon our silence, and promised to return as soon as the Prince should have reached his rooms. Mme. de Mortefontaine and I remained seated side by side, hardly daring to look at one another, lest we should give way.

Soon further news reached this room where pleasure was still predominant. I shall never forget its appearance: the groups farthest from the door gay and laughing, while those nearest successively received the sad news, and consternation spread from spot to spot, though slowly. No one would cry the news aloud, and it passed quietly from neighbour to neighbour. Those men who were able to rid themselves of their costumes rushed into the street to gather information, and those who had duties to perform hastened home to put on their uniform. Soon only the ladies and M. de Mun were left. M. de Mun was dressed like the doyenne of a château with lace collar, furbelows, and plumes, and was unable to rid himself of his costume. He thus remained dressed all night among the crowd of those who came and went: aides-de-camp, footmen, orderlies, and messengers of all sorts came in to us, but neither we nor the newcomers noticed him, so great was our dismay, that we only remembered the fact after reflecting upon the evening.

We learnt that it was impossible to carry the Duc de Berry to the Elysée, and that Mme. de Gontaut had received orders to take the little Mademoiselle to the Opera while the ladies of the Duchesse de Berry were to go and meet her there. At length, at four o'clock in the morning, we were informed by the watch at the Elyséee that better news had arrived; the Prince's wound had been dressed, he was easier, and was to be carried upon mattresses. Each of us went away with fear in our hearts; we had been waiting since seven o'clock to learn the end of this cruel tragedy. The accounts which I have received are scrupulously correct, and have been confirmed by too many mouths for me to doubt them for a moment.

The death of the Duc de Berry was that of a hero and a Christian; he thought of everyone with admirable courage, presence of mind, and coolness. It may be asked how this fact is to be reconciled with the want of resolution sometimes attributed to him. I cannot say. Men are full of these inexplicable anomalies. To show them as perfectly consistent is to draw only the portrait of a novelist's hero.

The Duc de Berry had just put his wife in her carriage, and the footmen were closing the door. He was going back to the Opera to see the last scene of the ballet and to receive from a member of the ballet the signal for a visit which he wished to make. He was followed by two aides-de-camp, and two sentinels were presenting arms at either side of the door. A man passed through all these people, and pushed so violently against one of the aides-de-camp that he said, "Take care what you are doing, sir." At the same moment he placed a hand upon the shoulder of the Prince, and with the other hand thrust an enormous knife into his breast below the shoulder which he left in the wound, and took flight; no one in the numerous escort had time to anticipate his action. The Duc de Berry thought at first that he had received a blow with a fist and said, "That man struck me"; then clapping his hand to his breast, he cried, "Ah, it is a dagger! I am a dead man."

The Duchesse de Berry, seeing the struggle, wished to go to her husband. Mme. de Béthisy, the lady on duty from whom I have these details, tried to keep her back. The footmen hesitated to lower the steps, and the Princess sprang out of the carriage without waiting for them. Mme. de Béthisy followed her. They found the Duc de Berry seated in a chair in the passage. He had not lost consciousness and merely said, "Ah, poor Caroline, what a sight for you."

She threw herself upon him, and he said, "Take care, you are hurting me."

They succeeded in carrying him up to a little drawing-room which communicated with his box. The men who had carried him then went out to get help, and he was left alone with the two ladies. The knife, which had been left in his breast, caused him dreadful suffering, and he insisted that Mme. de Béthisy should draw it out, after trying in vain himself. She was eventually induced to obey. The blood spurted forth abundantly, and her dress and that of the Duchesse de Berry were covered with it. From that moment until the arrival of the physicians with their bandages, he merely groaned continually, saying from time to time, "I am stifling; give me air." The poor women opened the door, and the music of the ballet which was in progress and the applause of the pit made a terrible contrast to the scene before their eyes. The Duchesse de Berry showed a calmness and a strength of character beyond all praise, for her despair was terrible. She thought of everything, prepared everything with her own hands, and the boarding-school girl of the morning became suddenly heroic.

I think that the Duc d'Angoulême was the first of the Princes to arrive, and was followed by Monsieur. The latter had thrown himself into the carriage of the person who came to bring the news. As yet it was unknown whether this assassination marked the outbreak of a wider conspiracy. There may have been danger of such an event. I have heard eyewitnesses relate that the progress of the old King through the corridors of the Opera, where he dragged himself along to receive the last sigh of the last member of his house, was all the more imposing by contrast to a similar scene in the interior of the palace. The touching details which accompanied this dreadful catastrophe, beyond dispute because of the number of witnesses, did much to restore the credit of the royal family in the eyes of France, and the death of the Duc de Berry was more useful to his family than his life.

The smallest incidents of that dreadful night were related to me by many who were there, especially by the Princesses d'Orléans. They were overwhelmed when I went to see them the next day. Mademoiselle told me that the King had said to the Duc d'Orléans, at the moment when the Duchesse de Berry threw herself upon her husband's body and refused to leave him:

"Duc d'Orléans, take care of her; she is with child."

The Duc de Berry entrusted to his wife two girls in England of whom he was very fond, who were daughters of his by a Mrs. Brown. They were sent for, and arrived in a condition that may be imagined; the Duchesse de Berry took them to her heart. She loyally kept her promise to the dying man, brought up the girls, provided them with dowries, married them, found them posts in her household, and showed them unbroken affection. We have seen them appear at court; first as Mlles. d'Issoudun and de Vierzon, afterwards as Princesse de Lucinge and Comtesse de Charrette. The Duc de Berry also entrusted to the kindness of his brother the care of a child he had recently had by an opera dancer, Virginie. The sobs of the Duc d'Angoulême testified to the readiness with which he accepted this charge. I do not know what became of this little boy, but I am certain that he was not abandoned by the Duc d'Angoulême.

The Duc de Berry had something appropriate and touching to say to everyone; he was under no illusion whatever as to his condition, and thought only of others. He fulfilled his religious duties with resignation and confidence, and surrendered his soul to God with a calmness wholly unexpected in so impetuous a character.

The death of the Duc de Berry was universally lamented. People who thought they were in no way concerned sympathised with the grief of the noble family, and the narrative of this cruel night brought tears to the eyes of even the strongest opponents. It is extraordinary that the ferocious Louvel,[4] who had been pursuing the Prince for some time, should not have found an earlier opportunity to strike him down. The irregular life of the Duc de Berry brought him almost daily and

4. Louvel was a saddler employed in the stables of Louis XVIII. He was executed on June 7, 1820.

without escort into places where it would have seemed far easier to attack him. Had the catastrophe happened at the door of some dancing girl or at the moment when he was leaving a cab, a very different impression would have been made compared with that produced by the sight of him in the arms of his young wife, who was covered with his blood, while he was surrounded with all that was due to his rank. From this point of view there was something providential in the manner of this great misfortune. The despair of the Palace of the Elysée was indescribable. The Duc de Berry, notwithstanding his fits of temper, was adored by his servants. He was kind, generous, just, and even affable as soon as anger had passed.

It is not sufficiently well-known that he was the first to introduce savings banks into France. He had founded one for his own household, to encourage saving among his servants. When any one of them had saved five hundred francs he doubled that amount. The details of this business were in his personal care. If one of these servants needed to withdraw his money, he inquired into the nature of his requirements and supplied him if the servant's needs were real and honourable. The attention which he thus devoted to their small interests secured him their passionate devotion, and his loss was bewailed with heartfelt tears.

If the Duc de Berry had been brought up by reasonable people, had been taught to conquer his passions, to consider public opinion, and to sacrifice his whims to social conventions, he would have become an accomplished Prince, for there was within him excellent material. As it was, his death was no loss to either his son, his family, or his country. My conviction of this fact has not, however, prevented me from mourning him sincerely, and my feeling was general. Whatever judgement may be passed upon him now, that tragic night was regarded as a national calamity. A long cry of grief rose throughout France, and was turned to such excellent advantage by party spirit that in three days it had changed to curses upon M. Decazes.

The first persons who expressed these views had merely wished to accuse M. Decazes of carelessness, but once the public was deceived no attempts were made to destroy the deception. It was asserted in the marketplace that M. Decazes had commissioned Louvel to act, and a deputy went so far as to denounce him in the Chamber as an accessory to the crime. These assertions would not stand a moment's investigation, but passion is unreasonable, and party leaders would rather profit from the blindness of the masses than attempt to enlighten them. On the other hand, an effort was made at the Château to use the grief of the Duchesse de Berry. Assuming that her repugnance was unjustifiable, could the King insist that she should see a man who inspired her with such repulsion? Was it not right to make allowance for her grief and her condition? Excitement grew so much that M. Decazes had reason to fear for his personal safety. Threatening murmurs were heard about him when he crossed the halls of the Life Guards, and his life was in danger at every turn. The King yielded. It was necessary to fill his place in the ministry, as Decazes was both President of the Council[5] and Minister of the Interior. Monsieur undertook to smooth away these difficulties.

Since M. Pasquier had replaced General Dessolle as Minister of Foreign Affairs, the Duc de Richelieu had given friendly and loyal support to the ministry of which M. Decazes was the head. In token of his goodwill he had just accepted a commission to compliment King George IV upon his accession. The death of his old father had made George IV sovereign of the country which he had been governing for fifteen years as Prince Regent. The Duc had planned to start out at the very moment when the Duc de Berry expired, and his journey was consequently delayed. The King suggested that he take M. Decazes's place, but he refused. Monsieur sent for him and begged him to accept; the Duc de Richelieu again refused and with greater energy when confronted with the Prince. Driven to extremes, he said at length that his strongest objection was the impossibility of governing on behalf of an invalid monarch who seemed constantly at the point of death, when the heir to the crown and all his friends were in opposition.

5. The office of President of the Council is equivalent to that of Prime Minister.

"If I were to accept, Sire, in one year you would be leading the opposition against my administration."

Monsieur gave his word of honour that he would support the measures of the Duc de Richelieu in every possible way, but the Duc still held out; finally he renewed his supplications on his knees in an absolutely literal sense, and begged him in the name of his misfortunes to come to the help of the family and to protect what was left of it from the assassin's knife. M. de Richelieu was much moved, but still hesitated. Monsieur continued:

"Listen, Richelieu, this is a matter between gentlemen. Should I find anything to criticise in your actions, I will promise to discuss it frankly with you alone; but I will loyally and constantly support the administration of your Government, and this I promise upon the bloodstained body of my son and upon my word of honour as a gentleman."

M. de Richelieu was overcome and deeply touched; he bowed respectfully over the hand which was held out to him, saying, "I accept, Sire."

Three months afterwards Monsieur was at the head of every opposition and at the bottom of every intrigue. Possibly, however, at the time he acted in good faith. In any case, he then led M. de Richelieu triumphantly to the King, who received him with no great cordiality. While Monsieur was doing his best to facilitate the retirement of M. Decazes, the King was striving to raise obstacles, in the hope that the uproar would die away, and that he would be able to keep the object of his affection near him. M. Decazes held a sounder view of his own position. He had attempted to bring public opinion to his side by proposing exceptional laws to fight crime, and by personally demanding the repeal of the election law, the very measure which he had formerly supported with so much warmth.

When these steps did not conciliate the public, he understood that the ambitious party leaders would not allow the excitement to cool, and that it would be impossible for him to defy the general resentment which was then overwhelming. M. de Chateaubriand was so ungenerous as to write that his feet were slipping in blood. He was indeed too enlightened to believe that M. Decazes was guilty of the murder of the Duc de Berry, but he wished to make his position, as Minister, untenable, in the hope that he himself might be called in.

As he was unable to make headway against the storm, M. Decazes extorted permission to resign from the King. The monarch only yielded with the keenest grief, and, as some alleviation of his royal vexation, he nominated M. Decazes peer, duke, and his Ambassador at London. Until he could take on his new duties, he went away to his estates in the south. The exasperation against him was so keen that it was not safe for him to travel in his own name. As his carriages were numerous enough to attract attention, he made use of the relays which had been ordered by the Duc de Laval Montmorency, who was returning to his post at Madrid. It was amusing to hear the fury of the latter at the idea that M. Decazes had taken to traveling incognito, under the name of Montmorency.

M. de Richelieu became President of the Council, holding no portfolio. Of all the administrations in my time, this was undoubtedly the strongest, the cleverest, and most united. In less than two years it was able to lay foundations of such strength that the Restoration could raise upon those foundations unharmed the follies that accumulated during the ensuing eight years. During the ninth year the centre of gravity was passed, and the structure fell with a crash.

The King was more deeply affected by the loss of M. Decazes than he had been by the death of his nephew. His affection had deepened with the disregard it had been shown, and he relieved his annoyance by continual petty, even ridiculous, outbursts. A portrait of M. Decazes, magnificently framed, was placed in his room. A miniature version stood on his desk.

The waters of Aix had done me so much good the previous year that I was anxious to revisit the town during the summer of 1820. I also wished to be present at the opening of a handsome institution which M. de Boigne had founded at Chambéry. This was Saint-

Benoît, which was intended to shelter forty middle-class persons who were over sixty years of age and without means. This provision was intended for ecclesiastics, old soldiers, retired clerks, and widows or spinsters who had lost their parents or were penniless. M. de Boigne had endowed this institution with a considerable income, and had been careful to provide everything which could secure for its future inhabitants an existence both comfortable and peaceful. I heartily approved of this noble idea, and had every satisfaction in doing the honours of the first meal given to the "refugees," as the inhabitants of the institution were to be known, and to the local authorities who had been invited upon this occasion. I spent that day and almost the whole of the next day with the new inhabitants, whose pleasure was a real happiness to behold. M. de Boigne had left nothing undone to secure their comfort.

The carriages of Queen Caroline of England were passing through Aix. We were informed that she had been staying in an inn on the Geneva route, and strange stories reached us from that quarter. Curious to know the truth about these details, I made inquiries a short time afterwards when I was following the same route. I stopped at an inn at Rumilly. A very respectable-looking girl was working in the kitchen, and I asked her a few questions about the Queen's stay. She replied with downcast eyes that she knew nothing. "The Queen did not stay here, then?" I asked.

"Oh yes, Madame, but I was not here."

The mistress of the inn then came up, and told me that the Queen had stayed a week at her house, but that after the first evening she had hastened to send away her daughters to one of their aunts.

"I was ashamed, Madame, of what I saw myself, and did not even like sending my servants to wait upon her."

It seems that the courtier Bergami had grown too lazy to satisfy the taste of this immoral Princess, although she still remained under his influence. Under pretext of a conference with the English Minister at Bern to arrange for her journey through Switzerland, she had sent him away and had spent the week of his absence in a perpetual orgy with her other servants. Indignation reached such a pitch in the little town which her presence had defiled that upon the day of her departure, when a quarrel broke out between one of her servants and a postillion, the Queen attempted to secure silence by her royal word, whereupon there was an explosion of popular indignation. The whole populace rose and threatened to stone her, and she ran some risk of being thus as- saulted. Such was the honourable person loudly claimed as sovereign by a large proportion of the English nation, a fact which provides fur- ther proof of the good faith of political opposition.

After spending some days in the delights which I was always cer- tain of finding at Geneva, I passed the Jura in the midst of snow, and reached Paris on the evening of the birth of the Duc de Bordeaux, on September 29, 1820. I do not deny that it caused me intense joy, and that I repeated all the Royalist exaggerations concerning this "mirac- ulous child," as we called him. Indeed, remembering as we did that his father's death had seemed to secure the extinction of the Bourbon branch, and that this feeble scion had survived all the mental and phys- ical agitation of his unhappy mother during that fatal evening on Feb- ruary 13, it was easy to see the finger of Providence in this event, and to count upon its protection.

At the same time, I remember well an incident which struck me at the time, and which we have often recalled since. I was walking in my drawing-room with Pozzo, and had been expressing my enthusiasm at this birth for an hour when suddenly he stopped, put a hand on my arm, and said:

"You seem very pleased, very happy, and very delighted. You hear those bells ringing? Well, I tell you they are tolling the death-knell of the House of Bourbon, and do not forget what I have said."

Pozzo's premonitions were only too correct. The birth of the post- humous child, who received the title of Duc de Bordeaux, induced his family to begin attempts for the reestablishment of the absolute monar- chy, and also deprived the people of their hopes that the older line, with which they were not in sympathy, would become extinct. Thus it is that the prophecies of weak mortals are often overthrown by the decrees of Providence and our cries of joy turn to lamentations. I must do Pozzo the justice to recognise that he was one of the few people who predicted this fact at that time. The Duke of Wellington expressed himself in almost similar terms upon the occasion of the marriage of the Duc de Berry: someone had said that the Duchesse seemed too feeble to have much hope of children, and he replied:

"It would be very fortunate for the Restoration. The best chance for the Restoration to establish itself is to leave some hope that the reigning branch may become extinct."

Party spirit set rumours in circulation concerning the birth of the Duc de Bordeaux which could not be maintained for a moment, in view of his public birth. I do not propose to give any details of this event, or that of the trial of the Queen of England.[6] All that I will say is that the reports of the maternal heroism of one of these Princesses and the scandalous life of the other made the newspapers so disgusting for several days that it was impossible to leave them lying about.

On May 5, 1821, Napoleon Bonaparte breathed his last sigh upon a rock in the middle of the Atlantic. Destiny had thus prepared for him the most poetical of tombs. Upon the confines of two worlds, and famous only for the name of Bonaparte, Saint-Helena became the vast mausoleum of his vast glory. The age of his posthumous popularity had not yet begun for France. I heard the newspaper sellers in the street crying, "The death of Napoleon Bonaparte, two sous; his speech to General Bertrand, two sous; despair of Mme. Bertrand, two sous"; and this produced no more effect in the street than an advertisement for a lost dog. I can still remember that the most thoughtful of us were greatly struck by this strange indifference, and repeated, "Vanity of vanities, all is vanity!" Yet glory is something; it has found its level once more, and centuries of admiration will recompense the Emperor for this moment of forgetfulness.

6. Upon his accession, George IV initiated a bill to annul his marriage with Queen Caroline.

I have no special details to give concerning the period of his exile. Details only came to me from fanatical partisans or detractors. I knew some of his entourage, but they were anxious to profit from what they had to say. Gourgaud was trying to sell his revelations, Bertrand to turn his fidelity to account, and in neither case were their stories worthy of credence. Still less was it possible to trust the version given by Sir Hudson Lowe,[7] who was overwhelmed by his responsibilities and had failed to understand his mission. He was constantly harassing the Emperor on petty details and giving way to him on essential points.

Lord Castlereagh went into the study of George IV and said to him:

"Sir; I come to tell your Majesty that your mortal enemy is dead."

"What!" he cried, "is it possible? Can she be dead?"

Lord Castlereagh was obliged to calm the monarch's joy by explaining to him that he was not talking of the Queen, his wife, but of Bonaparte. A few months afterwards the hopes of the King were realised, and it must be admitted that if such sentiments can ever be justified, they could be only by the conduct of Queen Caroline. Her death was a relief for everybody, and especially for the party which had undertaken the impossible task of repairing her honour. She died a victim of her excesses.

The Cabinet, under the guidance of the Duc de Richelieu, was now busily occupied. France was resuming her position among the nations, and was becoming a power worthy of consideration. The Eastern question was of growing importance and needed discussion. Domestic prosperity was increasing with the continuance of peace. Statesmanlike laws were in preparation, and everything pointed to a session which would be uneventful and serviceable to the country. The Ministry, immersed in business and composed of men out of touch with the court intrigues, either did not know about or disregarded them.

King Louis XVIII required a favourite. The retirement of M. De-

7. Sir Hudson Lowe was the Governor of Saint-Helena.

cazes had left a void which he desired to fill. If any one of his Ministers had been willing to take this place, the King would have readily fallen in with his wishes, but no member of the Government was suitable for the purpose. Chance brought Mme. du Cayla* into the monarch's purview. She retained some remnants of her former beauty, was a clever and intriguing woman, and utterly unscrupulous. The shameful methods by which she seduced the old King were only surpassed by the disgraceful salary which she received. If the Ministry had known more about her methods, it would have been possible to retain her as a paid subordinate. Her lust could have been entirely satisfied by money, but the Ministers despised her unduly. Thus she gained time to establish her influence, and prepared to use it for political purposes.

I do not know whether she conceived the idea of joining her fortunes to those of M. de Villèle* or whether he first thought of using this vile instrument; I am, however, certain of the fact that Sosthène de La Rochefoucauld, who had been for many years a more or less favoured lover of Mme. du Cayla, became the go-between of this most secret alliance. When once the alliance had been concluded, Monsieur was easily drawn into it, and the fall of the Richelieu Ministry was decided by this little council under the patronage of the Congregation.[8]

When it had become clear that the whole of the Ultra party, of which Monsieur was the leader, was working for the overthrow of the Ministry as actively as their chief, M. de Richelieu secured an interview with the Prince, and reminded him of the solemn pledge which he had given with so much earnestness the preceding year. Monsieur was in no way disconcerted.

"I would have given you many more pledges to have induced your acceptance at that time, for we were in so difficult a position that we were somewhat fortunate in being reduced only to yourself, and in being able to stop short at your shade of opinion; but you will understand, my dear Duc, that this could not go on."

8. The Congregation was a religious association founded in 1801. Banned by Napoleon, it was reconstituted in 1814 and regrouped Ultras of all kinds. Its different provincial branches made it a very powerful and secretive opposition. It was disbanded in 1830.

M. de Richelieu turned his back with little respect and much indignation. He called his colleagues together, and after a long conference they concluded that though it might be possible to resist the improvised coalition of the two oppositions and its victorious majority,
it was nonetheless impossible to continue their administration in the
teeth of the opposition of Monsieur.

Nothing would have been easier than to destroy Monsieur's popularity with the country by unmasking his intrigues and his proposals,
and to reduce him to the position of a party leader. The Cabinet, however, was composed of men too loyal and conscientious to ruin the popularity of the heir to the crown, whose accession seemed imminent in
view of the King's enfeebled health. Consequently, the Ministers decided to resign in a body, and the Duc de Richelieu was requested to
inform the King of their intentions. The King was much disturbed by
this explanation.

"Good Heavens!" he said, putting his head in his hands. "What
will become of me? What do they wish to do? What conditions will
they impose upon me?"

M. de Richelieu advised him to see Monsieur, and to arrange the
matter with him.

A few hours later he received a note from the King, requesting his
immediate attendance; he found him alone in his study, radiant with
happiness.

"Come in, my dear Richelieu; your advice was excellent. I have
seen my brother, and am perfectly satisfied. He is most prudent; everything has been settled, and you can retire when you please."

Such were the expressions of the royal gratitude for all the services
and devotion of the Duc de Richelieu. I have seen him smile when he
told the story, but it was a smile of sadness, and expressed deeply
wounded feelings. In the eyes of all the royal family, M. de Richelieu
had committed one wrong which nothing could efface. During the exile, when he was busily occupied with the foundation of Odessa, his
year of duty began as First Gentleman of the Chamber to Louis XVIII;
he begged his friend, the Duc de Fleury, who was settled at Mitau

with the King, to take his place, and did not go to perform his duty in the antechamber of the exiled monarch. In the opinion of the Princes of the House of Bourbon, personal service was always the chief duty of their subordinates. They never pardoned this mistake on the part of the Duc de Richelieu. He also displeased them because of his reputation for uprightness and for independence of character.

The King's anxiety to secure the resignation of his Ministers had become so great that he sent to demand it three times in the course of the evening. The difficulty of gathering all the Ministers together at an unusual time to decide upon their common action had delayed the transmission of the resignation. It was afterwards known that he had promised Mme. du Cayla that the resignation would be handed to her before she went to bed, and in fact she received the document at midnight.

Here the reign of Louis XVIII comes to an end; henceforward he was simply an instrument in the hands of Monsieur's agents, who, like himself, were dominated by the Congregation. When M. de Villèle attempted to throw off this influence, he fell like the rest.

France now suffered a real loss. The death of M. de Richelieu deprived her of a clever, upright, and respected man, around whom men of talent and honesty would have naturally gathered, and who would probably have been recalled to power by the force of circumstances before matters became desperate. Possibly M. de Richelieu might have been able to save the Restoration from itself. Heaven's ways are not our ways! Providence ordained the reign of Charles X, and may it grant that this decree be for the happiness of our nephews, seeing that it was not pleasing to contemporaries.

During the last months of his Ministry, and especially after his retirement, M. de Richelieu often came to see me. He had brought M. Pasquier, and it was at that time that my most intimate connection began with the latter. Both regretted their loss of power, which they felt themselves well fitted to wield, being thoroughly convinced that they had performed essential services to the King and to the country.

Both spoke freely upon the subject, and criticised, though in reasonable terms, the dangerous paths upon which those in power had entered. M. Pasquier was animated by only the feelings of a good patriot who was uneasy for his country and reasonable ambition. Though he was vexed to find his career cut short, there was no bitterness in his mind. The feelings of the Duc de Richelieu, who had been cut to the heart by the conduct of the Princes, were very different. Their ingratitude had wounded him in proportion to the depths of devotion which he had shown them, and though he was now disillusioned, old memories made him more sensitive to their actions. As the Duc de Richelieu was Master of the Hounds and First Gentleman of the Chamber, he continued to lunch at the Château from time to time, but always met with a very cold reception. The Duchesse d'Angoulême had just acquired the estate of Villeneuve l'Etang. She was much delighted with it, and had cream brought from it to her table. The cream was placed in a little jug which stood by her side, and as a mark of favour she would share it with certain individuals. One day she made a point of offering cream across the table to guests to the right and left of the Duc de Richelieu in so marked a manner that her neglect of him became a positive insult. I have heard the Duc de Richelieu himself relate this triviality with that tinge of irony which deep vexation, accompanied by disdain, may give. He was angry with himself for caring about such trifles, but his old courtier's blood overcame his common sense. In reality an intentional insult was hidden beneath this discourtesy at which he had every reason to be angry.

It was in this frame of mind that he found reason to suspect a man to whom he had shown kindness, of whom he was very fond, and who possessed his whole confidence, of a proceeding which in legal language is known as theft. The discovery staggered him, and he did not wish to make further inquiries. Before deciding upon his future action he felt that he needed some days' rest, and went away to his wife's house at Courteilles. He had recently spent considerable time there and had felt the better for it.

The infatuation of the Queen of Sweden for the Duc de Richelieu had not diminished; she pursued him as usual, and took up her abode in the little inn which served the château from where she could watch all his movements. The intrusion was the more intolerable to M. de Richelieu in his state of exasperation and he decided to return. The previous evening he had crossed a somewhat deep ford upon horseback, and had neglected to change his wet clothes. This caused the touch of fever and the invalid appearance which he showed as he entered his carriage. He refused to see Mme. de Richelieu's doctor, but promised to send for his own if he were not better the next day. He had hardly started when his fever increased. The Polish aide-de-camp who accompanied him became uneasy. At Dreux, the Queen of Sweden, who was in pursuit, caught up to him, and while the horses were being changed had her carriage drawn forward so that she could enjoy the happiness of seeing his face for a moment. She was so startled by the change in his appearance that she called the aide-de-camp and said to him:

"Sir, you must take the responsibility of having the Duc de Richelieu bled upon the spot." She repeated this injunction at Pontchartrain and at Versailles, and as a proof of the Duc's dangerous weakness, she pointed out that he had not troubled to pull down the blind of his carriage at the side where she was standing. Unfortunately the aide-de-camp would not make up his mind. The fever diminished between Versailles and Paris, and M. de Richelieu was not very ill upon his arrival. His sister, Mme. de Montcalm, was at home. He went into her room and asked for supper, but ate very little. He was induced to send for Dr. Bourdois; Bourdois was ill and sent Lerminier, a clever practitioner, but entirely ignorant of the Duc's temperament. Bourdois warned him that he had to deal with a man who was extremely nervous, and whose health was often affected by his mental condition.

"I have sometimes thought that he was about to have a serious illness," he said, "and two hours afterwards have found him in a normal condition."

Provided with this fatal information, Lerminier came to M. de Richelieu. He found him in bed half-asleep, and greatly irritated by the appearance of a newcomer. The doctor proposed various remedies, which were all rejected. At length he confined himself to ordering some cups of an infusion of orange blossoms to quench his thirst. The next day he would see what was best to be done. Lerminier returned to Bourdois to tell him of his visit and of the exasperation of the Duc, the only disquieting symptom. Bourdois said that he had always found him like that when he had a little fever.

Before going to his lecture, the Abbé Nicole went in at six o'clock to see M. de Richelieu. His servant said that he was resting after a very poor night. The Abbé went up to look at him, and was so struck by the change in his appearance that he resolved to send for the doctors. Several arrived, and all remedies were tried, but in vain. M. de Richelieu did not awaken from his sleep of death, and before midday he had ceased to live.

This sudden death, as no one knew that he was even ill, was a great shock. His friends, for he had real friends, lamented him bitterly; and every person with common sense mourned him then and still more afterwards. It was upon this occasion that M. de Talleyrand first uttered the observation which has since become so hackneyed, "He was somebody." The Duc d'Angoulême was the only member of the royal family who manifested any regret. These were his words to my brother: "I feel sorrow at his loss; he did not like us, but he loved France. His life was a resource, and his death will be a loss."

The King, Monsieur, and Madame were somewhat relieved to be no longer confronted with a man in whose presence they were ill-at-ease. The courtiers followed the example of their masters and did not pretend a grief which they did not feel. They too had their excuse, for M. de Richelieu felt neither esteem nor affection for them.

The despair of the Queen of Sweden was as excessive as her violent infatuation. She hired a pew at the Church of the Assumption, in which the body of the Duc de Richelieu had been placed until it should be carried to the Sorbonne; she spent days and nights there in unrestrained grief, and thus made amends for her previous foolishness.

I have already told how she pursued M. de Richelieu upon the high roads. She continued her persecution in Paris. She had rooms near his, and he could not appear at one window without seeing the Queen at another. As soon as he went out she went after him. Her carriage followed his. She stopped when he stopped, got out when he got out, waited for him whenever he paid a call, and continued this pursuit with a perseverance which had become an absolute nightmare for the poor Duc. If he went into a shop she followed him, waited until he had gone out, and then bought the object which he had chosen, and sent him another copy of it. The Queen constantly performed this innocent trickery in the flower shops, for the Duc sometimes sent flowers to a lady to whom he was attached; the Queen would innocently say that she was pretending to believe that the flowers had been chosen for herself, though she knew their destination very well.

M. de Richelieu required exercise, and often went to the garden of the Tuileries; the Queen pursued him there also, but she observed that her presence drove him away, and she did not wish to deprive him of his walk. One day she arrived at Mme. Récamier's house radiant with joy, and announced that she had arranged with her tailors to have a dress of different cut and colour for every day. Then M. de Richelieu would not recognise her at a distance, and would not turn away his head until she had had the happiness of looking at him for a moment in the face.

On one occasion when he was talking with animation, she had secured a bow by passing nearby and making him a bow which he returned before he recognised her. She came in delight to relate this triumph to Mme. Récamier, who gave me these details. Mme. Récamier made vain attempts to rouse a little natural dignity in the heart of the Queen of Sweden by reproaching her for continuing attentions thus constantly disregarded, seeing that the Duc's refusal was becoming as violent as the energy of his pursuer, and indeed bordered upon the brutal. But she liked him in that mood, "even when he was a little fierce." All the eloquence of Mme. Récamier was hopeless against this strange infatuation.

As for M. de Richelieu, he was irritated to the point of fury. Conscientious as he was about using the government for personal service, I am convinced that he could not resist the temptation of hinting to Stockholm that the Queen would be much more suitably settled there than in Paris. Her husband did continually urge her to return, but she answered his entreaties by sending doctors' certificates, and would not consent to join her husband on the throne until after the death of the Duc. I do not know any other case of so persevering and openly displayed love on the woman's side without the slighest encouragement and in spite of disdainful rejection.

A short time after the death of the Duc de Richelieu, Lord Castlereagh, who had become Marquis of Londonderry, put an end to his life. For some days his conduct had been eccentric. One morning he left the bedroom at his usual time, went into his dressing-room and came back half-dressed into his wife's room to fetch some pills which he took every day; after swallowing these he returned to his dressing-room and cut his jugular vein with a very small pocket knife so artistically that a most insignificant wound killed him almost upon the spot. Lady Londonderry heard him fall, and rushed to him at once, but he was already past help.

Attempts have been made to account for his suicide with political reasons, but there is no ground for such statements. Lord Londonderry was a cold, calm character, most unlikely amenable to such factors. His death can be attributed only to a fit of madness which was hereditary in his family. Anyone who knew the details of these events would regard the death of M. de Richelieu as more determined by mental affliction and consideration of politics than that of Lord Londonderry.

M. de Chateaubriand had been delighted with his appointment as Ambassador in England in the place of the Duc Decazes. His vivid imagination enjoyed the supposed contrast of diplomatic splendour in a country where he had led the weary existence of an obscure *émigré*. His happiness was not as keen as he had supposed, the more so as his personal glory was by no means established outside of France. Popular as his talents were among ourselves, he enjoyed little reputation abroad. Possibly the Revolution had drowned his loudest efforts; possibly, again, the daring of the school which he founded held no attraction for a people accustomed to similar methods in their own literature, and therefore unable to appreciate the charm which we recognised until the excesses of his disciples discredited the master. It must also be observed that the special merit of M. de Chateaubriand's writings depended upon certain artistic combinations of words, giving a flash and colouring to his style which foreigners were less likely to appreciate than his own countrymen. Whatever the reason may be, M. de Chateaubriand was not appreciated outside of France, and therefore it was always impossible for him to make a prolonged stay in other countries. He was as speedily and entirely disgusted with London as he had been with Berlin, and earnestly begged to be sent to the Congress of Verona. The Vicomte de Montmorency, who had largely befriended him elsewhere, would not listen upon this occasion, but immediately after the departure of the Vicomte for Verona, M. de Villèle, who had meanwhile taken over the portfolio of Foreign Affairs, secured his own appointment as President of the Council and began a close correspondence with the Vicomte de Chateaubriand.

As for Mathieu de Montmorency, he started for Vienna, where he was anxiously expected. Hardly had he left his carriage than he went out again on foot. Prince Metternich arrived at the Embassy soon afterwards, and was informed that he must have passed M. de Montmorency on the way to his own house. He went home again without finding Mathieu. A search for him was conducted throughout the town for six hours and people were growing anxious when he quietly returned. He had been entrusted with letters and little presents for some Parisian nuns who had a community at Vienna; his first care had been to deliver these messages and his visit to this house had lasted six hours. It is possible that he met some leader of the clerical party there but I cannot confirm the fact, and confine myself to details which I can positively state. This beginning did not increase his reputation in the diplomatic world, which was about to start for Verona, and nothing was more miserable than our political appearance at this Congress.

We had a considerable number of envoys there: MM. de Blacas, de Caraman, and de La Ferronnays had joined their Minister, while accompanying the sovereigns to whom they were accredited, and brought a multitude of secretaries and attachés with them. More Frenchmen were at Verona than members of all the other nationalities together; yet France did not play a leading part, and was the less likely to do so in view of the want of union and harmony among her representatives.

Monsieur and the Minister of Foreign Affairs were anxious over the war in Spain. The King and the President of the Council wished to avoid war, and the various Ambassadors were divided between these two opinions. M. de Villèle was persuaded by the declarations of M. de Chateaubriand that he would strongly reinforce his views, and gave him permission to go to Verona. He arrived fully determined to speak against the Peninsular war, and his despatches confirmed for M. de Villèle the idea that he had secured a powerful accessory. The Vicomte de Montmorency returned to Paris, where he found the title of Duc waiting for him. It is difficult to conceive the childish delight that this favour caused him and his wife, but it was not of long duration. The Duc Mathieu de Montmorency declared that he was bound to send an army into Spain. M. de Villèle declined to fall in with his views, and M. de Montmorency very regretfully resigned.

M. de Chateaubriand, who had arrived posthaste, took his friend's place, and as soon as he had secured a seat at the council, declared himself a more energetic partisan of the Spanish war than his predecessor had been. The flatteries showered upon him by the Emperor Alexander, when he had been left alone at Verona after the departure of his colleagues, must have produced a change in his ideas, or possibly he had hidden his real opinions up to that time. Whether he was false or fickle, the facts are as I have related them. Mathieu had no objection to seeing M. de Chateaubriand in his place, as long as he believed him to be of a different opinion. But he was furious when he saw that his successor followed his own policy as soon as he had secured his position, and expressed his views with extreme bitterness. I was present at a violent explosion in which he did not spare M. de Chateaubriand. All the cleverness and kindness of Mme. Récamier, who was almost equally intimate with both men, were required to avoid the scandal of a public rupture which M. de Chateaubriand had every reason to fear.

Mathieu's course in life was by no means ordinary. His father, the Vicomte de Laval, the youngest son of the Marshal, had married Mlle. Boullongne, the daughter of a financier and heiress to a vast fortune, which, however, she never received. She was extremely pretty, lively and attractive, and speedily secured the affection of the Duchesse de Luynes, her husband's sister. The Vicomtesse de Laval was extremely anxious for a position at court. Mme. de Luynes espoused the cause of her sister-in-law, and the matter had been almost arranged when the royal family declared itself against the claims of Mlle. Boullongne, and her request was coldly refused. The Montmorency family considered themselves insulted by this affront to a lady who was no longer Mlle. Boullongne but Mme. de Laval. Mme. de Luynes declared her dissatisfaction. I believe that she also ceased to act as Lady of the Palace until the misfortunes of the Revolution brought her back to the feet of the Queen.

The Duc and Duchesse de Luynes had an only daughter, who was destined to be the greatest heiress in France. The pride of the Duchesse in her own name made her anxious to marry her daughter to one of her nephews, and her friendship with the Vicomtesse induced her to give the preference to that lady's only son, and to disregard the four sons of her elder brother, the Duc de Laval. He, however, was devoted to the Vicomtesse, and supported the proposal. The union of Mathieu de Montmorency with the young Hortense de Luynes was thus arranged to the satisfaction of the two mothers and with the consent of the Duc de Luynes. An unexpected obstacle then arose.

Guy de Laval, the eldest son of the Duc, a red-haired, ugly, asthmatic, eccentric old man, at the age of twenty had married Mme. d'Argenson, whose charms formed a striking contrast with her husband, whom she had married for his title and his wealth. Young Mathieu was quickly attracted to her, and became infatuated with his charming cousin. He had been brought up hostile to the court by reason of his parents' irritation, and his education had been left to the care of the Abbé Sièyes*: thus prepared, he became intimate with the d'Argenson family, his revolutionary tendencies were increased in their society, as was his philosophical agnosticism, whose foundation his tutor had laid. However, his straightforward and passionate heart made him recoil from the idea of marrying Hortense de Luynes as long as he adored the Marquise de Laval. She was a clever woman, somewhat older than he, and perhaps less deeply in love: she clearly understood that the rupture of this marriage would be laid to her charge as a crime by the whole family, and secured the consent of Mathieu with her entreaties. He therefore led Mlle. de Luynes to the altar while she was still a child, and after the ceremony she went back to her convent. Mathieu almost forgot her existence in the society of the Marquise. However, time passed and the moment came when it became advisable to reunite the young couple. Once more it was necessary to use the influence of the Marquise.

Hardly had the matter been settled when the Duchesse de Luynes was confined of a son, after fifteen years of childlessness, while another event took place which affected Mathieu still more deeply: his cousin, Guy de Laval, died without issue, leaving a widow whom he desired more than anything. He was too honourable a man not to behave properly to his young wife, but his coldness crushed her, and to deaden his feelings he plunged headlong into all the revolutionary exaggerations of the time. His parents made no effort to stop him, and his mistress urged him forward. She was intimate with Mmes. de Staël, de Broglie, and de Beaumont; she shared their opinions and passed them on to Mathieu.

He showed considerable talent as a public speaker, though he concluded by denying with all the impetuosity of youth his origin and his God. He brought down upon himself the anger of the court and of the anti-revolutionary party, and also the blame of all sensible people.

At the time of the first Federation, excitement, or rather fashion, induced a certain number of fashionable women to go and trundle wheelbarrows in the Champs de Mars that they might give some actual help in the preparations for the so-called national festival of the Federation. The Marquise de Laval was among the foremost, and used to arrive in a beautiful gilded coach, followed by three lackeys wearing the Montmorency livery and the constable's sleeve, in order to declare her love for equality and to show her eagerness to belong to the ancient class of productive workers. A shower of rain soaked her thin clothes and her velvet shoes, and cruelly cut short her patriotic intentions: she caught pneumonia, lingered for a few weeks, and expired in the arms of Mathieu. Terrified perhaps at the course of the revolutionary movement, and brought back to sounder views by her grief and approaching death, she eloquently expounded her ideas to her cousin upon her deathbed.

This loss, which threw him into complete despair, checked for a moment the political career of Mathieu. It was then, however, that he began that intimacy with Mme. de Staël which no event could break or even cool. The public thought that the consoler had succeeded in making him forget the Marquise. I am persuaded that the contrary was the fact. This pure friendship was born in tears, and preserved the purity of its origin.

While Mathieu was entirely absorbed in his grief, the Revolution proceeded from crime to crime, and no honest man could approve it. I cannot say if it was immediately after the death of Mme. de Laval that my cousin became inspired with religious feeling. I remember, however, that I found him a few years later leading an ascetic life in Switzerland and expiating the errors of his early youth with remorse. He had left his wife, the Duchesse de Luynes, who was with child, in France with his mother. She bore him a daughter, who was afterwards married to Sosthène de La Rochefoucauld. When time had somewhat healed the wounds of Mathieu, the entreaties of Mme. de Staël brought him to Coppet, where her kindness completed the cure.

When France had once more been pacified, he was induced to return by the desire of seeing his country and of fulfilling those duties which the violence of his passion had made him badly neglect. If Mme. de Montmorency had suffered from his coldness before the exile, she repaid him for it by her haughtiness and ill-temper upon his return. During her long imprisonment under the Terror, Hortense had grown passionately attached to a chambermaid whom she had either taken with her to prison or found there. She lived with her, exclusively devoted to the little cares of religion, which alone would bend her iron character. Her daughter occupied but a small part of her life, her parents even less, and her husband no part at all. Conscious that he had wronged her, and anxious to find in lawful affection an object for the warmth of his feelings, M. de Montmorency bore with admirable patience the cold reception which greeted him, and attempted to mollify his wife's harshness. Soon his daughter was sent to a convent to remove her from his affection, and Mme. Mathieu declared that while she was in prison she had taken a vow of chastity in order to save her own life and that of her parents. Mathieu yielded: his only resource was to follow her example and to lead a wholly ascetic life. He devoted himself to good works, to mortification of the flesh, and became a religious fanatic, as he was forbidden all family affection. For twenty years he pursued this mode of life, and was treated so disdainfully by his wife that, when she was dining away from home, she did not take the trouble to inform him of the fact, and he would come in to find that no meal was laid and that the servants had been forbidden to prepare any. He had no money of his own, and Mme. Mathieu did not give him a halfpenny, even when she inherited vast wealth at the death of the Duc de Luynes. I have seen him travelling outside a coach because he had no money to pay for an inside place. To her outward discourtesy was added real coldness and severity, and only the inexhaustible patience of Mathieu could have borne such conduct.

He had an attractive and noble face and was an amiable and witty character, made to please. His exaggerated affections were divided between religion and friendship. Ambition was added to these motives after the Restoration; it was that fanatical ambition which can lend itself with a clear conscience to the lowest intrigues with the certainty that its aim for power is intended only to promote the glory of God. Mathieu, who had been thrown into the hands of priests by his desire to expiate the errors of his youth, had for a long time been a disciple of the Little Church, and easily became a member of the Congregation, which urged him to lend his support.

The Duchesse d'Angoulême showed him marked favour, and when M. de Damas, her knight of honour, died in 1814, Mathieu took his place. He had great influence with the Princess, and also with Monsieur. These marks of court favour produced some kind of reconciliation between Mme. Mathieu and her husband: she no longer declined to provide him with dinner, and sometimes lent him her horses.

Duc Adrien de Laval, who alone of the four brothers in the elder line had any children, lost his only son, aged nineteen, and the branch of Montmorency Laval was left without an heir. The age of the Duchesse de Laval left no hope of male issue, and the family council therefore had recourse to the Mathieu household. I have seen the correspondence between the husband and wife upon this subject, and I am forced to admit that the letters of Mathieu were so tender in their affection, so gracefully expressed, with such purity of style, that I read them with real interest, though I felt certain that they would inspire me with disgust and scorn. Mme. Mathieu was persuaded. The couple sent a courier to Rome to secure the removal of the vows which separated them, and his return was awaited with much exaggerated impatience. From that moment Mme. Mathieu was seized with a violent infatuation for her husband. She was unable to live apart from him, and the change was one that is usually confined to fiction. The face of the heroine at the age of forty-five, ugly, awkward, and excessively vulgar, completed the ridiculous element in this absurd honeymoon, which Mathieu endured with his usual resignation.

It has been said that the attentions of Mme. Mathieu shortened her husband's life. In any case, she was perfectly happy for a few months in his love, in the importance of his position, his Ministerial post, and her title of Duchesse. Her vexation at leaving the residence of the Foreign Minister, with its beautiful drawing-rooms, was soon compensated for by her husband's nomination as guardian to the Duc de Bordeaux, with the prospect of apartments in the Tuileries. Unfortunately, Mathieu's health grew steadily worse, and he suffered from attacks of pain which his patient resignation concealed. He was better, and it was hoped he was cured, when on Good Friday in 1826, as he had not been well enough to attend divine service, he went out to accompany his wife and daughter to the Adoration of the Cross at the church of Saint Thomas d'Aquin. He was kneeling against the chair, and his prayers were unduly prolonged; Mme. de La Rochefoucauld advised him not to remain any longer on his knees. He made no answer. She waited for a moment, repeated her words, then attempted to raise him in alarm, and found that he was dead. He was carried into the sacristy. All efforts to restore consciousness were fruitless. Heart disease had cut short his life at the foot of the Cross which he had so earnestly, and I believe so sincerely, invoked for the last thirty years.

A picture was made of him which was a striking likeness, and recalls the features given to the Christ of the Spanish painters, especially that of Murillo. In my opinion, Mathieu's expression lost something of its beauty after ambition entered life. I can remember him in 1810 in the chapel of Saint Bruno in the desert of the Grande Chartreuse, where he made a poetical and touching picture. He was absorbed in prayer, and his beautiful face was lighted by a beam of sunlight. All who were present were astonished, and in a more credulous age we should certainly have believed that his head was encircled with a halo of divine light.

I was always fond of Mathieu, and lamented his death, but I felt some comfort in the fact that he had died the death of the righteous at a moment when he was surrounded by intrigues and intriguers who would almost certainly have sullied his reputation. His connection with Mme. du Cayla had already stained it. The despair of the Duchesse Mathieu was extreme. She was a strange person, and in her narrow mind there was room only for passion. She was not devoid of intellectual power, could tell an amusing story, and counted her money with great accuracy. As money had always been the chief affection of her life, she assumed that her deity shared her tastes, and when she wanted anything she would go to the altar and promise to devote to religious purposes a larger or smaller sum in proportion to the importance of her desires. If her prayers were heard she paid conscientiously, but if she was unsuccessful she gave nothing.

Thus the second Restoration of 1815 cost her thirty thousand francs. She had promised fifty thousand if Mathieu got well; this she did not pay. She gave the amount of alms prescribed by the Gospel, but with very laughable restrictions and without the smallest enthusiasm. She asserted that she had been born with most worldly inclinations, and with strong tastes for dissipation, and that she had been obliged to stifle this passion, as she could not subdue it. She survived her daughter as well as her husband, and spent her time managing the religious institutions which he had founded.

Monsieur greatly regretted the loss of Mathieu. Madame's enthusiasm for him had wholly cooled; she could not pardon him for preferring the post of Foreign Minister to that of her knight of honour. Here we have another proof, as I pointed out in the case of the Duc de Richelieu, of the importance which the Princes of the House of Bourbon attached to service to their persons.

In 1824, the King's health became steadily worse. He fell into a kind of stupor, from which he recovered only to receive the visits of Mme. du Cayla. Upon those days he invariably gave as the password "Sainte Zoé," accompanying this confidence with a smile which he attempted to make indiscreet; the Duc de Raguse has often told me that it inspired him with even more pity than disgust. The King detested Saint-Cloud. His favourite physician, Father Elisée,* whom he had brought back with him from exile, felt bored when out of Paris and had persuaded the old monarch that the château was damp. Hence he had been accustomed to say every year, for Princes are always ready to repeat polite formulae, that he could not wait there for his birthday, but would come back to Paris for the "Festival of the Cats." It was a piece of the courtiers' art to appear not to understand, in order to give him the pleasure of explaining that he referred to the middle of August.[9]

A strange anomaly in this strict and religious court was the presence of Father Elisée. He had been a monk and was a somewhat clever doctor. During the Revolution he threw away his cassock, and plunged into all the extravagances of the time with the appetite of a man long under restraint. He found some amusement in introducing his successive mistresses under the title of "Mère" Elisée. By some means he discovered a considerable number of pretty girls, whom he then passed on to his friends or patrons. This business of his, with its accompanying disgraceful scenes, extended to the apartments of the King's palace, beneath the very eyes of Madame. She was aware of it, but that made no difference in her treatment of him, though so scandalous a life, especially in the case of an old monk, would have met with just reprobation anywhere. But Father Elisée enjoyed the privilege of a man without character, whose actions pass unreproved because the actor is unashamed.

It was only in view of the absolute necessity of having the Tuileries cleaned that the King consented to leave this palace for a while. It was inhabited by more than eight hundred people who were by no means invariably clean in their habits. There were kitchens on every floor, and an absolute lack of cellars or sinks; consequently all kinds of filth collected and made such a smell that one was almost suffocated when going up the staircase of the Pavillon de Flore and crossing the corridors on the second floor. These appalling odours eventually reached the King's rooms, and made him decide to stay the shortest possible time at Saint-Cloud. He would leave Paris only when driven to extremes. I have heard that one of those visionaries, of whom the King was always ready to ask questions, had told him during the exile that he would return to the Tuileries, but would not die there. The worse his health became the more earnestly he clung to the place where he

9. Mid-August is *mi-août* in French and sounds like meow.

was not supposed to die. It must have been at Ghent, during the Hundred Days, that the King told the story of this prophecy. I cannot recall how the story reached me, or how credible it is. The fact remains that he preferred the Tuileries to any other dwelling. Monsieur and the Duc d'Angoulême liked it very well. The Duchesse de Berry did not object to it, and was ready to follow her family. Madame was the only person who preferred Saint-Cloud, and regretted that the court did not stay there longer.

On the festival of Saint Louis, 1824, I went to pay my respects to the King. I had not seen him since the month of May, and I was much shocked by the great change in his appearance. He was seated in the same armchair, and in his usual costume, a uniform brilliant with gold lace and studded with orders. The gaiters of black velvet around his legs were twice as large as before, and his once noble head was so diminished in size that it looked quite small. It dropped so low upon his chest that his shoulders rose above it; he could only raise his face with an effort, and then showed features so changed and lifeless that there could be no doubt of his condition.

He spoke a few kind words to me when I made my bow. I was all the more touched as I considered that I was then seeing for the last time this old monarch, whose wisdom had been put to the test so often, and who would perhaps have triumphed over the difficulties of his position if his infirmity had not made him helpless in the hands of those against whose foolishness he had struggled for thirty years.

Louis XVIII was accustomed to say that a King of France should only take to his bed in order to die. He proved loyal to this principle, for between August 25 and September 10, the last day of his life, he appeared again in public and held his court on two occasions. Possibly a more personal motive stimulated his courage. I had this account from Dr. Portal, his chief physician. The preceding year, the King had asked him what would be the manner of his death. Portal had attempted to change the subject, but the King declined to be put off.

"Do not treat me like a fool, Portal. I know very well that I have not long to live, and I know that I shall suffer much, perhaps more than at this moment. What I wish to know is whether the final crisis will take place in unconsciousness, or if I shall be obliged to spend several days in agony."

"Why, Sire, so far as can be seen, your Majesty's illness will be slow and gradual, and may last many years."

"Slow and gradual," said the King with some temper; "that is not what I want to know. Is there no prospect that I shall be found dead in my chair?"

"I do not think there is any likelihood of that."

"Then it will be impossible to keep out my brother and his priests," growled the King between his teeth, after a moment's silence. Then he turned the conversation.

It would seem that his prejudices had in no way diminished, for he received with marked coldness all the hints of those about him that he should attempt to seek relief from his sufferings in the good offices of the Church. When the Duchesse d'Angoulême ventured to advise this step more directly, he replied in a severe tone:

"It is not yet time, niece; make your mind easy."

However, the danger became more imminent, and the anxiety of the family increased proportionately.

Mme. du Cayla, who was not likely to be deterred by any sense of false delicacy, decided that there was no harm in hurting the feelings of a dying man in order to gain some power over the living. She arrived unexpectedly to see the King on the evening before his death, with the result that after a long conference the royal almoner was summoned to the King's side. Temporal affairs, moreover, were not forgotten during this last conversation.

Marshal Mortier* possessed in Rue de Bourbon a magnificent residence which he announced was for sale. That same morning a businessman came to offer him eight hundred thousand francs. The Marshal gave his consent, and immediately after the visit of Mme. du Cayla to the King, the eight hundred thousand francs were paid out to him in cash. An order, signed with the name "Louis" barely legible, had induced the Duc de Doudeauville to pay this considerable sum. The

King was still breathing, and under strict law could still sign a monetary order. However, Mme. du Cayla was always somewhat ashamed of this acquisition, and of the time when she secured it. She never ventured to live in the house, and a few years afterwards she sold it to the Duc de Mortemart.

As soon as the King's resolve was taken, he showed the greatest firmness. He personally gave orders that all the ceremonies should be carried out with all the usual forms which his prodigious memory could recall in the smallest detail. A few hours before his death the royal almoner made a mistake in reading the prayers for those *in extremis*. Louis XVIII interrupted him, and corrected the mistake with a presence of mind and calmness which never left him for a moment. The family was assembled at the end of the room, and was deeply affected. The doctors, the attendants on duty, and the clergy were around the bed. The First Gentleman of the Chamber held the curtain; when the chief physician gave the sign that all was over, he let it fall, and turning round, bowed to the Princes.

The Duc d'Angoulême, now direct heir to the throne, left the room sobbing, and Madame prepared to follow him. Hitherto she had always taken precedence over her husband as a King's daughter but now when she reached the door she suddenly stopped, and through the heartfelt tears with which her face was streaming she said with difficulty:

"Take precedence, Monsieur le Dauphin."

He immediately obeyed, without any hesitation or any remark. The First Gentleman announced, "The King!" the courtiers repeated, "The King!" and Charles X reached his rooms. The carriages were waiting, and he immediately left the palace with his family to go to Saint-Cloud, according to the custom of the Kings of France, who never stay a moment in the palace where their predecessor has just died.

The Princes of the House of Bourbon have been warmly criticised for their sacrifices to the laws of etiquette, but it is obvious that this was a tendency inherent in their character. Certainly the Dauphin's

wife was deeply affected by her uncle's death; and even if she had not
been attached to him, the terrible scene at which she had been present
would have been enough to move her deeply. Only a few seconds had
elapsed, and the dying man's last groan was still ringing in her ears; yet
nothing could distract her attention from a matter of pure etiquette under circumstances when no one would have noticed any breach of it.
On this sad occasion the Dauphin had not claimed his right, but had
simply accepted it without any display of astonishment or impatience.
A man so enslaved by forms will naturally impose the same duties on
others and may at times reach a point that seems ridiculous to people
brought up with other ideas. My brother, who was on duty in the service of the Dauphin, was an eyewitness of the last moments of Louis
XVIII, and it is from him that my account is taken.

The late King's apartment was draped in black, and decorated as a
chapelle ardente.[10] Masses were said there throughout the morning. The
senior officers undertook the duty of watching beside the body, which
lay in state for several days. The public were admitted by ticket, and
the scene was said to be extremely beautiful. My usual idleness and a
slight dislike for spectacles of this kind prevented me from going or
from being present at the funeral in Saint-Denis.

I received an account of the spectacle the same day from many of
the eyewitnesses, and especially from the Duc de Raguse, whose lively
imagination had been struck by the ancient feudal customs in which he
had been called to play his part. He described them with a happiness
of expression which he attained more often in speaking than in writing, and which made his conversation delightful.

I can remember, among other things, how he described the moment
when the chief herald took, one after the other, the helmet, the buck-
ler, and the sword of the King, and threw them after him into the
vault. They could be heard rolling from step to step, while the herald
said three times in each case, "The King is dead!" After this death cry,
nine times repeated in a mournful voice, amid the silence of the con-

10. A *chapelle ardente* is a chapel lit by candles where a dead person lies in state.

gregation, the door of the vault was closed violently, and the heralds turned around to the people with the simultaneous cry, "Long live the King!" All who were present repeated the cry. I will admit that throwing the helmet and sword of Louis XVIII might seem to be a ridiculous procedure, but when the Marshal described the sound of these weapons falling into the depths of the royal tomb, he inspired the same emotion in me he had felt at the time.

King Charles X said a few kind words to M. Brézé, Grand Master of the Ceremonies, thanking him for the excellence with which he had prepared and organised the details of the funeral.

"Oh, Sire," he replied modestly, "your Majesty is very kind, but there were many mistakes; next time we will do better."

"Thank you, Brézé," replied the King with a smile, "but I am not in a hurry."

Thereupon M. de Brézé collapsed. Upon assuming the title of Dauphine, the Duchesse d'Angoulême abandoned the title of "Madame," which she had hitherto borne. The Duchesse de Berry desired to appropriate this latter, and asked for the King's authorisation. He replied very dryly:

"By what right? I am alive and you are a widow. The thing is impossible."

In fact, if the Duc de Berry had been alive, he would not have become "Monsieur" until his brother's accession. Some courtiers attempted to speak of "Madame" during the first days, and the Duaphine replied severely: "Do you mean the Duchesse de Berry?"

The King expressed himself in similar terms, and the title was used only by those attached to the household of the Duchesse de Berry, by some familiar friends, and by subordinates who wished to curry favour. Mme. de Gontaut, though the governess of the children, declined to use it, and this began the coolness between the Princess and herself.

Charles X had not inherited the ill feeling of Louis XVIII for the d'Orléans family, whom he treated with kindness. The sincere friendship between the Dauphine and the Duchesse d'Orléans had modified the prejudices of the daughter of Louis XVI. The King conferred upon the Princes d'Orléans the title of "Royal Highness," which had been extinct for two generations. Only a Prince, and one who had been long exposed to the petty vexations resulting from difference in rank, could appreciate the joy which was felt at the Palais-Royal. Notwithstanding their claims to enlightened Liberalism, this title was received with as much happiness as it could have been during the period described by Saint-Simon. Old instincts take in consideration neither claims, nor times, nor circumstances, whatever efforts may be made to overcome them. The d'Orléans family were and will be Princes and Bourbons, whatever may happen.

The day following the death of the old King, Charles X received the chief bodies of the State at Saint-Cloud. He made a declaration of principle, and gave assurances so much more Liberal than might have been expected, that delight was both keen and widespread. These words were repeated in the evening, and printed the next day in the *Moniteur*. In Paris, and soon afterwards throughout the provinces, they excited general enthusiasm for the new ruler. His popularity was at its height on the day when he made his entry into Paris in a pouring rain which could neither diminish the number of the spectators nor drown the warmth of their cheers. The King was on horseback, getting wet with the best grace in the world, with the pleasing and open countenance which charmed the citizens of Paris in 1814.

CHAPTER THREE

Charles X

1824–1830

The Dauphin enters the Council ~ Popularity of the Duchesse de Berry ~ Coronation at Rheims ~ Influence of the clerical party ~ Death of Emperor Alexander ~ Signature of the ordinances ~ Carnival of 1829 ~ Fall of the Martignac Ministry ~ Outcry against the Polignac Ministry ~ The court of Naples in Paris ~ Ball at the Palais-Royal ~ Death of General de Boigne ~ Capture of Algiers ~ July Ordinances ~ Incapacity of Jules de Polignac

*T*he nation, always desirous of something new and ever ready to be entertained, welcomed the new reign with satisfaction. All the distrust of Monsieur, Comte d'Artois, which had been accumulating for years, was dispelled in a moment by a few phrases which Charles X pronounced in honour of the Constitutional Charter. He had only to turn these favourable feelings to further advantage. He fully appreciated them, for it was ever his instinct to seek popularity. He wished to please, and if he repulsed popular affection, he did so with reluctance. He was carried away by the clerical and political partisanship which dominated both himself and his Council. I might have wished to deceive myself in the belief that the weight of the Crown had changed the course of his ideas, but I knew him too well. I remember at that time that I discussed the matter at length with Mathieu de Montmorency, M. de La Rivière, and some others of the Ultra-Royalist party.

"You assert," I said to them, "that France does not know what she wants, and that there is no public opinion. Well, you will admit that Monsieur was most unpopular, and that, on the contrary, Charles X is very popular. Hence you infer that the nation is both fickle and prone to exaggeration, and that its impressions are not worth consideration. At the same time, a change has taken place during the last week; the unpopular Monsieur was regarded as hostile to the new laws of the country, whereas the popular Charles X has proclaimed himself their guardian. Would it not be logical to conclude that France is unanimous upon one point, namely, the maintenance of the new interests and of the Constitutional Charter which she has secured by thirty years of suffering?"

"Good gracious!" they replied, with some disdain, "no one wishes to interfere with their Charter or with the interests of the Revolution. They will be left untouched. But it is not right to sacrifice to them the few advantages that have been left to the upper classes, and, besides, we must have the power to govern."

M. de Villèle took advantage of the new regime to remove the censorship, which was causing him great trouble. He did not gain much as a result, for permitted attacks are just as sharp as forbidden ones.

The Liberal tendencies were not of long duration. The King and his councillors reverted to their former habits, and hostility to the Government increased as hopes which had been so readily entertained upon such slight grounds were deceived.

I have reason to believe that the prudence shown at the outset was due largely to the influence of the Dauphin. M. de Villèle, who knew by experience what could be effected by the heir to the Crown, realised immediately the strength which a reasonable Opposition under his leadership might gain, and attempted to neutralise any such movement. Pretending great admiration for the sound judgement of the Dauphin, he requested him to enlighten the Council with his presence. The Prince perceived the snare, and those who were honoured by his confidence advised him to refuse. But the King commanded, and the son obeyed as he obeyed every order from his father, including the order to lose his crown. At the same time he was relieved by the fact that he was not supposed to take responsibility for the acts of that Council in which he consented to take a seat. He offered criticism of their decisions, but ostentatiously took no part in them.

For instance, on the day following an important decision which had been taken against his opinion, as he walked past the Council table he put his hand upon his chair, saying: "I often have a very comfortable nap in this chair."

On another occasion at Saint-Cloud, addressing a crowd of courtiers who were standing around him:

"Gentlemen," he said, "which of you can tell me, at once and without counting, how many volumes there are in this bookcase?"

Several people made a guess.

"Lévis is the nearest," said the Dauphin. "I am quite sure of the number, for I counted them all again during the last Council. I usually spend the time that way when I do not go to sleep."

These words were repeated as they were spoken, and for so reserved a Prince they seemed to denote absolute opposition to the step taken by the Ministers. But these disavowals were known to only a small circle, and the Dauphin's popularity suffered greatly from his entrance to the Council.

Next to hunting, the Dauphin liked nothing so much as playing at being a soldier. This amusement was permitted the more readily as he cared very little about matters of military organisation. After he had drilled a few battalions, had severely reprimanded some clumsy execution, had pointed out a mistake in a uniform or in the handling of a weapon, he imagined that he was a great General, and went home delighted with himself.

The Dauphine had a much better idea of the part he should have played. There was not an officer whose face and name she did not know; she was aware of their circumstances, their hopes, and their family connections, and she paid no attention to the notes of the Almoner, notwithstanding her sincere piety. She would put forward the Dauphin's name whenever she gained a favour, which in most cases was nothing more than an act of justice. She was almost a mother to the young officers of the Guard, and did her best to procure them amusement as well as promotion. On many occasions she secured the suspension of orders which interfered with the amusements of the Carnival. Hence she was adored by these young men for whom she relaxed the usual severity of her countenance. Though she thus appeared the patroness of the young army, she was never able to identify herself with the glorious remnants of Napoleon's *Grande Armée*.

The Dauphin showed less aversion in this direction. As for the King, his *émigré* tendencies were impossible to keep in check. Louis XVIII was constantly reminding the officers of the Empire of the anniversaries of those battles in which they had taken part: his incredible powers of memory were often displayed in his narratives of marches and manoeuvres which the soldiers themselves had often forgotten amid the number of their military experiences, while he often brought forth memories agreeable and flattering to those with whom he spoke.

Charles X, on the other hand, would never speak of the wars of the Empire. Marshal Marmont, who was often summoned to play whist with him, sometimes took pleasure in noting the anniversaries of brilliant exploits performed by the French army. But the King invariably disputed their brilliance with much vivacity, and described them as they appeared in the accounts which he had read abroad. If the Marshal or anyone else attempted to place the facts in their true light, he showed much displeasure and anger, and his partner in the game felt the consequences, for he was a very bad loser.

When he ascended the throne he declared that a King's reproaches were too important to be expended over a game of cards, and that he would lose his temper no more. However, he was not one of those men who can control themselves. He was extremely obstinate because he could not understand explanations, and he had no force of character. After a few weeks of constraint his old tendencies took the upper hand, and his anger exploded.

He was vexed, and even a little ashamed of himself in consequence, and did not care for too numerous an audience. He usually played his game of whist in the rooms of the Dauphine, and practically no one was present except his partners. They were not particularly anxious to repeat the discourteous words which the King let fall in his anger, as they knew that their turn might come the next day.

Sometimes, however, such comical scenes took place that stories of them reached the outside world. Among others I remember one evening that the King, after uttering a thousand insults, called M. de Vérac a *driveller*.

M. de Vérac, red with anger, rose and said with much vehemence: "No, Sire; I am not a *driveller*!"

The King, who was also very angry, raised his voice and replied: "Well, sir, do you know what a *driveller* is?"

"No, Sire; I do not know what a *driveller* is."

"Well, sir; no more do I."

The Dauphine could not refrain from a burst of laughter, in which the King joined, together with all the company. The Dauphin used to play chess, and withdraw at an early hour to the Dauphine's room, the doors of which were then closed. The Princess was left alone with her tapestry work. Every day she invited two or three ladies from her own household or from that of her husband to join these evening gatherings, at which full dress was obligatory. My sister-in-law was invited somewhat oftener than others, as she was a favourite; the ladies on duty had no right to be present without an invitation. The Dauphine was by no means pleasant to her ladies, and permitted no familiarity. From time to time the Duchesse de Berry would come to the apartments of the Dauphine. She took part in the King's game, and was scolded quite as much as the others.

This kind of court was sometimes held at her house, and was then a little more numerous. When the Dauphine was absent, the King would transfer his game to the rooms of the Duchesse de Berry. At Saint-Cloud they met in the King's drawing-room; this way of life continued without the smallest change until July 31, 1830.

The Duchesse de Berry did not share the monotonous life of the other Princes. For some time she had thrown off her mourning and plunged into every available distraction. Her mourning had been a pretext for surrounding herself with her own court, and she had been careful to choose young and cheerful members. The funeral monument and a charitable institution which she was founding at Rosny to receive her husband's heart often brought her there during the early days of her grief. Her constant appearances in this district became visits; she received some visitors, and began to seek amusement. Soon the journeys to the château of Rosny became diverting festivities. Nothing was simpler in character, though I could never reconcile myself to the Princess's interest in shooting. Mme. de La Rochejaquelein had taught her this pastime. They used to shoot rabbits and to mark those which they had killed by cutting a bit of the ear with a little knife which they carried for that purpose, putting the fragments in their bodices. When they returned to the château, they counted these bloodstained trophies. This always seemed to me disgusting.

Mme. de La Rochejaquelein wore an almost entirely masculine costume upon these occasions. The Duchesse de Berry was delighted with this dress, and when she proposed to imitate it was checked by the dry answer of her lady of the wardrobe, the Comtesse Juste de Noailles, whom she had ordered to get a similar one made:

"Madame had better apply to one of these gentlemen, as I do not understand trousers."

Gossip quickly became rife about the conduct of the Duchesse de Berry, but suspicion pointed to M. de Mesnard, who was thirty years older, and whose attendance was determined by his post as knight of honour to her; the public, who regarded him as a kind of mentor, would not believe the scandals which went around the court. The royal family, however, was persuaded of the extreme indiscretion of the Princess's conduct. The King was often heard upbraiding her with the utmost violence: she attributed these scenes to the influence of her sister-in-law, and their mutual dislike constantly increased. Neither Mme. de Noailles nor Mme. de Reggio were among the favourites of the Princess. In this way discord entered the Pavillon de Marsan, with Mme. de Gontaut and M. de Mesnard struggling for the favour of the Princess. The latter, however, won the day, and the consequent coolness towards the governess tended to estrange the mother from her children.

The Duchesse de Berry troubled herself very little about them, and hardly ever saw them. When the Duc de Bordeaux was suffering from a severe attack of measles which caused some anxiety, she did not think of postponing a journey to Rosny. The King and the Dauphine were displeased in consequence, and expressed their feelings loudly. Yet they would have been the first to blame the Princess if she had asserted her rights as mother against those which etiquette assigned to the governess. Every day the governess brought the children to the King when he awoke, and I do not think that the Duchesse de Berry received much consideration during these daily interviews.

I have heard at various times that her numerous indiscretions caused much commotion. In any case, the matter is unimportant; I was entirely outside the circle where this royal gossip caused disturbance, and am but the uninformed historian of it.

I have never seen the Duchesse de Berry except as a sulky, unformed schoolgirl. Her misfortunes had taught her nothing in this respect. I remember that, at the last concert at her house at which I was present, some forty ladies who were in her salon, including myself, had stayed behind after the concert was over. She allowed us to stand around the room, spent twenty minutes whispering and giggling with the Comte de Mesnard and then, taking him under her wing, retired to her own room without addressing a single word to anyone else. People went away somewhat vexed at the foolishness of her behaviour. I am, however, persuaded that her behaviour was merely that of a spoiled and untrained child.

Though she often deeply displeased those who came from a distance to pay their respects to her, she was very greatly loved by her intimate friends. She was cheerful, natural, and of a gay and clever disposition; she was a good mistress, and was adored at Rosny, where her bounty was intelligently distributed. She also enjoyed a certain popularity among the middle class of Paris. Her chief merit consisted in her difference from the rest of the family. She was fond of art, liked the theatre, and gave entertainments. She used to walk in the streets, indulged her fancies, and went into shops. She paid much attention to dress, and brought a little movement into court life; this was sufficient to secure her the affection of the shopkeeping class. The banking class liked her because she would appear in public and be present at every small festivity without etiquette. She would have been less disposed than the Dauphine to insist upon distinction of rank. The artists she employed, and whose work she appreciated with the intelligent tact of an Italian woman, also praised her and contributed to increase her popularity.

M. de Villèle relied on the influence of the Dauphin against that of the Congregation under circumstances when the success of the intrigues begun by the Congregation would probably have forestalled the catastrophe of 1830 by some years. The Congregation wished to omit from the coronation oath the promise of fidelity to the Charter, on the pretext that this compact permitted liberty of worship. The King was disposed to make this restriction openly. The Congregation party in the Council approved, and the clergy, led by the papal nuncio, urged him forward. M. de Villèle was under no illusions as to the consequences of such conduct, and asked the Dauphin for help. The latter succeeded in persuading his father to abandon this dangerous project, but only with some difficulty. The whole of the night preceding the ceremony was spent in altering and discussing the various forms of oath.

In accordance with my idle habits, I felt no temptation to go to the coronation at Rheims. If I had thought that the holy ampulla was to be used probably for the last time on the coronation of a most Christian king, possibly my curiosity would have been aroused. Notwithstanding the magnificence beneath which the clerical and feudal mummeries were concealed, they excited some comment. Charles X, in a white satin shirt lying on the ground to receive through seven openings in his vestment the drops of holy oil, was not regarded by the multitude as sanctified by the anointing of the Lord, but rather as a personage made ridiculous and discredited by this ceremony. The birds released in the cathedral as a sign of emancipation merely proved a nuisance, and no one thought of shouting "Noël! Noël!"[1]

On the other hand, when the King, magnificently dressed in the royal cloak, pronounced the oath from the throne, when the doors of the cathedral were opened with a crash, and the heralds announced to the people that their King was crowned, when the cheers from without joined the acclamations within, and answered the heralds with the universal cry, "Vive le Roi," a deep impression was made upon all there.

In these old ceremonies there are always some customs which are merely antiquated and best forgotten, and others which invariably make a strong impression. Tact is required to tell the difference between the two and intelligence to choose. The Emperor had been able to make this choice. His coronation had been most solemn and religious, and had been accompanied by none of those prostrations which the Church claims and the spirit of the age rejects. I am well aware that the Prince who performs them professes to humiliate himself only before his Lord, but the priest seems too strongly in evidence to be completely left out of count in these ceremonies, whose mystical meaning is hidden beneath material forms.

Upon his return from Rheims, the King made a magnificent entry into Paris. The procession was superb. I happened to see it as it was returning from Notre-Dame to the Tuileries. The King, in a coach with seven windows, was accompanied by his son and by the Ducs d'Orléans and de Bourbon. The d'Orléans Princes were in the coach of the Dauphine with the Duchesse de Berry. The carriages of the different Princes followed. Those of the Duc d'Orléans were both elegant and magnificent. Notwithstanding this pomp in magnificent weather, we

1. Traditionally, one shouts Noël when something long hoped for finally takes place.

noticed that the King was rather coldly received. There were none of those heartfelt cheers which had welcomed him months before amidst the pouring rain.

The court of Vienna had never consented to recognise the Italian or the German titles which the Emperor Napoleon had distributed to his Generals. On the other hand, the court of France did not wish to order the Generals to renounce their titles, and the difficulty between the two Governments remained undecided, though the holders of the titles themselves were not concerned. Since 1814 the Austrian Ambassador, Baron von Vincent, had avoided the difficulty without raising any disturbance. As he was unmarried, he gave no evening parties, and his hospitality was confined to dinners. He used to give verbal invitations to M. le Maréchal or M. le Duc without adding the title. When he expected one of these doubtful titles, he was careful to stand so near the door that the footman was not obliged to announce the name. This proceeding seemed so natural that the device was continued for a number of years without attracting attention.

On the arrival of the new Ambassador, Count Apponyi, there was a vast change. He proposed to live in great style, and to make a brilliant entry into society. Invitations were sent to Marshal Soult, to Marshal Oudinot, and to Marshal Marmont, et cetera. No one took offence, and everybody went. Their wives were more accustomed than the marshals to use their titles exclusively. Eventually it was necessary to notice the fact that when the servants gave the title of the Duchesse de Dalmatie or de Reggio, the footman announced the Lady Marshal Soult or the Lady Marshal Oudinot. The fact became more noticeable when those ladies, who had never used anything except their titles, found that they were not accepted, and that the Duchesses de Massa and d'Istrie were announced as Mmes. Régnier and Bessières. An explanation became necessary.

There was a general outcry of dissatisfaction, and military society in a body deserted the salons of the Austrian Embassy. In all justice it must be said that even people of extreme Ultra politics showed the greatest annoyance at this insult to our new titles. The quarrel might have been avoided easily, but Count Apponyi was by no means tactful, while the Baron de Damas, who was then Minister of Foreign Affairs, and as narrow-minded as he was exclusively *émigré* in opinion, could not understand why this incident should arouse such a disturbance. Charles X showed no offence, and even insisted that the courtiers attached to his person should not desert the Austrian Embassy. Louis XVIII would have resented this political affront, and therefore the court of Vienna made no attempt of the kind during his reign. After a great deal of outcry, and after a great many social dissensions and quarrels, the splendid balls and excellent lunches brought the greater part of society back to the Countess Apponyi. The position of the Ambassador, however, remained unpleasant. Many people would not go to his house, and were displeased because the King took no notice of the incident.

The Emperor Alexander died at Taganrog of a fever, endemic on the shores of the Sea of Azov, to which he had very imprudently risked exposure in 1825. His last years had been poisoned by suspicions which had reached the point of monomania and crushed the naturally generous feelings of his heart.

Mme. de Narishkine had been recalled to Saint Petersburg for the marriage of a daughter whom she had had by Alexander, and whom she passionately loved. This young person died a few days before the date fixed for the marriage. The Emperor was in despair, and their common grief renewed the intimacy between these old lovers. Mme. de Narishkine told me the most extraordinary details of the Emperor's condition. At one time he had been the most trusting of men, but recently he not only feared for his personal safety, but if he heard a laugh in the street, or surprised a smile among his courtiers, he was persuaded that people were laughing at him, and would implore Mme. de Narishkine, in the name of their former affection, to tell him for what reason he excited the ridicule which pursued him everywhere. One evening when she had a young Polish relative with her, tea was served, and the Emperor hastened to pour out a cup for Mme. de Narishkine and then another for the young lady. Mme. de Narishkine leaned towards her cousin and said to her:

"When you go back to your father's estate, you will be able to boast of the distinction of your tea-maker."

"Yes, indeed," the girl replied.

The Emperor, who was deaf, did not hear the conversation, but saw the smile upon their faces. His own immediately grew dark, and as soon as he was alone with Mme. de Narishkine he said to her:

"You see how ridicule pursues me everywhere. Even you who are fond of me, and on whom I can rely, cannot help laughing at me. Tell me what I did to provoke your laughter."

She had the utmost difficulty in soothing his diseased imagination.

The Emperor trusted no one but Prince Metternich, and maintained an almost daily correspondence with him. The Austrian was far deeper in his confidence than his own Ministers, and the Emperor gave implicit belief in particular to his police reports. He constantly carried with him a little list sent by Prince Metternich containing the names of every political suspect in the whole of Europe: the names were arranged in alphabetical order, with the reason for suspicion attached to each. When a new name was pronounced before the Emperor, he immediately consulted his list, and, if he did not find the name, he listened benevolently to anything that people had to say. If, unfortunately, the name was there, nothing could overcome his prejudice. Mme. de Narishkine told me that she had often seen him consulting these oracular pages.

The last years of the Emperor were poisoned by these anxieties, possibly aggravated by intrigue, but hereditary in origin. In any case, his death caused much sensation and grief in Paris. He had shown magnanimity in 1814, and had been very useful to France in 1815.

In 1826, Talma died, at the height of his talent. He had created several parts in plays of no great merit in which he was sublime. His best were Sylla, Leonidas, and Charles VI; in the latter he invariably maintained his kingly demeanor amidst all the misfortunes of the man. I doubt if the actor's art could be carried to a higher pitch; our fathers, however, assured us that Le Kaïn was highly superior to Talma. Hitherto we have had no opportunity to boast of his supremacy to the new generation, for no one has appeared to take his place.

Talma in France and Mrs. Siddons in England have always seemed to be absolutely perfect upon the stage, because they completely identified themselves with the character which they represented. Both, moreover, were so handsome and so graceful, and their voices were so harmonious, that their attitude was a picture as agreeable to the eye as their words were charming to the ear. One of my vanities—who has not many?—is to pride myself upon my lack of exclusiveness, and I should therefore be delighted to hear an actor or actress who could give me as much pleasure as Talma or Mrs. Siddons, but I doubt if any such will be found in my time.

I have now reached events highly important in view of their consequences. I cannot explain them, for I do not understand them, although they took place beneath my eyes. Perhaps someone will someday reveal the more hidden motives which prompted the facts I have to relate. I shall speak only of those motives which I have been able to discover.

I have already noted the prudence manifested by the Dauphin during the Ministry of M. de Villèle. I have also referred to the confidence which he gave to the supporters of the new Ministry, and M. de Martignac* in particular, who had previously accompanied him during the Spanish campaign. No sooner, however, had this new administration been appointed under his auspices than he seemed to withdraw his support and to stand perceptibly aloof from his usual advisers. M. Pasquier, and especially M. Portal, who had hitherto been frequently called to intimate conferences with the Prince, suddenly ceased to receive these messages. The notes which he continually used to ask them to write in order to enlighten his opinions were no longer demanded. These facts would be quite understandable had he given his confidence to the new Cabinet.

The Dauphin made the mistake of desiring a portfolio for himself, instead of simply maintaining his influence at the Ministry of War, where he used to do whatever he liked. But he had wished for some tangible responsibility, for offices and for definite work to do: the jealousy of place thus took hold of him, and he soon felt for his "colleagues" the petty rivalries which were carefully fostered by the inferior agents of his Ministry. On the other hand, all those officers who had not immediately secured what they desired could no longer appeal to the Prince against the Ministers, and therefore blamed him. Thus the Dauphin began to lose the popularity which he had formerly enjoyed in the army. These results had been foreseen by the previous counsellors of the Dauphin. They had attempted to dissuade him from his administrative whims, and his coolness towards them was probably the result of their efforts. I have already said that he was very reluctant to countenance the entrance of M. de La Ferronnays to the Council over which he presided. That gentleman has told me that throughout his Ministry the Dauphin never spoke to him directly, though they were often at cross purposes in the Council. The point of keenest dissension was the Duke of Wellington.

The Dauphin wished to adopt a measure recommended by the Duke of Wellington, of which M. de La Ferronnays disapproved, because, as the Prince said, "The Duke of Wellington is attached to our family, and as he likes us he will only recommend actions for our good."

M. de La Ferronnays, justly incensed by this innuendo, replied hotly that the Duke of Wellington was an English Minister, who would naturally regard politics from an English point of view; that it was the business of the Council of the King of France, composed as it was of Frenchmen, to weigh these proposals and to decide whether they were in French interests, and not to be led astray by questions of personal intimacy which certainly had no influence upon the British Government. He shattered the Duke's arguments which M. de Polignac had undertaken to propound, won the King over to his opinion, and carried his proposal in spite of the Dauphin's opposition.

This discussion took place at the close of the year 1827. But other circumstances had already embittered the feelings of the Prince. Of these, one of the earliest was the question of replacing the Duc de Rivière. The King wished the post of Governor of the Duc de Bordeaux to depend solely upon his nomination. The Council wished to be consulted, while the King's claim was supported by the Ultra party. The country as a whole took the side of the Ministers. The Dauphin vigourously supported his father's point of view, and insisted that in the choice of a Governor for his grandson, he would use that independence of judgement which belongs by right to every head of a family. With his usual want of tact, he said that it would be an impertinence to refuse the King this right. The Ministers, however, insisted, and the King undertook to make no choice without informing them. They proceeded to look about for a suitable person. The Duc de Mortemart was sounded out, but while negotiations with him were in process the King informed his Ministers individually about his decision, saying that at ten o'clock in the evening the nomination of the Baron de Damas would appear in the *Moniteur* the next day. This was what he called making no choice without informing them. They had mistaken the sense of his words, for when the rumour of this nomination was going about the chamber, I know that M. de Mortemart was told of it by M. de Glandèves, who replied that the appointment was impossible as the Council would never consent. The King's device was entirely successful, for the Ministers had no time to meet or discuss their plans or address a remonstrance to the King. None of them dared take the responsibility of stopping the printing of the *Moniteur*, and the nomination was inserted. The Cabinet entered a protest, but its influence then received a blow from which it did not recover.

M. de Damas was an extreme member of the Congregation. It was obvious to everybody that there was a clique in the Château whose influence was superior to that of the Ministers, and which was in the King's confidence. The Dauphin detested the Congregation, cared nothing for M. de Damas personally, and should have been opposed to his nomination. The Dauphin, however, was convinced that the choice of a Governor for the Duc de Bordeaux was the King's exclusive privilege, and that if he were not allowed to exercise it, he would be shorn of a civil right which every private individual should have. One day at lunch, one of his aides-de-camp ventured to say that the education of a child whose birth had been a national event should be regarded as a Government question. The Prince burst into a fury which quickly shamed him so much that he apologised. At the same time, he afterwards perceived that the nomination of M. de Damas produced an extremely bad effect upon the country, which led him to support the ordinances directed against the Jesuits and the little seminaries.

I shall not relate these great events in detail. I know history only as gossip and through connection with personal acquaintances, but as I shall probably have to refer to these so-called June ordinances,[2] it is necessary to mention them, and also to note the energy which the Dauphin had brought to the task of drawing them up.

The King kept the ordinances for a fortnight before signing them; they were submitted to the inspection of his spiritual directors. The leaders of the Jesuits gave their consent, understanding that any resistance at that moment would have caused their overthrow. They thought that it was more politic to yield, as they could rely upon the assistance of the King when circumstances might seem favourable for a counterstroke. The King therefore appended his signature with a clear conscience and with the full authorisation of his secret counsellors. But he was deeply annoyed, and we saw traces of this feeling.

As for the Dauphin, this was his last sensible act. Thenceforward he steadily abandoned the ideas which he had hitherto professed. The election of General Clausel as deputy for Lille finally drove him into the hands of the Ultra party. He had never been able to forgive this officer his role during the Hundred Days and his exasperation at this appointment reached the pitch of monomania. From this time onwards

2. The ordinances of June 16, 1828, brought under university government certain institutions conducted by the Jesuits, and also maintained that thereafter no one should be allowed to teach or to lead an educational establishment if he had not previously declared that he belonged to no Congregation not legally authorised in France. Moreover, the number of pupils which might be admitted to the little seminaries was limited to twenty thousand, and rules for supervision were included.

not a glimmer of the sound sense upon which France had set her hopes for many years was to be found in him. This change, which became speedily well-known, as well as the subject of the education of the Duc de Bordeaux, roused public passion against the older branch of the Bourbons, and procured the overthrow, accomplished in three days, because every root had been cut through months before.

I have said what I know of the motives which may have actuated the Dauphin. Possibly there are some others that I do not know about. Certain people have believed that Nompère de Champagny, one of his aides-de-camp, a distinguished young man and a zealous member of the Congregation who seemed to follow the ideas of the Prince, might have influenced him. Possibly also the continually increasing demands of the Liberal party led him to fear the advance of demagogues who must be crushed if one would not fall a victim to them, and it may be that he had been persuaded that a system of concessions merely served to strengthen their claims. I cannot say what was at the bottom of his heart, but the consequences were only too obvious.

The military council over which the Dauphin presided had resumed its sittings, and Marshal Marmont told me daily that the Prince was constantly proposing obsolete theories and absurd claims. I remembered his earlier praises, and I will admit that I attributed this change of tone to the fickleness of the Marshal. Unfortunately, he was not the only man who disturbed our peace of mind by such remarks, and all our evidence contributed to show that the Dauphin had joined the most violent reactionary party.

I labour this point, which history will perhaps neglect, because, in my opinion, it was this circumstance which destroyed all hopes, exasperated all minds, and drove both parties to excesses.

The King made a journey to Alsace during the summer of 1828. He was thoroughly delighted with his excellent reception. However, every address complimented the ordinances against the Jesuit establishments, and M. de Martignac pointed out this fact upon every occasion. The King conceived an additional dislike for his Minister, and attributed the demonstrations of the inhabitants throughout his triumphal progress to their personal affection for himself. Some petty German sovereigns came to pay their respects to him at Strasbourg, and he thought of himself as a second Louis XIV.

The Ministry continued a painful existence: it was forced to combat the opposition of both the Left and the Right, composed of Ultras, Congregationists, courtiers, and the King. Possibly the Ministry might have held out, notwithstanding these obstacles, if the supporters of peace and order had openly united to help, but everyone had different views and wishes and used his right to blame and to criticise.

While the leaders were thus playing pitch and toss for the Crown, the amusements of the capital were nonetheless brilliant, and the Carnival of 1829 was very splendid. The young d'Orléans Princes were growing up, and the Palais-Royal became correspondingly cheerful. Concerts and dinners were succeeded by theatrical performances, by balls and quadrilles. The Duchesse de Berry took advantage of this fact, and gave very handsome entertainments. The most agreeable and pleasant of these were held in the apartments of her children, and were given in the name of Mme. de Gontaut. This device enabled the Duchesse to dispense with the rules of etiquette and to choose her guests from the most fashionable society. Masked balls were given where the magnificence of some of the costumes delighted the eyes, but which were not a beautiful spectacle on the whole. The Duchesse de Berry thought that if she allowed her guests full liberty in dress, she would succeed better, and she was in fact entirely successful.

The appreciation for the Middle Ages was becoming fashionable. The Duchesse conceived the idea of representing the Renaissance court of François II. All the youngest and most fashionable members of society were given a place in this company, for which marches, evolutions, and dances were composed; the remainder of the guests in ordinary costumes were spectators. The Duc de Chartres, the son of Louis-Philippe, representing François II, was the object of general admiration. It was his first public appearance, and his charming face and graceful bearing were much admired; those who had been admitted to rehearsals no less readily praised his politeness and the fine tact which governed his every action. The master of the ballet had prepared a throne for the Duc de Chartres above that of the Queen, who was represented by the Duchesse de Berry. The Duc de Chartres refused to take this place, and conducted Mme. de Podenas, who was taking the part of Catherine de Medici, to it. This little incident gave the utmost delight at the Tuileries. The Dauphine pleasantly related it as an action "in excellent taste on the part of Chartres." Could it have been that some instinct told him that the throne of the Tuileries would be placed within his reach? Upon that occasion he did not seem inclined to exercise the "good taste" of renouncing it.

We were informed that the Dauphine had strongly objected to the Duchesse de Berry's choice of Mary Stuart as her part. The role of a queen who had been beheaded was perhaps somewhat tactless to assume in the palace of Marie-Antoinette. The Duchesse de Berry, however, was less far-sighted. The King did not forbid the quadrille and the Princess, as usual, disregarded her sister-in-law's disapproval. The latter had been present at the masked ball in costume and bedecked with jewels, but she did not appear at the quadrille and sent no excuse on the grounds of health. However, she did lend her diamonds to the lady who took the part of Marie de Lorraine, mother of Mary, Queen of Scots.

Generally speaking, the women were well-dressed, and were beautifully set off. The men, with few exceptions, looked like masked street ruffians. The Duc de Chartres wore a magnificent costume to excellent effect, and the little Duc de Richelieu looked better than I have ever seen him before or since.

The Queen of the festival, the Duchesse de Berry, looked appalling. She had had her hair arranged in a tier, a fashion perhaps entirely classical, but which suited her abominably; dressed in a long ermine cloak with the fur turned inwards, she looked like a drowned dog. The heat of this costume had reddened her face, her neck, and her shoulders, which were usually very white, and no one was ever more successful in her efforts to look a fright. The little Mademoiselle, her daughter, was present at this entertainment, and went from bench to bench gathering expressions of admiration for the Duc de Chartres. Her own enthusiasm seemed extreme. She displayed an affection for him which was quite touching in view of her age, for she was not more than ten years old. This young Princess promised to be highly accomplished rather than pretty. I never had the honour of her intimate acquaintance, but sometimes saw her in Mme. de Gontaut's rooms, and she seemed to me very pleasant. She overwhelmed the Duchesse d'Orléans with caresses, and often said:

"I am very fond of my aunt. She is very kind, and then she is the mother of my cousin Chartres."

She was continually holding up this cousin as an example to the Duc de Bordeaux, whom she dominated with all the superiority of her age and of her mind. She took an interest in public affairs when quite young, and she knew enough to show marked politeness to a politician, though she had not been specifically told to do so. Mme. de Gontaut understood that the child of a Princess should not be kept as ignorant as the child of a private person, and encouraged conversation of any kind before Mademoiselle, who soon showed a keen interest. In any case, it was necessary to occupy her lively imagination, and above all to instruct her that her haughtiness of character was unsuitable to our age.

Mme. de Gontaut told me that when the Duc de Bordeaux was taken from his sister's entourage, so that his education might be entrusted to men, she took the little Princess to the King the following day, according to daily custom. When they crossed the guard-room, the Life Guards did not present arms. Mademoiselle stopped short in astonishment, and seemed much displeased. When she went out later in the morning, there was no escort for her carriage. The next day the sentry, who had received no orders on that point, turned out the guard when he saw her coming.

She stopped, bowed to him, and said:

"I thank you; but you are mistaken, it is only myself."

She refused to take her usual drive. Mme. de Gontaut understood that she did not wish to go out without an escort. She watched the child carefully but said nothing. Mademoiselle, beginning to weary of staying in the house, asked her governess if she could not go out with her brother, and added that it would be more amusing to go to the park of Bagatelle with him than to walk about at her side.

Mme. de Gontaut answered coldly:

"Think the matter over for half an hour, and if you can then tell me that you wish to go with the Duc de Bordeaux, merely for the pleasure of seeing Bagatelle, I will undertake to arrange the drive."

A few moments afterwards the young Princess came in tears to admit to her "dear friend," as she called Mme. de Gontaut, the weak pride of her young heart and her sorrow at discovering that Bordeaux was "everything" and that she was "nothing." It was not difficult for a clever woman like Mme. de Gontaut to make so clever a child understand the pettiness of such claims. A short time afterwards Mademoiselle was anxious to make amends by walking on foot, giving her arm to Mme. de Gontaut and followed by a footman, through the streets of Paris.

I have narrated this anecdote to show how early the royal instincts assert themselves, and how natural it is that etiquette should be necessary to Princes as they grow old.

In any case, Mme. de Gontaut had exceeded her powers in saying that she could arrange the drive to Bagatelle, as the Baron de Damas, in his wisdom, had resolved to separate the two children. He feared the effects of female influence on the young Duc de Bordeaux, and his bigotry, which I thought utterly indecent, had already forbidden the eight-year-old Prince to kiss his sister, who was nine. His education as a whole was conducted upon generally enlightened principles, apart from the gymnastic exercises, which he was obliged to practise as if he intended to appear with the Franconi circus. The poor little Prince was brought up like a monk and bored to distraction. Public indignation at the training which the future sovereign underwent ultimately alienated the affection of the people from the reigning monarch.

The health of M. de La Ferronnays had been very poor for a long time, and now became so bad that he was obliged to resign the Ministry of Foreign Affairs. Several persons were asked to take his place, among them M. Pasquier. He again declined, convinced that the King's prejudice would prevent any confidence between them.

This prejudice was long-standing. In 1814, when Monsieur had reached France before Louis XVIII, and had governed the country for some time as Lieutenant-General, M. Pasquier had spoken to him of the state of the country, the strength of parties, and the importance of individuals with a frankness which the *émigré* Prince had been unable to understand, and which those about him had labelled as hatred for the Restoration. Nothing could be more absurd. M. Pasquier had heartily fallen in with the new order of things, necessitated by safety for the country, and he merely wished to turn it to the best account. Accustomed as he had been to serve under the Emperor, he was only continuing his previous methods.

Napoleon not only desired but insisted that everyone should tell him the whole truth, and should support their opinion against his own. In personal discussion he would permit argument to the point of contradiction. He invariably acted as he pleased, but he never bore ill feeling for any opposition to his views in the Council or in the Cabinet. Monsieur could not understand this method of treatment: anyone who offered objections, even in his own interest, was regarded as an enemy. M. Pasquier took so long to discover this frame of mind that his own zeal steadily worsened his position; even when he realised the truth he nonetheless continued doing what he considered his duty.

When he became a Minister of Louis XVIII, he was suddenly brought into collision with the Ultra party, and displeased Monsieur as a result. These views did not allow him to enter the Council of Charles X, and he pointed out to the Ministers who desired his cooperation that he would be of no help to them if he sat at their Council, and could be more useful to them in the Chamber of Peers. He did not share the discontent which most of our party felt for the weakness of the Martignac Government, but openly declared that it was foolish to demand from the Government what could not be extorted from the King's prejudices. It was not the fault of M. Pasquier that the Ministry fell, for he supported it most frankly and by every means in his power.

During the last days of the session of 1829, M. de Villefranche, a peer and member of the Congregation, delivered a violent but somewhat clever speech, which he obviously had not composed himself, vigourously attacking the King's Ministry for its general policy and especially for the so-called June ordinances. M. de Martignac replied with his usual talent, and spoke with great eloquence and wisdom upon the subject of the ordinances. In the evening he was with the King, and met with an excellent reception. The monarch complimented him upon his success in the Chamber of Peers. The next day there was a change: M. de Martignac came to work with the King, who received him most coldly, and the Minister could not imagine how he had given offence. At length, when their work was ended, he was addressed as follows:

"Why on earth did you want to speak yesterday?"

"What, Sire! How could I allow the invective of M. de Villefranche to pass without reply?"

"Well, the session is nearly at an end, and it was not worth your while."

"It is precisely because the session is at an end that the King's Government should not be left to bear the weight of all these calumnies."

The King began to walk up and down the room.

"At any rate, you might have avoided any reference to the ordinances."

"M. de Villefranche began it, Sire, and I was naturally obliged to explain a measure which was the work of your Majesty as well as the Council."

"Explain! Explain! To begin with, M. de Martignac, they will never pardon you—you may be certain of that."

"What, Sire?"

"Oh, I know what I am talking about. Good day to you, Martignac."

The Minister who was thus dismissed was obliged to withdraw without realising that his overthrow had been determined. He had not long to await his fate.

As a contrast to this anecdote which M. de Martignac told me, here is one which I have from M. de La Ferronnays. I am anticipating a little, in order to bring the two cases together.

When M. de La Ferronnays took the place of M. de Chateaubriand at Rome under the Polignac Ministry, he told the King that he could not accept the embassy if there was any proposal to revoke the June ordinances: they had been proposed under his administration, discussed at the Council of which he was the president, bore his signature, and that he could not announce their repeal. The King flew into a rage, asked what reason he had to believe him capable of such recantation, asserted that the June ordinances were his work quite as much as the work of the Ministry, reminded him that he had kept them three weeks before signing them, and seemed very angry that he could be suspected of such weakness. Such was the account of M. de La Ferronnays at the time, and we may ask how his story can be squared with that of M. de Martignac. I do not propose to undertake the task; I quote the words as I received them, and have stated my authorities.

I remember that in the course of that summer of 1829 I was staying in the country with Mmes. Nansouty and de Jumilhac, and the Duc de Raguse. We were amusing ourselves by recalling the events of the Empire and comparing our various impressions of them. The Marshal spoke from the point of view of the army, Mme. de Nansouty as a member of the imperial court, Mme. de Jumilhac as one of the absolute Royalists of the Opposition, and I myself as a Constitutional Royalist. We kept saying to one another: "What! You believed that?" "You hoped this?" "It was ridiculous." "I quite agree."

This examination of our political consciences pleased us so much that two o'clock in the morning found us in warm discussion, and we were informed of the time only by the lamps which suddenly went out. We said to one another:

"The moral to be drawn from our conversation is that the period of revolutions is past. When people of every party can thus meet together and laugh at their own absurdities, there can no longer be political divisions in society, whatever may happen. Party spirit is dead and personal hatred worn out."

Alas! How utterly false were our prophecies! I by no means expected that the keenest animosity of discord was about to rise around me, to break even the bonds of friendship and to divide families.

New Year's Day was notable for the speech of the papal nuncio to the King, in which he seemed to offer advice for the furtherance of an Ultramontane policy, to which his Majesty's reply gave a ready response. This circumstance caused a revival of the rumours which had been in circulation to the effect that this nuncio, Lambruschini, assisted by Cardinal de Latil, had, with the authorisation of the Pope, released Charles X from the oath[3] which he took upon his coronation. I cannot assert that such a ceremony took place, but well-informed people believed the fact.

That same New Year's Day, the King's Court of Justice, led by its president, M. Séguier, called upon the wife of the Dauphin. The president was about to address the customary congratulations, when she cut him short, saying in a most haughty tone, "Pass on, gentlemen, pass on."

These two events caused a great sensation and gave rise to much gossip. So studied an affront to the magistracy of the country and so benevolent a reception of antinational advice were two mistakes of serious import; however, the time had arrived when such errors followed in rapid succession.

The winter was extremely severe, and the population suffered proportionately; hence public charity attempted to relieve its miseries. The idea was then first conceived of giving a ball at the Opera, with

---

3. The oath demanded the respect of the Constitutional Charter.

tickets at the price of one louis each, in order that luxury might thus be induced to help poverty. The ladies of the court and of the town took equal part in this good work, which was entirely successful and brought in a very considerable sum. The inhabitants of the Tuileries had been among the first to contribute, but no one appeared in the box reserved for them. On the other hand, the box reserved for the Palais-Royal was occupied by the whole family of the Duc d'Orléans. The Duc d'Orléans and his son went down and mixed with the dancers. The Duc de Chartres took part in several dances. This gesture was highly approved, and contrasted strongly with the desertion of the royal box, which alone remained empty in the whole theatre. It was by such small attentions that the d'Orléans family secured that popularity which the other branch rejected even while they desired it.

Usually I am by no means curious to see those ceremonies to which the public throngs, but circumstances had made the opening of the session so important that I wished to be present at the royal sitting. This was held at the Louvre, and the details of the spectacle have remained in my memory.

The Duchesse de Duras, of whom I have so often spoken, had at length succumbed to the illness which had long earned her the title of imaginary invalid and had entirely exhausted the patience of her husband. He had just married as his second wife, a kind of Swiss-Anglo-Portuguese woman of whose origin I know nothing; she possessed a considerable fortune, which had been able to buy the title and the name of Duras. Some weeks after the marriage her behaviour had induced her husband to exclaim, "Ah! my dear, you cannot understand how pleasant it is for a husband to find himself more intelligent than his wife." It is certain that the first Mme. de Duras had given him no opportunity for this kind of enjoyment. It was beside this bride that I found myself on the day Charles X made his last speech in public. I could not restrain a feeling of terror when he pronounced the fearsome words, which I cannot precisely recall, asserting his intention to maintain his Ministry in spite of the Chambers.

The second Mme. de Duras asked what was the matter with me.

"Alas! Madame, do you not hear the King declaring war upon the country? And yet it is not for the country that I fear."

Five minutes afterwards, as we were about to go away, she said to me:

"You must have misunderstood. The Duc"—as she called her husband in her middle-class way—"told me this morning that he had read the King's speech; that it was excellent, would put an end to all difficulties, and silence all those who cried out against the King."

"So much the better, Madame."

It is not on account of any personal importance attached to these words that I relate this dialogue, but in order to show the state of feeling within the the Tuileries. M. de Duras was at that moment serving as First Gentleman of the Chamber, and his wife lived in the palace with him. Confidence in that quarter was as complete as it was blind.

King Charles X was entirely gracious in a drawing-room, and held his court in noble style, but at public functions he was completely undignified. His brother Louis XVIII, notwithstanding his strange bearing, succeeded much better on these occasions. Charles X had a shrill voice without resonance, did not pronounce his words clearly, and read his speeches clumsily—his usual gracefulness abandoned him. Accidental circumstances also contributed to hamper him: as he was very short-sighted, his speeches were written out for him in a large hand; hence it was necessary for him to be turning pages constantly, which did not add to his dignity. On that day when he reached the threatening phrase, he attempted to raise his head in a more imposing manner while he turned the page. During this gesture his hat fell off and the weight of its diamond ornaments brought it to the ground at the feet of the Duc d'Orléans. The latter picked it up, and held it until the end of the speech. This circumstance was remarked on by many people.

In the evening I went to the Palais-Royal and mentioned the incident of the hat. The Duchesse d'Orléans caught my arm.

"Oh, my dear, do be quiet. Can it have been noticed?"

"The Dauphine has also observed it. I did not dare to look at her, but I am sure she was vexed. I hope that there will be no talk about it."

Mademoiselle added, "Let us only hope that the newspapers will not make the matter a subject for silly comment."

This little incident caused even more sensation at the Palais-Royal, for the following reason: on January 6 of each year the Princes were accustomed to go to the King's house to share the Twelfth-Night cake for the Feast of the Magi. Upon that occasion the bean had fallen to the lot of the Duc d'Orléans, and the Dauphine had shown some ill temper at the fact. Thus a kind of presentiment had been formed which was shared by the whole country. When they saw the deplorable entanglement into which the members of the elder branch gaily plunged, people who were very far from desiring their overthrow could not help crying out, "Cannot these people see that they are paving the way to the throne for the d'Orléans?"

The arrival of the court of Naples in the spring of 1830 gave the signal for festivities. The Duchesse de Berry seemed delighted to have her family in her own house, and I have never seen her to better advantage than under these circumstances. Her father, the King, seemed to have been brought to premature dotage by the inroads of disease, and went out as little as possible, preferring the calmer atmosphere within the residence of his sister, the Duchesse d'Orléans.

The Queen of Naples, however, who was fat, plump, radiant, and ready to be amused in every possible way, availed herself of the good offices of the Duchesse de Berry to go around the whole of Paris and visit all the sights. Thus our two French Princesses were able to share in the reception given to their relatives. There were festivities at court, and for the first time we saw the d'Orléans family appear in the royal box. The evening before the performance the King had expressed a slight regret that the box was not sufficiently large to contain them as well as their near-relatives, the visitors. M. de Glandèves, Governor of the Tuileries, happened to overhear these words, made his carpenters work all night, and reported to the King the next day that there was room in the box for the d'Orléans Princes. The King was astonished for a moment, and then gave way with good grace. The delight of the Palais-Royal was infinite, and their gratitude to M. de Glandèves was so sincere that I have constantly found signs of it, even when the situation had entirely changed after the events of July.

The Duchesse de Berry gave a magnificent ball in her rooms and in those of her children at the Tuileries. I have never seen an entertainment better organised. The arrangement of the apartments necessitated the use of two stories, but the staircase, which was not that by which arrivals were admitted, had been beautifully decorated; the landings had been transformed into comfortable drawing-rooms, and the few steps which separated them were so hidden by hangings and flowers that the staircase was as crowded as any other room, and seemed to form an integral portion of the apartments.

Notwithstanding the exquisite elegance of this ball where a brilliant company was gathered in large numbers without any confusion, notwithstanding also the excellent arrangements and the satisfaction of the mistress of the house, gaiety was checked by an instinctive apprehension which weighed upon every mind.

The ball was followed by a most magnificent journey to Rosny. I heard many stories of its splendour, but as I was not myself present, I shall say nothing of it. I wish I could also pass over in silence the entertainment given at the Palais-Royal upon the return from Rosny, for my recollections of this festivity are by no means agreeable. As King Charles X had consented to accompany the King of Naples to the ball, it seemed only natural that the entertainment should be given in their honour, but the result was very different.

When I reached the Palais-Royal the neighbouring streets were thronged with people. Carriages advanced with much difficulty amid the curses of the crowd. My coachman was obliged to turn down ten different streets to make his way to the door. When at length he reached the little door in the Rue du Lycée, the police, orderlies, et cetera, were obliged to make a kind of chain and join hands with my attendants to deliver me from the crowd and secure my entrance to the palace. Within, the throng was only slightly less overpowering. Any-one who had cared to ask for tickets had received them, and it was with the utmost trouble that the aides-de-camp of the Prince, together with those of the King and the officers of the Life Guards, were able to keep a space of a few feet around the royal party. For a long time it was impossible for their Majesties to pass from room to room. I was driven by the crowd into the reserved space, where I had had no intention of venturing, and was nearly thrown into the arms of the Prince of Sa-lerno, the brother of the King of Naples. The Duc de Blacas, who was on duty, and with whom my relations were not too cordial, took pity on me and protected me while one of the waves of this multitude passed by.

I then had an opportunity to examine the bearing of the Princes. The King seemed to be in a good temper, the Neapolitans were as-tonished, and the Dauphine seemed displeased, which I could under-stand. The Duchesse d'Orléans was vexed and Mademoiselle was em-barrassed, while the Duc d'Orléans seemed satisfied. This satisfaction displeased me, I cannot precisely say why, but I felt afraid, vexed, and anxious to go away.

I returned home at ten o'clock, and my mother feared that some acci-dent had happened when she saw me arrive back so early. I told her that I was too fond of the d'Orléans family to be pleased with the en-tertainment, and that for the first time I could not help suspecting some ulterior motives on the part of the Duc d'Orléans.

His rooms had been thronged to suffocation by those most displeas-ing to the King at a time when he was supposed to be giving an enter-tainment in the King's honour. Also all the gardens were brightly lit and thrown open to the multitude at a time when the unpopularity of the Crown was well-known to everyone. He continually appeared on the terrace in order that the multitude might shout, "Long live the Duc d'Orléans!" These proceedings went beyond mere popularity-hunting; they were vulgar and wounded me the more as they were entirely inappropriate. It would have been quite natural for the Duc d'Orléans when receiving the Kings of France and Naples to pay special attention to his royal guests. A kind of political preoccupation was thus manifested by this transformation of an entertainment for kings into an entertainment for the people, and I was hurt by his attitude.

In any case, his action bore its fruit. That night may be considered the first demonstration of the year 1830, so fertile in unrest. The crowd admitted to the gardens and the galleries without supervision eventually became excited by the exhortations of certain agitators, and grew so turbulent that it was necessary to drive it out by armed force. Must we hence conclude, as I asserted in my ill temper, that the Duc d'Orléans entertained ulterior motives? The answer may be both negative and positive. I am persuaded that there was no actual plan of conspiracy, but he was nursing what he called "his popularity," and he was always anxious to "follow his own road," to use the expression of the poor Duc de Berry.

The day following this ball a letter from Chambéry informed me that M. de Boigne had been ill and was growing worse, and that his doctors were anxious. I knew him too well to venture to pay him a visit without his permission. I wrote to him at once in such a way as not to alarm him, asking that I might go and see him. He sent a reply stating that he had been very ill and was too weak to write himself, but that he was now better and that as soon as he could bear the journey he would go and take the waters in the Tarentaise, as his doctors advised. He begged me to delay my visit until his return at about the end of July. Reassured by this letter and by others, but not desiring to go out into society, I settled in the country at the beginning of June. I then learnt that M. de Boigne, who was said to be convalescent, had succumbed on the 21st to a fresh attack of the disease which he had suffered from for many years. This final attack lasted only a few hours, and I was assured that there had been no time to send me warning. Nonetheless, I regretted that I had not insisted more strongly upon a visit to Chambéry in the month of May, despite the patient's objection.

The elections of a new Chamber took place, with results more and more hostile to the Ministry. The two hundred and twenty-one members who had voted for the address[4] were all reelected by acclamation, and in the other colleges the retiring deputies were for the most part replaced by Liberals. The Cabinet began to grow uneasy, and anxiously awaited the successive nominations, news of which arrived by courier or telegraph. When an election which seemed to be favourable was heard about in the course of a day, the King usually took the name of the town for his password, adding to it an epithet of satisfaction.

The college of Montauban elected M. de Preissac, who had voted for the famous address. But the town mob, at the instigation of some members of the Ultra party, attacked the electors, pursued M. de Preissac, broke into his house, insulted his old mother, and wounded those who attempted to defend her. M. de Preissac owed his safety only to flight and the firmness of the Duc de La Force, who protected his retreat.

Everybody was furious at this brutal violation of constitutional right. Charles X conceived the idea of taking the name of Montauban as the password, and smiled in satisfaction at his choice. The Duc de Raguse drew himself up with so affronted an air that the King became red and stammered:

"Mont-Mont-Montpellier."

"Yes, Sire, I understand; Montpellier," replied the Duc. Nothing further occurred, but the two men understood one another, and their displeasure was mutual. The Duc de Raguse related this incident to me the same evening. It seems to me that little touches of this kind often reveal men much better than long and detailed accounts of their actions.

As the results of the elections became known, the rumours of a proposed coup d'état increased. The Duc d'Orléans had had a long conversation with Charles X upon this subject at Rosny, and the King assured him with such apparent frankness that nothing would induce

4. The address of March 15 in reply to the speech from the throne. Speaking of the harmony that should subsist between the political views of the Government and the wishes of the people, the address contained the famous phrase, "Sire, our loyalty and our devotion condemn us to tell you that this harmony does not exist."

him to take any unconstitutional measure that the deception was complete. Notwithstanding all the weapons prepared for legal resistance to Polignac, a Minister who was detested by the country, and notwithstanding all the possible trouble that might arise, the Duc d'Orléans was persuaded both then and afterwards, as I know from his own lips, that the Crown itself was in no danger as long as it abided by the letter of the Charter. The Charter, the whole Charter, and nothing but the Charter: such was the desire of the country, as expressed by him.

The lengthy stay of the Neapolitan sovereigns, who were established in the Palace of the Elysée, began to weary the King, who wished to leave Paris for Saint-Cloud. The Dauphine undertook to ask them when they would start home, under pretext of setting the day when she could start to take the waters. The sovereigns were deeply wounded by this mode of dismissal and named an early date. The Dauphine had one excuse for this apparent inhospitality. Her journey had been announced, and she could not have abandoned it without difficulty; at the same time, she wished to return before the meeting of the Chambers could give the signal for those extreme measures against which she alone fought with perseverance. It is strange, and yet entirely accurate, to say that she and her husband had exactly reversed roles. The more he followed the violent moves of the Ultra party, the more moderate and temperate she became. I was not sufficiently initiated into the secrets of their households to learn the reasons for this change of conduct, but it is certain that at this time the Dauphin was in favour of extreme measures, while his wife was opposed to anything of the kind. She had no confidence in the Polignac Ministry, upon which all her husband's hopes seemed to be set. The Princess went away with the King's promise that no important decision would be taken in her absence. The ordinances of July have proved how this promise was kept.

Private business had brought me to Paris, and I happened to be in the street at the moment when a salvo of cannon announced the capture of Algiers.[5] A loud cry of joy ran through the town, and I was much struck by the general enthusiasm. I had heard these triumphant cannon fired many times before, with little effect as far as the citizens were concerned, on occasions of far greater importance under the Empire, and was therefore much astonished at the personal interest taken by everyone in this success. Every door or shop was full of the household inhabitants, and passers-by stopped people whom they did not know to express their satisfaction. It may have been the long disuse of this kind of announcement that now made it all the more precious; or possibly the fatigue of the long wars of the Revolution and the Empire, and the sacrifices which they had exacted from almost every family, had made it impossible to strike so directly a note of national pride. Yet, in my opinion, the popular delight at the entry into Algiers was keener than it had been over the entry into Vienna or Berlin. I am giving only my own impressions, and do not guarantee their exactitude.

The King wished to return thanks to God for the success of his armies, and a solemn *Te Deum* was sung at Notre-Dame. Charles X arrived with all the pomp of royalty, and was received with high ceremony by the Archbishop of Paris. His sermon, which was faithfully reproduced in the *Moniteur*, promised the King the support of the Holy Virgin in the crusade which he urged him to undertake as well as against those of Africa. This appeal from the ecclesiastical or Ultra party was heard far and wide and exacerbated the people's patience. The words of the prelate must be added to those circumstances which more immediately contributed to provoke resistance to the Government of Charles X.

This success at Algiers and the hope of turning the general satisfaction to account, possibly also desire to profit by the absence of the Dauphine, who had announced her return, decided the Council to sign the

---

5. Algeria had been under Turkish law since the sixteenth century. A slight diplomatic incident between the Dey and the French Consul provoked a military expedition ordered by Charles X. Three weeks were sufficient for the French force to occupy the whole country. Algeria would remain French till 1962.

historical ordinances,[6] which the King's secret advisers had long advocated and which Charles X desired with all his mulish obstinacy. Indeed, it might be said of him with perfect truth, "He has learnt nothing and forgotten nothing."

I have been told that at the last Council, which was held on Sunday, these fatal papers were on the table: their purport had been discussed and settled the preceding Wednesday. The moment came to sign them but all hands seemed to be paralysed. The King's name had been placed beneath them, and in impatience at the general hesitation he left the room. Thereupon M. de Polignac, whose heart invariably took precedence over his intellect, seized the pen and wrote the name of Polignac beneath that of Charles. "Now, gentlemen," he said, "the signature of the King is legalised and ours is no longer necessary; you may sign if you like, but I myself do not fear the responsibility of my actions." All hastened to sign forthwith.

Notwithstanding the secrecy which surrounded this deplorable decision, enough was known to provoke serious anxiety. At the same time, those in charge of public affairs were so indifferent that the indiscretions of the Ultras and of the King's friends did not attract sufficient attention. Yet several priests had spoken, even from the pulpit, of the approaching humiliation of the impious. The Jesuits showed themselves more exultant than ever, while the council of the King's conscience did not hide its satisfaction, and M. Rubichon had revealed to M. Greffulhe the actual text of the ordinances, but had been unable to persuade him of their reality. The proceeding appeared so extravagant that no one would believe it, the more so as nothing showed that any measures had been taken to support the proposed revolution in the Government of the country.

M. de Rothschild, a state banker who believed that he was in the

6. The ordinances of July 25, 1830, were four in number: (1) The suppression of the liberty of the press except where authorisation had been secured; (2) the dissolution of the Chamber which had not yet met; (3) a new electoral law providing election in two stages and modifying the right of amendment; (4) convocation of the electoral colleges for September 6 and 18, and of the Chambers for September 28.

confidence of the Government, went to M. de Peyronnet to ask what he was to think of the rumours in circulation. The Minister expressed his astonishment that so sensible a man could attach the least importance to them; they could only have been spread by ill-intentioned persons, according to him. "Moreover," he added, "if you wish for material proof of their falsity, look here," and he pointed to his desk, which was covered with the letters he was signing to summon the deputies to the opening session. Most of these letters were in fact sent off by that day's post. M. de Peyronnet left M. de Rothschild and went to Saint-Cloud, where the ordinances were signed, while M. de Rothschild went to the country to dine with Mme. Thuret, together with the whole of the diplomatic body.

His visit to the Minister of the Interior and the letters he had seen upon his desk were the one topic of conversation at that dinner, and reassured the minds of the guests. Some of the guests stopped by my house as they went home and told me what they had heard. The *Moniteur* of the next morning contained the ordinances. M. de Rothschild was not the only man deceived. M. de Champagny, Under Secretary of State to the War Office, who was directing the Ministry in the absence of M. de Bourmont, was in the country: he did not receive the *Moniteur* until Tuesday evening, and could not reach Paris before Wednesday. Thus the Dauphin said, rubbing his hands:

"The secret has been so well kept that Champagny will learn it only from the *Moniteur*." The Duc de Raguse, who was secretly supposed to be the man to enforce these unsupportable measures, had been kept in the same state of ignorance.

M. de Polignac had surpassed himself by the utter incapacity which he had displayed throughout this incident. Almost all the chiefs of the Royal Guard were away on leave, and the military authorities were out of Paris. Three of the regiments of the Guard had been sent to Normandy to deal with disturbances begun by arsonist outbreaks. In a word, foresight or preparation was nonexistent, and the Government plunged into these rash measures carelessly and without precaution. The fact is that their narrow minds were unable to see beyond the limits of their own partisanship: neither the King nor his Ministry had foreseen any possible obstacles, and had taken no measures to arm themselves for a struggle which they considered unlikely.

Such is the explanation for their conduct, and possibly its excuse. They thought that they could guarantee the passing of measures adapted to the moral interests of France, and flattered themselves that they would be supported in this pious enterprise by such a large part of the country that its handful of opponents would not venture to display any resentment. Unfortunately, they discovered that the whole nation was opposed to them. I say the whole nation, for at the outset no single voice, not even among those who accompanied Charles X to Cherbourg, ventured to justify the steps which had plunged him into this abyss. Never was a sovereign overthrown by greater unanimity of popular feeling.

CHAPTER FOUR

Revolution of July

1830

The following pages were written in July 1832 at an earlier date than the preceding chapters, and at a time when I had no idea of beginning this work for my own distraction. When I had continued my narrative to the outset of the Revolution of 1830, I proposed to read through these pages and to compress them into a final chapter. But after reflection I have decided to leave them unchanged.

I am well aware of their defects, and if I have not sufficient cleverness to remove their faults, I have sufficient intelligence to perceive them. The style is slipshod, and the narrative lacks proportion. However, I probably could never correct faults due to my ignorance in the art of writing; I should also be afraid of depriving this narrative of one merit which it does possess, if merit be not too ambitious a word, and which is obvious at any rate to myself. This merit consists in the fact that I have gone back to events, and have so vividly recalled my impressions of the moment as almost to have relived those July days, with their fears and anxieties, with their hopes and their illusions. A narrative of such great events must, I think, be marked in the first place by sincerity, and often by the trivial detail which helps to give the stamp of truth which I seem to find in my story. If I attempted to prune away what now seems useless, I could not be sure of not removing precisely those touches which give actuality and truth to the narrative. In any case, the events described are too important in themselves to require anything more than a faithful historian.

On the other hand, if I reconstructed these pages there would also be the danger that I might no longer describe those days in July as they appeared to my observation. Today, seven years later, we are feeling the difficulties which spring from a revolution directed against the whole organisation of a society. We are deafened by the hissing of the serpent which the movement has brought forth; I would be tempted to look beneath the pavements of Paris, and to examine the filth in which these monsters were born, in which case I would no longer be the careful chronicler of the impressions of the moment. Throughout my narrative I have been careful to avoid any presentation of events judged in the light of history, and have always endeavoured to show them from the point of view as they were seen when they occurred. This is the impartiality I wish to preserve in the case of the July Monarchy.

Now my task comes to an end. Hitherto I have related events as seen from the audience, but from 1830 onwards I have been behind the scenes, and the intricacy of the threads which have been woven before my eyes would make it difficult for me to choose between them, and still more difficult for me to preserve that impartiality at which I aim. Sincerity would on occasion become revelation. We may relate what we have seen or guessed at, or even what we have been told, but never what we have been told in secrecy. I therefore propose to conclude my work with July 1830. Possibly the habit of scribbling which I have now contracted may induce me to draw up some notes upon particular events, though such is not my intention at this moment.

March 1837

In the memorable days of July 1830, I played no special part and was swayed by no special feelings. I shall only relate what I have seen for myself or learnt by my own observation; therefore, I think that I can be entirely impartial.

I have sometimes regretted that I never wrote down the events of the month of March 1814. Then, as in 1830, I enjoyed a close-up view of events by reason of my intimacy with several of the actors in these great dramas. However, in 1814, either because I was younger or because of the opinions with which I had been brought up, I was more strongly influenced by enthusiasm and by party spirit than in 1830, while my position brought me into contact only with the victorious party. In 1830, on the other hand, I stood midway between the two parties, inclined to the one side by my position, to the other by my reason, and to both by sympathy.

In these events I was greatly struck by one point: during the first three days in 1814 and in 1830, generous feelings, loyalty, disinterestedness, and patriotism were predominant. But from the fourth day onwards, evil passions, ambition, and personal interest became paramount, and were able in twenty-four hours to taint all those influences which previously had appealed to the loftiest hearts. The selfishness of certain individuals poisoned the generosity of the masses, and here we have the only point of resemblance between these two catastrophes. Neither the actors nor the scenes nor the results during the rapid fall of two suicidal Governments bear any resemblance to each other.

On Monday, July 26, 1830, I was the only member of my family in Paris, and was busy rearranging rooms in the Rue d'Anjou. I was speaking to the workmen early in the morning, when I was informed that the Duc de Raguse was in my study. I had never received him in the morning before, but as he was living at Saint-Cloud, his visit did not astonish me.

"Well," he said, "this is a nice business."

I thought he was jesting about the complaints which he might have heard me address to my workmen. I replied with a smile, and we exchanged several phrases at cross-purposes.

Soon, however, I recognised my mistake. His face was greatly changed, and he began to speak of those insane ordinances. He told me how the news had come to him at ten o'clock by one of his aides-de-camp, who had met an officer from Paris expressing the extravagant joy at the court of Saint-Cloud.

After giving me details, he added: "The Bourbons are ruined; they know nothing of the country or of the age. They live outside the world and the country. Wherever they go, they carry their own atmosphere about them and all attempts to enlighten them are hopeless. We are at the end of our resources."

"But you are ruined also, my dear Marshal; you will be dreadfully compromised by all this. It will destroy your only explanations of the events of 1814. You understand, as you say, that you were obliged to sacrifice yourself in order to obtain liberal institutions for the country. Where are these institutions now?"

The Marshal sighed deeply. "Doubtless my position is unpleasant," he replied, "but while I am sorry for what has happened, and especially regret the calamities which are about to fall upon us, in view of the good that might so easily have been accomplished, I am personally much calmer after reading the *Moniteur.* I do not propose to take any part except insofar as my military position may oblige me. Resistance, however, will be entirely constitutional and moral: they will refuse to pay the taxes and the Government will collapse if the Ministry is not driven out, for which latter event I dare not hope. Supposing, however, that open resistance should require the interference of the troops, this event could only take place at the time of the elections, which are set for September 3, and my period of duty finishes on August 31. The next day, I shall be twenty stages on the road to Italy, and shall remain in that country for the whole winter. I do not wish to find myself a second time in a position where there is a conflict of duty. Therefore you need not feel any special anxiety for myself; all our anxiety should be devoted to current events."

We continued our lamentations, our fears, and our apprehensions, foreseeing disaster for the country, but our prophecies were certainly removed from reality. He left me promising to come and spend the following Saturday at my country house. I did not see him again!

I went out as usual, and was much struck by the look of gloomy curiosity on all the faces I saw. Acquaintances stopped to speak, while strangers exchanged questioning glances as they passed. When an unmoved countenance appeared, people thought to themselves, "There is a man who knows nothing yet." This description is so true to fact that the next day, when everybody knew, everybody exchanged glances, and their course of action was thereby agreed upon. There was no other form of conspiracy. It was this very unanimity of indignation which produced the extraordinary magnanimity by which this popular uprising was marked. The people saw partisans everywhere, even in the soldiers who fired upon them. But I must not anticipate events, which were proceeding quickly enough.

In the evening I saw certain people opposed to the Polignac Ministry but attached to the Restoration. All were in despair, confused by conjecture and expecting violent but constitutional resistance. The letters of summons had been sent out to the deputies, who arrived at intervals. Was this summons the result of habitual carelessness, or were the deputies assembled in order to be the object of hostile fulmination? There were many subjects for discussion, and we talked about them at great length.

On Tuesday the 27th, I learnt from thirty workmen, all of different professions who were working at my house and came from various parts of the town, that the ferment was beginning to spread. There was much agitation among the workmen, but based upon such excellent reasoning as to surprise me. Here I must put down an observation made at this time. I had furnished a house in 1819, and had employed the same kind of workmen as in 1830; but within these ten years the manners, habits, dress, and language of these men had so entirely changed that they no longer seemed to belong to the same class. I had already been greatly struck by their intelligence, their politeness, which was in no way servile, the ready and scientific method of taking their measurements, and by their chemical knowledge of the ingredients they used. I was still more struck by their arguments concerning the danger of these fatal ordinances, of which they understood both the range and the probable results. If our Governors had been half as foresighted and prudent, King Charles X would still be living quietly at the Tuileries.

Doubtless such a population could not be made the milk cow of a privileged caste. Any ruler, however, who had wished to consider the real interests of the country would have found the people as docile as they were intelligent, while the common sense of the masses would have supported the Government against the extravagance of certain agitators. Unfortunately, the King and the nation were of incompatible temperaments.

The stories which I had heard had not so far alarmed me as to induce me to remain at home. At four o'clock I went out in my carriage with the object of doing some shopping in the Rue Saint-Denis. One of my men asserted that there was some disturbance in this direction. I resolved to continue my drive and pay a visit to Neuilly, the d'Orléans residence. For a few weeks I had been in full mourning for my husband, and before going back to the country I wished to thank the Princesses for the kindness which they had shown me upon this occasion.

The Duchesse d'Orléans was walking in the park, and I had no news for her of sufficient interest to provide an excuse for following her. I found Mademoiselle at home in despair about the ordinances, much disturbed by the popular agitation of which I spoke to her, and very apprehensive lest her brother's name should be compromised. These were her actual words:

"Had it not been for those two ceremonies, the Mass of the Holy Spirit and the opening of the Chambers, at which we were obliged to be present, and the wretched snare which was set for us, we should have started for Eu[1] on Saturday, and should now be out of all this turmoil."

If her intention was to mystify me, she was entirely successful, for even now I am persuaded of her good faith. She admitted that the ordinances were bound to produce a catastrophe. But, like everybody else, she anticipated resistance from a class which does not immediately take to stone-throwing. A refusal to pay taxes and the impossibility of carrying on the Government in the face of general opposition mani-

1. Eu was the d'Orléans's estate in Normandy.

fested by all legal means seemed to her to be the danger of the situation into which the King had plunged. We discussed the matter at great length, but no mention was made of the remedy which Neuilly was to provide eventually for so critical a situation.

From Mademoiselle I went on to Mme. de Montjoie, the lady-in-waiting. I found her also in a state of great anxiety and uneasiness, and much downcast because they were not at Eu. This, indeed, seemed to be the impression of the whole household. I went somewhat further with her, and we spoke of the possible results which such a series of mistakes might produce. She repeated what she had said to me a thousand times: that the Duc d'Orléans was the most faithful subject of the King of France, but that he would not again follow him into exile abroad. We were obliged to admit the possibility that his name might be put forward at such a time even without his knowledge and against his will. During the previous year I had heard people say twenty times in speaking of the King and his Ministers, "They are paving the way for the d'Orléans."

Mme. de Montjoie told me with reference to this subject an incident which had happened the preceding Wednesday. The Duc d'Orléans had a bad cold, and when he came out on the steps after a large dinner he had put on his hat, making some excuse. M. de Sémonville had replied aloud, "We will allow you your hat, Sire, while waiting for the Crown."

"Never, M. de Sémonville, unless it comes to me by right."

"It will be by right, Sire. When the Crown is on the ground, France will pick it up and will oblige you to wear it."

"Can you imagine M. de Sémonville speaking in this way?" added Mme. de Montjoie. "I heard his words, and ten people could have heard them just as easily."

"I understand," I replied, "that he considers the game as lost even more than we do."

"Yet if the King were willing, he still has great resources."

"Yes, but unfortunately he will not be willing."

"Then what will happen?"

"Who can tell? Doubtless many misfortunes."

"Supposing there is a civil war—what about the Duc de Chartres, who is serving in the army? What will he do? It is enough to drive one wild."

Our conversation continued for some time, but the Duchesse d'Orléans did not come in, and it was getting late. I therefore left my kind regards for her with Mme. de Montjoie, and returned to Paris.

There was no premonition of the evening's tumult in the districts through which I passed. The streets were perhaps somewhat less crowded than usual. I heard that there had been some disorder at the Porte Saint-Martin, and gatherings of people in several other quarters. We were so persuaded that this was not the kind of resistance to be feared that I attached little importance to these facts. None of the workmen employed at my house had come back since dinner-time. A coach-builder, a blacksmith, and a locksmith opposite my house had also been without workmen for three hours. This was the first incident which roused my apprehensions.

Soon every quarter of an hour brought fresh news of those grave events with which the future was pregnant. The same people who had gathered at my house the evening before came in one after another, and all brought news of a character more and more alarming. I heard that the Duc de Raguse was established at the Tuileries. About six o'clock, as he drove through a group of people in his tilbury, he had run some risk on the boulevards. Barricades had already been constructed. They had indeed been destroyed by the Guard, but this only seemed to incite the general agitation. It was even said that gunshots had been exchanged. M. Pasquier went to the house of Mme. de Girardin,* where there were always plenty of visitors, to learn the news. Pozzo, the Russian Ambassador, arrived. One of his secretaries had seen a dead man on the Place de la Bourse and people making speeches around the body.

Pozzo himself might have acted as orator. He grew excited and gave us a speech on the irrevocable right of nations to oppose the overthrow of their institutions and to chastise perjured kings. He was astonished that a single man could be found to oppose an insurrection which was so obviously lawful and blamed Marshal Marmont for attempting to check it. His vehemence impressed us all. We have often remembered it since, when we heard him use very different language while accusing the Duc de Raguse for not firing on the inhabitants of Paris that same Tuesday, when there was nothing more than some excitement and a few gatherings.

M. Pasquier had found the Girardin household alone. The wife was depressed and very sad, the husband bombastic and loud-voiced, saying that this mob must be dealt with once and for all, that the malcontents must be silenced with terror, and government conducted by the sword, that this was a small temporary incident which would have no consequence, et cetera. At the same time he confirmed the news that the police had charged, and that several people had been killed and wounded. A barricade had been constructed by the people with an omnibus and some overthrown carts at the entrance of the Rue de l'Echelle, and the barricade had been destroyed by the Guard. Blood had been shed in front of the Palais-Royal, and M. de Girardin expected the most successful results.

At the same time we learnt that the Place Louis XV, the Place Vendôme, and the Carrousel were full of artillery with guns loaded and matches lighted. I was not greatly disturbed by the news. I had often heard the Marshal say that in times of popular agitation a great display of force must be made, to strike men's imaginations and to avoid violent measures. We separated about midnight, after hearing the reports of two men who had been sent, one to the Place de Grève, the other to the gate of Saint-Denis. All was calm. We were undoubtedly extremely anxious, but no one, I think, expected the events of the next day.

Wednesday the 28th, as I went into my house, I was informed that none of my workmen had appeared; my neighbours were in the same situation. I did not, however, consider this sufficiently serious to change my plans, and as I was to go back to the country the next day, I wished to call at my bankers, MM. Mallet, where I had some business to transact. I resolved to go out immediately, thinking that if there was to be any disturbance it would occur later. I ordered the horses to be readied and entered my carriage about ten o'clock. I was going into the Rue de Mont Blanc,[2] and I told my coachman to go down the side streets instead of following the boulevards, and to turn back if he saw any crowds. I was, however, considerably alarmed.

From the middle of the Rue des Mathurins and in all the side streets, the lamps had been shattered and were lying in fragments on the pavement. At every door there was a group of women and children with terror-stricken faces. The royal ensign which decorated the shop of Despilly, the stationer, had been torn down and trampled underfoot. The porter of MM. Mallet objected to opening the carriage entrance: at length he gave way, my carriage went in, and he closed the gates with a rapidity which did not calm my anxieties. I went up to the office, where the partners were much astonished to see me. They advised me to go home and to stay there.

While I was signing certain necessary papers they told me that at about six o'clock in the morning several bands of considerable size had invaded the armourers' shops and plundered them without opposition. Street lamps had been smashed everywhere, and the royal ensigns torn down from the shops over which they were placed. The proprietors, indeed, had offered no resistance but even helped in the work. There was some talk of reestablishing the National Guard to protect people and property. MM. Mallet had already been to the Mayor's house on this business. They proposed to return and hoped that before the end of the morning an improvised National Guard would be on foot in every quarter. It was not intended to assist the troops, but to protect peaceable people and to prevent the pillaging which the events of the morning gave every reason to fear.

I went home again more frightened than when I had set out. I found my own street entirely calm. By way of precaution the inhabitants were taking down the lamps, locking them up, and removing the royal arms wherever they were placed.

A note was handed to me from M. Pasquier. He asked whether I

2. Now the Rue de La Chaussée d'Antin.

had any means of communicating with the Duc de Raguse, and begged me to let him know that well-informed people considered that any military resistance to so general a movement would produce frightful catastrophes, whatever the ultimate result. His opinions and his sympathies were known, and it was considered that his best position would be to act as mediator by reporting the difficulties, greater perhaps than he imagined, with which he was surrounded to Saint-Cloud, and by advising concessions which might even now save everything if they were proclaimed forthwith.

I enclosed his note in a hastily written letter of my own, but did not know how to send it. My doctor happened to be there, and, seeing my anxiety, he undertook to deliver my letter himself. He was successful, for a short time afterwards I saw M. de La Rue, the Marshal's aide-de-camp, come into my room. The Marshal had sent him to say that it was too late. All attempts at conciliation had been tried in vain. His orders from Saint-Cloud were imperative, and all that he could do was conduct the military operations. Moreover, matters had gone too far, and it was necessary above all to crush the insurrection. M. de La Rue added that he had just given the order to the columns to advance; that they were to go forward sweeping all before them; and that probably I would hear the roar of the cannon within half an hour.

"Heaven preserve us!" I cried. "I do not know what the result will be for the monarchy. But if the monarchy escapes such a crisis, it will be obliged to abandon all those who shoot down the Parisian populace in a cause so hateful to the nation.

"If the Marshal," I added, "should fire a single cannon shot he had better commit suicide, for his life will be nothing more than a series of misfortunes."

I was greatly excited, and succeeded in persuading La Rue. His despondency increased, and he continually exclaimed by way of reply:

"But what are we to do? We are being fired on, and the business has begun; the best thing we can do is to go through with it and to bring these people to reason. Besides, it is impossible to get a word with the Marshal. He was obliged to take me into a window corner to give me the message which I bring you, and he had the utmost difficulty in finding a moment to read your letter."

"Why so?"

"Why, the Ministers are at the Tuileries with him. M. de Polignac and his people surround him, and supervise him so carefully that though he is nominally in supreme command, he cannot say a word or make a gesture except under their surveillance."

"Nonetheless, try and make him understand how utterly useless his self-sacrifice is. And especially remind him of the danger to the country to which he is so devoted."

"I will attempt to convey your words to him, for mine would have no influence. He is accustomed to command us and not to listen to us, and advice from our lips would have little effect on him."

"Do your duty as much as you like, but tell the Marshal if he permits a serious engagement he must consider all as lost. The troops can do nothing in the town against a unanimous and exasperated populace. There will be some moral hesitation at the beginning, but when people once feel that they are entirely compromised, they will fight desperately."

Immediately after the departure of M. de La Rue I began to consider what he had said to me concerning the want of consideration which any words from his mouth would receive. Knowing that no one had so much influence with the Marshal as M. Arago,* I wrote to him, begging him to go himself to the staff forthwith and to use his influence to save the country, the throne, and his friend from the imminent ruin with which they were menaced. I ordered a man to go on horseback to the Observatory by way of the outer boulevards.

Hardly had he set forth when I heard the first cannon-shot. I cannot describe the effect which it produced upon me: I uttered a cry and, hiding my head in my hands, I remained motionless for some moments. All our efforts had been in vain; the die was cast, the country, the throne, and individuals were hanging in the balance. Nothing could be done but to await with fear and trembling the result of these gloomy prospects. I spent all my time at the window. Soon I saw a patrol of soldiers arrive. As soon as they entered the streets they fired a dozen shots, although the calm was absolute. Count Karoly, as he was leaving my house, was nearly struck by a bullet which hit the frame of the door. There was no casualty in the Rue d'Anjou, but a carter who was quietly driving his wagon was killed in the Rue de Surène. This useless demonstration greatly excited the people in my neighbourhood. Hitherto they had been standing silently at their doors or windows. From that moment the houses were abandoned, people formed groups in the street, and every able-bodied man prepared for defence. This was the signal for the outbreak of hostilities. The imprudent patrol soon joined a larger body in the Rue du Faubourg Saint-Honoré, and we heard a long and vigourous fusillade provoked by confusion over the need for a National Guard.

As I had learnt from MM. Mallet, the more important citizens had gone to their mayors with the idea of reviving a kind of National Guard for the purpose of protecting peaceable citizens, but with no intention of unconstitutional action. The ruling powers, ill-instructed or badly advised, had sent out troops everywhere to drive these persons from the mayors' houses. Resistance was offered, and these simultaneous attacks at a dozen points throughout the capital had completed the exasperation of a populace already raised to the highest pitch of excitement by the noise of the fusillade.

After this episode I saw my doctor, Chavernac, coming towards the house, staying close to the walls. He came to say that he had given my letters to one of the Marshal's aides-de-camp. I was aware of the fact, as I had received the answer. He had gone back to his own house and told me that a considerable gathering of common people, headed by a man dressed, or rather undressed, like the rest of them, had come to knock at his door. He had gone down to speak to them. The leader had asked him very politely if he had any weapons to lend them. He had answered that he had none, as the house was only inhabited by himself and some women. They made many excuses for thus disturbing him. Not to be behindhand in civility, he also expressed his regret that he had no weapons to offer to these gentlemen.

"Ah, sir, we are quite sure of it. What Frenchman is not on our side in this noble cause, at any rate at heart?" Chavernac saw the same band go and knock at the next door, where a dozen large pistols and some bullets were handed out to them. They already had a dozen guns and as many pistols, which had probably been collected in the same way. In any case, similar collections were made in almost every quarter of Paris. What is almost as remarkable as the meekness with which refusals were received is the fact that a week afterwards almost all of these weapons, many of which were valuable, had been brought back to their owners.

About this time or a little earlier, a small sheet published by *Le Temps* was circulated; it gave an account of events and urged resistance to the soldiers, promising victory. It was not without influence. My man brought back an answer from Arago; he was about to go to the staff with no great hopes for success, but that he might have no subsequent ground for self-reproach as a Frenchman and as a friend.

The roar of the cannon seemed to slacken. Suddenly it began again with greater vigour and simultaneously on several sides. Small-arm firing also began again but at some distance from us. Women, children, and a few men appeared upon their thresholds: several had resumed their positions in the mayor's house, which the troops had been forced to evacuate after a short occupation. At that moment I saw a man passing by with a covered basket such as cake-sellers carry. He was distributing cartridges: everybody took them and everybody hid them. All of this great city seemed to be animated by one thought, one will, and one plan of operations. It was already plain that intelligent leaders were directing the masses of the populace. The tactics pursued were too generally identical not to be the result of preconcerted design.

A numerous body drew up before the columns of the guard of the line; then many of them who had weapons advanced and fired upon the troops. The latter replied. If any of the army of insurgents were put out of action, others immediately advanced and took their guns and their ammunition. After several shots had been exchanged, part of the group ran forward, while the others rushed into the carriage entrances, the doors of which opened before them. They then went upstairs to the windows and fired upon the column whilst it passed. They next came down to the street, threw up a barricade behind the column, left it in charge of a few guards and all the neighbouring inhabitants, and went off down the side streets at a run to rejoin the original band, the numbers of which steadily increased, and began to arrest the progress of the column a hundred paces farther forward by a repetition of the same manoeuvre. The result was that the troops found it extremely difficult to advance and entirely impossible to retreat. It was not until midnight, after making wide detours, that they were able to regain their headquarters.

About midday a general distribution had been made of war munitions: a powder magazine, guarded by only two veterans, had been seized by a trick. Carts carried the powder through the streets, and in the centre of the town women were busy making cartridges at their doors without any attempt at concealment. I heard a man call out to his neighbour through the window, showing him two cartridges, "When I have six, I shall start." A moment afterwards I saw him in the street with his gun on his shoulder. He was rejoined by his neighbour; after a short conversation the neighbour went into his house, came out again with a sword and a long pistol, and followed the same route. These people were quiet and orderly family men. I cannot sufficiently repeat the fact, for it is the explanation of every event throughout these days, that the whole population was electrified. Everybody took an active part in events, and many showed unexampled courage, energy, and devotion.

At the descent from the Porte Saint-Martin, one of the most disputed points, a regular battle took place. A man who was unarmed happened to be standing beside one of the populace who carried a gun which he did not know how to use.

"My friend, will you lend me your gun?"

"Certainly, sir. Rest it upon my shoulder as you will find that more convenient."

One or two shots were fired, to the admiration of the owner of the gun. Eventually the marksman noticed that his acquaintance was shielding him with his body, and also saw him call up one of his comrades in order to mask him entirely.

"Look here, my friends; stand aside a little, please; you are making me appear ridiculous."

"Good gracious, sir, what does it matter if we are killed? We cannot shoot, as you see. But you are much more important."

This story was told to me the next day at the house of the Russian Ambassador, who thought it splendid.

I return to the events of Wednesday. The streets were unsafe, and communication was barely possible; however, I saw two or three times during the day M. Pasquier and the Duc and Duchesse de Rauzan, whose house adjoined mine, as did that of M. de La Fayette. We exchanged such information as we had, which for the most part consisted of vague rumours, and the explosions of the cannon remained the clearest reports which came to us. Towards nightfall the sound of the tocsin from all the bells of Paris was joined to the roar of artillery, and seemed to us even more gloomy and appalling.

It was a magnificent moonlit night, terribly hot, without a breath of air. The ordinary noises of the great city were silenced or drowned in the sinister and monotonous tolling of the tocsin, the continuous discharge of small arms, and the constant roar of cannon. From time to time a red glare would rise above the roofs, signaling some conflagration and increasing our apprehension. By the moonlight I saw that a large black flag had been hoisted upon the Madeleine. I cannot say at what moment it had been raised, but it was a complete expression of our feelings.

I spent the whole evening wandering about the courtyard and the staircases, looking out of the windows onto the street, collecting news which my servants brought in from the neighbours, which grew steadily more alarming. Several parts of the town had been burnt; the Duc de Raguse was mortally wounded; General Talon had been killed; not a single lancer was left; the river was red with blood, et cetera.

About eleven o'clock the firing died away. Half an hour afterwards the tocsin stopped, and a most impressive silence reigned. It was so solemn that I caught myself speaking in a whisper to one of my servants who volunteered to go out and reconnoitre. Two others, under the stimulus of their warlike ardour, had gone out to fight, and had not returned. The last messenger, an active and intelligent man, came back before midnight to tell me that soldiers and people alike were resting but remained under arms: the crisis was by no means over. The battle would begin the next morning with greater vigour if the troops remained faithful. He had been assured that two regiments had already gone over to the people. Though but little calmed by this report, I decided to lie down for a few hours, though I did not expect to get much rest.

On Thursday the 29th, at six o'clock, the stillness remained unbroken. My butler had gone out at four o'clock and had traversed much of the town; he had seen no troops, but many barricades guarded by armed men who had spent the night at their posts. These barricades were the meeting points for those who were going to rejoin them. General obedience was shown to the Polytechnic[3] students; they alone were in uniform and had secured authority. My butler had seen one driving into the Place de la Bourse, seated upon the front of a two-horse cart, waving a sword and shouting continually, "Out of the way, this is gunpowder! Out of the way, there is danger here!"

This gunpowder, which had been simply tossed into the cart, was handed out to men and women, who sat down upon the steps of the Bourse and began the work of making cartridges. Several persons, no less enthusiastic, went out to distribute the cartridges throughout the barricades, to which the neighbours brought provisions and refreshments. Everywhere the wounded were cared for and sheltered, while the dead simply served to arouse enthusiasm. It must be added to the honour of the Parisian populace that, though they were animated as one man by this spirit of resistance, and though they concentrated their efforts to defeat the troops, they showed no animosity to the

3. The nation's most prestigious military school, which trained artillery officers.

soldier as such. Attentions were showered upon the wounded soldier, although while he had arms in his hands his death did not evoke the smallest regret.

The man who came in confirmed the reports of the previous evening with reference to the speedy resumption of the conflict. He had met one of my grooms, and had made a vain attempt to bring him home; the man had already been fighting and wished to continue. Another groom came in to water his horses and intended to start out again; however, I detained him, as I was thinking seriously of leaving Paris.

As I foresaw that the task of crossing the barriers would be very difficult, I wrote a very gloomy note to the Duc de Raguse, asking him for a pass, and issued orders for my departure. I wished to rejoin my family at Pontchartrain. I also wrote to M. Pasquier bidding him farewell, and asking him if he had any message for me to take. While I was making my preparations I was informed that Mme. de Rauzan had returned. She had started half an hour before, but her carriage had been stopped on every side by barricades, which could neither be crossed nor avoided.

The Marshal's answer was brought back to me, containing a pass countersigned by M. de Choiseul. The Marshal had himself handed the pass to my man, whom he knew, saying to him:

"Louis, this is what Mme. de Boigne desires; but tell her not to be in a hurry. I hope that in a few hours everything will be over just as she wishes, and I expect I shall be able to come and see her during the day."

Poor man, he was greatly deceived! I informed M. Pasquier of this message, and he strongly advised me not to attempt to leave Paris. I was tortured by the fear of causing anxiety to my parents, and was still hesitating when the firing broke out again. It may have been eight o'clock in the morning, and at the same time the sound of pickaxes reechoed in the street. I put my head out of the window, and saw two or three men beginning to tear up the pavement of the Faubourg Saint-Honoré; soon there were twenty-five or thirty of them, a number which speedily grew to fifty. In less than a quarter of an hour there was a strong double barricade in the street of the Faubourg, which was accompanied by a transverse barricade in the Rue d'Anjou. Similar precautions were immediately taken at the crossing of the Rue de Surène, and probably throughout the quarter. In the Allée de Marigny the trees were soon cut down to make stockades in the Place Beauvau. I saw these barricades in course of construction, and apart from the zeal and energy with which the work was conducted, I can assert that no extraordinary excitement was manifest. They were raised for the most part by the inhabitants of the street; there was no shouting and no quarrelling; order and activity were predominant. When the work had been finished, several men remained to guard it under arms and the rest went away. I saw nobody in command, and these actions seemed to be directed by inspiration. By each of these barricades a narrow passage had been left for people on foot; anybody was allowed to pass without hindrance. I am speaking only of the barricades which I saw constructed; there were others differently made and very difficult to pass through. It was impossible to think of leaving the town now, and I was correspondingly relieved. Nothing is more difficult in such circumstances than to come to a decision.

My chambermaid brought a certain Mme. Garche into the house. She was a shopkeeper in the Rue du Bac. This woman had a married daughter in the district of the Halles, and had heard on Wednesday morning that the young woman was about to deliver her child and was in danger. Twice she started to go to her, but was unable to pass any of the bridges, upon all of which fighting was in progress. At length towards midnight she had reached the Carrousel. Attempts were made to send her back, but she contrived to slip along the walls. When she reached an open space where the moonlight cast no shade, she was seen, and an officer attempted to turn her back. She was begging him to let her pass, when she heard someone giving orders to turn her away with an oath.

"That's the Marshal," said the officer. "Off with you, and quick!"

With the courage of a mother, the poor woman ran straight to the Marshal. She explained her situation, and he turned round to an aide-de-camp and said to him:

"Go and tell the guard to let no one pass."

Then he turned to Mme. Garche.

"Come, Madame, give me your arm." He accompanied her to the last sentry, and added when he left her, "Now be quick. Take the smallest streets, and do not leave them. God protects good mothers." Eventually she reached her daughter without mishap, and found that the child was born and that all was well.

As she attempted to return to the Faubourg Saint-Germain by the Pont d'Iéna, she was stopped by my chambermaid, who was her friend. She spoke of the Marshal with tears in her eyes, and when so many were cursing his name it was a pleasure to his friends to hear these blessings.

The firing seemed to be slackening. M. Pasquier came to my house and explained the message of the Marshal. The ministers had gone to Saint-Cloud, and in the Place Vendôme a declaration had been read announcing the suspension of hostilities and the withdrawal of the ordinances. The fact has since been denied, but a proclamation was certainly made by General de Wall, the military commander of Paris, on the Place Vendôme. At last it was possible to expect some settlement of this dreadful crisis. A moment afterwards Arago arrived with his son and told me that he had made vain efforts to reach the Tuileries, as hostilities had recommenced around the Louvre and the Faubourg Saint-Germain. In any case, he did not expect to be more successful with the Marshal than he had been the evening before. He had exhausted his arguments, but the Marshal persisted in seeing nothing but the military situation, and had said to him:

"My friend, I have at one time sacrificed the soldier to the citizen, and on this occasion I intend to sacrifice the citizen to the soldier. The results may be no more successful than before. But I have suffered too much from the previous situation, justifying the motives which inspired my action, to be willing to expose myself to any further possibility of the kind. Do you wish people to say Marmont is always on hand when any treachery is required?" and he clapped his hands to his forehead with a gesture of despair. "Can I be so unhappy as to find myself a second time in a position involving a cruel conflict of duty?"

Arago also confirmed the report of M. de La Rue concerning the obstinacy of those in attendance upon the Duc de Raguse and the difficulty of gaining a moment's access to him. He also told me of the absurd answer of M. de Polignac, and the silly manner in which he had replied:

"Well, if the troops should join the people, we shall fire upon them as well."

I then gave Arago the Marshal's message, and told him that the Marshal had received no answer from Saint-Cloud in reply to the step which the commissaries had taken the evening before.

"If the Marshal has no news from Saint-Cloud," said Arago, "I am more successful than he. The Dauphin has sent me a messenger bearing a note from his own hand."

"Really! And what did he say?"

"He asked me the precise thermometrical measurements for yesterday."

Such a revelation is overwhelming. Lest it should be treated as fictitious, it should be remembered that in private life the Princes of the royal family paid much attention to the weather, not in the interests of science, but to learn the prospects for sport. They were accustomed to communicate their meteorological observations to one another every day, and the exactitude of their thermometers and barometers had become a kind of preoccupation, especially in the case of the Dauphin. In their most princely existence nothing could disturb these futilities, which had become a kind of etiquette.

The man whom I had sent in the morning to headquarters had provided himself with a card for the return journey, and asserted that with the aid of it he could go back again. We observed, in fact, that the card bore a free pass in the service of the Marshal. Arago proceeded to write a letter telling the Marshal that the whole city was in revolt, that every class had joined the movement, and that the political organisations were lending their support. He knew many of the leading figures in the movement, and proposals had already been made to him; a provisional Government was required, and the tricolour cockade had been demanded. The only prospect for the King was to give way to these desires, and to proclaim the abandonment of the system of absolutism, which would certainly produce a civil war in which he would be overthrown. As for the Marshal himself, he might, if he would, adopt the fair position of mediator, but he had not a moment to lose. The retirement of the Ministers had left him sole master at Paris. He should immediately proclaim an amnesty for all that had been done and induce the King to grant those conditions, and should save himself by enabling the troops to join a side which would consider the real needs of the country. I added a few words to Arago's letter and gave it to my man, advising him to be careful and not to expose himself unnecessarily.

Hardly had he started when the rifle firing broke out once more, and grew louder as it approached us. We heard a very vigourous fusillade in the direction of the Place Louis XV. We rushed to the window and saw people running in the Rue du Faubourg Saint-Honoré. A band of soldiers appeared before the barricade and was obliged to retire. Firing was heard in the Champs-Elysées. There was a halt for a moment around the Allée de Marigny, several consecutive volleys were fired, and then the firing grew distant; the whole affair lasted barely ten minutes. We were unable to understand these proceedings.

My messenger, upon whose account I was growing very anxious, returned. He brought back our letter. He had reached headquarters without difficulty, had found the rooms deserted, and had even reached the Marshal's room. All the doors were open, and he found no one to give him any information. Going to the window, he saw the gates of the courtyard closed and the troops rapidly marching under the clock tower. The people were masters of the Carrousel. As he went downstairs, he had met M. de Glandèves, the Governor of the palace, whom he knew; he was rushing into a subterranean passage which communicated with the palace beneath the watch-house: my man asked him where he could find the Marshal. M. de Glandèves, who seemed greatly agitated and in a violent hurry, replied:

"The Marshal is probably in the garden of the Tuileries, but it is impossible to get to him, and I should advise you to go away as quickly as possible."

Profiting by this advice, he had come back without any further attempt to fulfil his mission, and he knew nothing more.

We speedily learned the news of the capture of the Louvre, the abandonment of the Tuileries, and the complete evacuation of Paris after a moment's check at the barrier of l'Etoile, and the march of the troops upon Saint-Cloud. The dissemination of this news produced the most instantaneous effect upon the populace: it was as if a pot of boiling water had been taken off the top of a stove; all disturbance was calmed in a moment. Other passions may have disturbed the minds of certain factious people and found expression around the Hôtel de Ville; the rest of the city became calm.

The only authority generally recognised was that of the students of the Polytechnic School, who had been assigned to different posts throughout the city. Apart from the bravery which they had shown in the combats of the previous evening and morning, they owed their importance to the fact that they alone wore uniforms. The defenders of the barricades called each student "My little General" and obeyed the students the more implicitly as their line of study had made them very useful in directing the rapid construction of barricades. They helped in both making and defending these obstacles. In any case, it is a somewhat remarkable circumstance that the populace at this time should have given so much consideration to people who seemed to belong to the upper classes of society. Anybody wearing a coat and willing to join a band could easily secure the command of people in waistcoats.

I am wrong, however, to use the word waistcoats: the popular costume was a pair of canvas trousers and a shirt with the sleeves turned up. Indeed, it must be said that the heat was suffocating. Often this scanty clothing and even the arms of the wearer bore traces of the conflict. Faces were blackened by powder, yet were in no way terrifying: they proclaimed the calm courage of defenders and the consciousness of right. Once the heat of combat was over, the city was pervaded by a spirit of brotherhood.

M. Arago left me. Some visitors came in as the streets were being reopened to people on foot. M. de Salvandy* arrived from Essonnes, where he had been the previous evening.

About three o'clock I decided to go out. M. de Salvandy gave me his arm. He did not expect any attack during the night. I was living in one of those places which were greatly exposed if one returns by the same route as one sets out. I did not wish to alarm my household by sending any member of it with this message, and went myself to Mme. de Jumil-hac in the Rue Neuve-des-Mathurins, to warn her porter to open to me if I should come and knock during the night. As I returned, I visited the boulevard, which was blocked by felled trees and everything that could be found in the neighbourhood for the construction of barri-cades. The barricades themselves were very difficult to cross; it was necessary to climb over some and to crawl under others. Everywhere, however, those in charge of them offered a ready and obliging assis-tance, calling up the cleanest of their number in order not to soil the clothes of the ladies. There were no coarse jokes, and never were politeness and courtesy more paramount in Paris. A secret instinct seemed to warn them that the least shock might produce an explosion. In any case, the idea of an opposition to current events occurred to no one.

I reached the Rue de Rivoli. Barely three hours ago furious fight-ing had been in progress. The gates of the garden of the Tuileries were closed and guarded by sentinels wearing the costume I have described. In the street I saw a very lofty barricade composed of garden chairs. As I passed, a considerable number of ladies had pulled down part of this barricade. They had seized some of the chairs, and in their best dresses, wearing hats adorned with feathers and flowers, were calmly seated under their parasols in the shade of the barricade as if they had been under the trees in the garden of the Tuileries. This curious spectacle continued until that Sunday when the chairs were returned to the garden.

I called upon the Russian Ambassador, whom I had not seen for forty-eight hours. I found him much disturbed: he had been a witness to the rout of the troops and gave me a detailed account of it. He was both surprised and indignant that he had received no message from M. de Polignac at such a time. He was equally indignant at the delight of Lord Stewart, the English Ambassador, who had expressed it to the point of indecency. Pozzo also thought that an attack on Paris was probable, and was greatly disturbed about the position of his residence. He was swayed by no sense of partisanship, and was alarmed, disturbed, and apprehensive, and explained that his haggard appearance was caused by illness.

I went home again and sent out to buy a few hams, a sack of rice, and a sack of flour. I had expected these provisions to have gone up in price, but there had been no change, so great was the public confidence.

Standing at my window, I saw an old street singer coming up the Rue de Surène. He stopped at the barricade of the Rue du Faubourg Saint-Honoré, where some fifty men were gathered. There, while pretending to help them replace the paving-stones which were continually thrown out of position by the passers-by, with an excellent voice and a good diction, he struck up a song in five couplets in honour of Napoleon II, the refrain of which was, as far as I can remember, "Without overshadowing him, the son will be as good as his father." He caused not the smallest sensation, and hardly anyone seemed to listen to him. When the song was over he crossed the barricade to look for another audience, whom he probably found equally inattentive.

I have already spoken much of this barricade, and shall have more to say. From a window where I habitually stood I could see and hear everything that went on. This point had become a meeting place, and neighbours gathered around the twenty-five or thirty men on guard. These latter never left their posts until they were relieved by a Polytechnician and replaced by others after twenty-four hours of duty, during which the inhabitants of the quarter were careful to provide them with food and drink. I have undertaken to relate merely what I have seen with my own eyes and heard for myself, and therefore I have no scruples on entering into these details. Moreover, the events which happened upon this little stage were repeated at every crossroads in the town, and may give a fairly accurate idea of the general situation.

I can positively affirm that throughout this and the following days I heard no cries except "Long live the Charter!" and no other cry was ever reported to me. A strong line of demarcation must be drawn between the actual temper of the city and the manifestations which might break forth about the Hôtel de Ville. In that quarter, faction leaders were calling for a revolution; elsewhere the sole desire was to remove the people who claimed to establish absolutism. Charles X would have been drawn around the city in triumph on that Thursday if he had repealed his ordinances and changed his Ministry. Whether he could have continued to reign after such a concession is a question which I can neither decide nor discuss; I merely claim that the Charter as established satisfied all desires at that moment.

I return to my story. I soon heard loud cries which appeared to be joyful, though any uproar was then terrifying. Climbing onto a terrace, I was able to perceive an enormous tricolour flag hoisted upon the summit of the unfinished church of the Madeleine; it replaced the black flag which had been floating there the evening before. Afterwards I saw a plank on which was written in rude letters, "Long live Napoleon II!" It remained there for several days, and neither its appearance nor its removal attracted the smallest attention. About seven o'clock fresh cries coming from the street recalled me to the window. I saw a numerous body of people engaged in making a passage through the barricades for a man and his horse, who were both covered with dust and sweat and panting with weariness.

"Where does General La Fayette live?" he cried.

"Here, here!" cried fifty voices.

"I have come from Rouen in advance of my comrades; they are coming. Here is the letter for the General."

"This is the place."

He learnt at the door of the house that the General was staying at the headquarters of the National Guard, but that he would be more likely to find him at the Hôtel de Ville.

"The Hôtel de Ville!" cried everyone, and the courier in his waist-coat with his noisy escort started off throughout the town, relating his mission at each barricade.

Towards the close of the day I heard a well-known voice asking if I were at home. I went out upon the staircase to meet M. de Glandèves. My man had seen him in the morning at the moment when the Château had been invaded. I had been very anxious on his account and was de-lighted to see him. We met with real joy. He told me that he had found his room empty. His cook had shown great presence of mind, had quickly adopted the universal costume, placed a gun upon his shoul-der, and stood sentry before his door, refusing admission to everybody with the words, "I am on guard, and you cannot pass!" Thus he had gained time to take off his uniform and collect his money and his pa-pers. Two quartermasters of the palace, in trousers and shirts with sleeves rolled up and guns on their shoulders, had escorted him to the Rue Saint-Honoré, whence he had reached his sister's house in the Rue Royale. There he proposed to remain hidden, but as he saw everyone so peaceful he had attempted to come to my house, and had arrived by way of the barricades and the politeness of their guardians. He gave me an account of all the foolishness of the wretched Polignac during these days: of his obstinate and stupid confidence, and also of his tendency to cruel and arbitrary measures, his discontent with the Marshal, who re-fused to keep as hostages the deputies who had come to him as a depu-tation on Wednesday morning.

Glandèves also said that during Wednesday evening, the King had been playing his game of whist with the windows open. The noise of the cannon and of the small arms could be distinctly heard. At each ex-plosion the King gently flicked the tablecloth as if to remove a speck of dust. He gave no other sign to show that he was aware of what was go-ing on. The game proceeded as usual, and no courtier ventured to make the smallest remark upon the situation. When giving the password,

Charles X had avoided speaking to anyone who came from Paris, and etiquette was so strict that, although an arrangement had been made beforehand for M. de La Bourdonnaye and General Vincent to tell him the truth about what they had witnessed, neither of them, nor any of those who were to support them, had ventured to take the initiative. When the game and the evening had concluded as usual, General Vincent had returned to the Tuileries, furious with the scene he had witnessed, disgusted with his post as equerry, and bursting with the desire to tell Glandèves what he had seen, who was himself unable to control his tongue. At such moments people do not weigh their words, and even courtiers speak the truth.

The fact is that the King, wrapped up in his mystical ideas and encouraged by the correspondence of M. de Polignac, was persuaded that everything was proceeding admirably, and would not be turned from the path he believed, with great piety, that the Holy Virgin had marked out for him. The Comte de Broglie, Governor of the military school of Saint-Cyr, reached Saint-Cloud on Wednesday afternoon, greatly disturbed by what he had heard and seen as he passed Versailles. The King listened to him patiently and took the trouble to reassure him at great length. When he saw that he was withdrawing no less anxiously than he had come, he took him by the arm and said to him:

"Comte de Broglie, you, at any rate, are a man of faith. Therefore have confidence. Jules[4] has seen the Holy Virgin again last night. She ordered him to persevere, and promised that all would end well." Though the Comte de Broglie was a religious man, he nearly collapsed at this revelation.

Etiquette was not always so strictly rigorous. Among the excellent reasons which I expounded on Wednesday morning to M. de La Rue, to prevent the Marshal from ordering the troops to fire on the people, I remember that I especially emphasised the eminent service which he would render to the King and to the royal family.

4. Jules de Polignac, his Minister.

"At any rate, it would not be their opinion," he answered, "for yesterday evening the Marshal, instead of returning to Saint-Cloud, sent word to say that he thought it his duty to spend the night in Paris with the King's permission, though the rioters had been dispersed and peace established. The officer who brought this message was shown in. The King was playing at whist with the Duchesse de Berry. When the officer had delivered his message, the Princess asked him:

'Did the troops fire?'

'Yes, Madame.'

'Willingly?'

'Yes, Madame.'

'Then I must embrace you for this good news.' She rose from the table, and the King said with a smile, 'Come, come, sit down; no childishness.'"

Friday, July 30th, so fertile in great events at the Hôtel de Ville, at the Luxembourg, at the Palais-Bourbon, at Saint-Cloud, and at Neuilly, has left me with fewer memories to relate than those of the other days. This is natural, for the scene of events was no longer on the street, open to every eye, and the actors were too absorbed in their parts to have any time for relating details.

I should note that on that Friday all the workmen who were employed at my house returned to work in the most peaceable manner. Several of them had taken an active part in the conflicts of the two preceding days, and related their experiences with heroic simplicity. I also saw the workshops in my neighbourhood reopened. However, the defenders of the barricades remained at their posts, and could be seen with guns on their shoulders and loaves of bread under their arms. Some, with the object of increasing their warlike appearance, stuck their bread on the end of their bayonets; but all were quiet and polite.

I was recalled to the window which I had just left by the sound of a drum. At that time any sound was alarming, and doors and windows were consequently thronged with people in a moment. We saw a band of armed men, preceded by a drummer, slowly advancing and escorting a stretcher upon which was a mattress, on which reclined a man in

the attitude of an actor. He made a gesture with his hand to still the acclamations which no one seemed inclined to raise in his honour. As he
passed beneath my window this modest individual raised his head and
I recognised the ugly face of M. Benjamin Constant. I cannot describe
the impression which the sight of him caused. The days of nobility and
heroism seemed to be over, while falsehood and intrigue were about to
enter the scene. My instincts were not deceived.

I return to the events of those earlier days, over which I linger with
the greater pleasure as later days have somewhat obscured their due
rights. On leaving me the previous evening, Arago had been stopped
by some workmen who required him to help them with a barricade.
He thought it prudent to lend a hand with a show of willingness,
though he was exceedingly anxious to get away. One of the workers
observed that he had been there for eighteen hours without food or
drink, that he was exceedingly hungry and had not a halfpenny. Arago
thought that this was an excellent opportunity: he drew a crown from
his pocket and the workman stretched out his hand, but one of his
comrades stopped him:

"Are you going to take it? It is dishonourable."

The other withdrew his hand, thanking Arago very politely and
saying, "You see, sir, that it cannot be done." Then a discussion arose
between them, in the course of which M. Arago attempted to prove
that, as he was richer than they, it was reasonable that he should be
allowed to contribute his money as well as his labour to the common
cause. This argument shook their resolution, even that of the former
spokesman, and Arago reproduced the crown, but he suggested that
they go and spend it in drink, and this ruined the whole business.

"What, drink! You are probably an enemy who wants to make us
drunk. Drink indeed! We need possession of all our faculties. It is
quite possible that we shall be attacked tonight. Comrades, we are
hungry and thirsty, but that is nothing; we shall eat tomorrow. Put
your money in your pocket and pick up that paving-stone."

Confidence was not sufficiently established for Arago to venture a
reply, so he silently resumed his task. Soon one of his students from

the Polytechnic School arrived to inspect the work. He showed the utmost respect for his professor and consulted him with regard to the orders that he gave. The hero of the paving-stone listened to them attentively, and then addressed the pupil:

"My little General, is this gentleman one of us?"

"Certainly he is, my friend."

"Sir, will you have the kindness to give us what you offered us just now? We will drink your health most willingly, for we are mortally thirsty."

A man in society, M. de Bastard, saw a workman on sentry duty at one of the gates of the Tuileries on the point of fainting. He said that the authorities had forgotten to relieve him, that he had been there for twenty hours and felt exhausted.

"Then you must go and take some refreshment."

"But who will guard my post?"

"I will."

"You, sir? That is extremely kind of you. Well, here is my gun."

"Very good; and here are five francs to pay for your dinner."

"That is too much, sir."

After a quarter of an hour the workman came back to his post, bringing with him three francs, as he had only spent two upon his dinner.

Stories of this kind might be endlessly repeated. In several parts of the town people had gone into the houses in order to fire through the windows, had found tables laid and valuables lying about, but in no case throughout these disturbances was the smallest theft committed. There was, however, some pillaging in the rooms of the second-in-command at the Tuileries. But it is very possible that it may have been committed afterwards by the subalterns of the Château. They were suspected by those who inhabited the rooms. At the outset scruples went so far that the mattresses taken from the Archbishop's house, as well as the silver plate, were carried in procession to the hospital.

A further characteristic of this time, upon which I cannot insist too strongly, was the spirit of universal toleration. I went out that morning with M. de Salvandy; neither of us wore any fragment of tricolour. Many people, including those who were most opposed to the course of events, were bedecked with tricolours. Women, who took their stand by preference near the barricades, were carrying tricolour cockades in baskets and offered them to the passers-by just as they usually sold flowers. The common phrase, "Buy a flower for the lady," had been replaced by the words, "Here, sir, a tricolour for the lady." M. de Salvandy continually declined with some appearance of ill temper, but without producing more effect than if he had refused a bunch of lilies.

I went to the house of the Russian Ambassador; he had made great progress since the evening before. Disgusted at the neglect which Saint-Cloud showed towards the diplomatic body, he loudly proclaimed the impossibility of reentering a capital which had been stained with blood. According to him, the attempt to form a new Government led by M. de Mortemart was futile and too late to succeed. The cowardice of the rulers was equalled only by their incapacity, and it was necessary to look towards the d'Orléans family. Only upon that side was there safety, and everybody should join them, et cetera. There were several people in the room where these phrases were uttered. I believe that Baron von Werther, the Prussian Minister in Paris, was there, though I cannot be certain of the fact.

I do not precisely remember the hour, but it was late in the morning when I reached home again and found Arago waiting for me. Since his last visit he had heard that energetic efforts were being made on behalf of a republic, and said that he had just been arguing against this ridiculous project. The chances of success of Mortemart's Ministry were disappearing, but some decision must be taken rapidly if we were not to fall into the disorder of complete anarchy. He was to meet the leaders in the evening and would attempt to bring them to reason. He could answer for the Polytechnic students for a few hours, but for only a few hours. Those gloomy revelations served only to increase my anxiety.

I was with Mme. de Rauzan when we heard a great noise in her courtyard. The yard was soon filled by a crowd of people dragging a cart

filled with straw, upon which a cannon was comfortably placed. The
sovereign people proposed to present this cannon to their leader La
Fayette. This crowd was sent away to the staff quarters of the National
Guard in the Rue de Mont Blanc. They committed no excesses, but
were hideous to behold, uttering frightful yells, and there were dreadful women among them. They were not like my friends at the barricades. Poor Mme. de Labédoyère nearly died of fright. However, there
was no danger; they were only cries of joy and triumph, though of a repulsive character.

I was much surprised to see M. de Glandèves, who had started in
the morning for Saint-Cloud with the intention of remaining there. He
had been deeply wounded by his reception. Possibly the fact that he
had shaken hands with Casimir Périer[5] had been denounced. The fact
remains that the King had received him most coldly, and had ostentatiously declined to speak with him, though he was a kind of favourite.
After he had vainly waited for an opportune moment, he at length requested an audience. The King moved into the recess of a window. M.
de Glandèves attempted to speak to him of the situation in Paris, but
the King insisted in replying in a voice sufficiently loud to be heard
by the Baron de Damas and two or three other faithful members of the
Congregation who were in the room. M. de Glandèves then said to
him:

"I see that the King does not wish to listen to me; I will therefore
confine myself to requesting his orders for my future movements."

"Go back to your Tuileries."

"The King forgets that they are invaded and surmounted by the tricolour flag."

"In any case, it is impossible to put you up here."

"Then, Sire, I will return to Paris."

"The best thing that you can do."

"Has the King any other orders for me?"

"No, I have none, but you had better see my son. Good day to you."

5. A liberal-minded politician.

M. de Glandèves went off to the Dauphin.

"Sire, the King has sent me to ask if you have any orders to give me for Paris, as I am returning there."

"I? No. What orders should I have to give you? You are not one of my army."

With that the Dauphin turned his back on him. In such a way was one of the most faithful servants of the monarchy dismissed on July 30th. He was heartbroken. He had heard M. de Polignac reply to Mme. de Gontaut, who overwhelmed him with reproaches, "Have faith, have faith; none of you have faith enough." He also heard him repeat this remark several times: "If the sword had not broken in my hands, I would have established the Charter upon immovable foundations." This phrase was no easier to explain than the rest of his conduct, but in any case he seemed to be perfectly self-satisfied. On the other hand, the poor Duc de Raguse was in despair at events in Paris and crushed by all that he saw at Saint-Cloud, although his scene with the Dauphin had not yet taken place.

Pozzo came to see me. M. de Glandèves gave him the details of his visit to Saint-Cloud, and recommended his litany of the morning and of the evening before.

"They are ruined and done for. Neuilly contains the only resource which can save the country."

Nobody desired a republic. But it became an imminent possibility if some decision were not promptly taken, and whatever form it assumed, a decision could proceed only from Neuilly. There were vague rumours that some steps had been taken in that direction. At length, M. de Fréville came to tell us that the Duc d'Orléans had arrived at the Palais-Royal. It had been decided to form a provisional Government: the Prince was to be at the head of it, the Ministers had been nominated, and General Sébastiani[6] had been appointed Minister of Foreign Affairs. I cried out that this was a fatal choice: I knew Pozzo's ha-

6. A Corsican officer who had served Napoleon.

tred for him and the intensity of his Corsican feelings. The mention of this name would have been enough to make him as hostile to the Duc d'Orléans as he was then favourable. His great influence upon the diplomatic body would have been an enormous obstacle. Everybody recognised the fact and the importance of explaining it to the Palais-Royal. I was urged to undertake the task, but it was midnight, and the nominations were to be published, it was said, the next morning!

Here begins the small political part which I was able to play in these great events. It was neither foreseen nor prepared, and lasted but one day. The Carlist party[7] learnt of it, and was unduly indignant with me in consequence. I was dragged into it without premeditation, by the force of circumstances. Possibly, however, I was able at this early moment to facilitate the establishment of the new royalty, for which the Russian Ambassador had openly declared. I should have kept unbroken silence upon the whole of this affair, if the Ambassador himself had not been the first to speak of it.

On Saturday, July 31st, at daybreak, after careful reflection throughout the night, I decided to write to Mme. de Montjoie; I reminded her of the remarks of M. de Sémonville and of our conversation on Tuesday. It was strange to observe that what had been the gossip of two women on Tuesday should have become history on Friday. I then asked her if the authorities at the Palais-Royal were aware of Pozzo's profound aversion for General Sébastiani, and of the extent to which his nomination would certainly alienate the Ambassador, who was at present most favourably disposed. I added that if I could hear of a time when I should not be intruding, I would be tempted to run the risk of the barricades and pay her a visit to continue our conversation of Tuesday.

I sent this note to the Palais-Royal. An answer was returned to the effect that everybody was at Neuilly, but that my note would be sent there. I thought that M. de Fréville had been mistaken when he told us

7. Mme. de Boigne means the party faithful to Charles X.

the previous evening that the Duc d'Orléans had arrived at the Palais-Royal. As a matter of fact, he was there, but nothing had yet been decided, and the fact of his arrival was kept secret.

I received a letter from my mother, which was brought to me by Moreau, the steward of Pontchartrain. He had left his carriage outside the barriers, and was anxious to take me away if I would consent. My mother begged me to leave urgently. She thought she would see one of her children besieged and reduced to starvation by the other. Her vivid imagination carried her back to the time of the Medici Princes. These misfortunes, however, seemed less probable as Moreau told me that Saint-Cloud had been abandoned. The King was withdrawing; the road to Versailles was jammed with troops in disarray, while deserters were crowded together on every side. I went to take this news to M. Pasquier and found the Duc de Broglie with him. He had already heard of the retreat to Rambouillet. Both of them advised me strongly to remain in Paris, as being the spot where I should be safest for the moment. The Duc de Broglie had summoned his wife and children to the town. I was easily persuaded, for I took too great an interest in current events to be anxious to withdraw. I therefore returned home to write to my mother and explained my objections to leaving, and especially to following the road and surmounting the many obstacles over which Moreau proposed to take me.

While I was writing to my mother, visitor after visitor came in. Everybody was in despair, for nothing was decided and no news had been published. The same people who have since asserted, maintained, and printed that the Duc d'Orléans was so necessary to the country that he might have held out for a long time in order to secure the most advantageous conditions were then terrified and in despair at every hour's delay. They were loudly impatient because he did not immediately plunge into the movement.

"Let him begin by seizing power," they said; "explanations can come later." This was the general opinion, and I admit that I shared it.

Anarchy was coming upon us from every side, and seemed to me to be the worst of all evils.

Arago arrived completely bewildered; his efforts had been in vain. He had just left a meeting of young men who were preparing to proclaim the republic. Then the Duchesse de Rauzan came in with the same news. Moreau had also heard this rumour in the street, and used it as a further argument for taking me away. However, I continued to decline and sent him off with my answer. At that moment I received an answer from Mme. de Montjoie.

"Your note," she said, "only reached me at ten o'clock, and is now in the hands of the Duc d'Orléans. Come quickly, my dear; you are expected here with the most eager and touching anxiety."

I wished to question the messenger, but he had gone back. The note was dated from Neuilly at half past ten. How was I to get there? Any journey in carriages was impossible. Arago and Mme. de Rauzan alike urged me to go and explain the situation, and to hasten a solution. After a few moments of hesitation, I decided to start on foot. Arago gave me his arm and Mme. de Rauzan helped me to put on my hat in her hurry to see me start. As she tied the strings I said to her:

"You are my witness that I am not going to Neuilly as an Orléanist, but as a good Frenchwoman who desires the peace of the country."

She wished me every success, and told me that my mission was a deed of charity.

When we reached the Place Beauvau, we heard a proclamation read aloud from the Lieutenant-General of the Realm.[8] It was a proclamation which asserted, "The Charter will henceforward be a reality." The man who was making it public stopped every hundred paces to read it again. Groups formed about the reader, and the effect was as

---

8. In the course of Friday, sixty deputies who had met at the Palais-Bourbon had decided to offer the post of Lieutenant-General of the Realm to the Duc d'Orléans, with the restoration of the national colours. The peers, thirty in number, had met and declined to take any action. The Prince had returned from Raincy, where he had gone during Friday night, and did not receive the deputation until Saturday morning. He accepted the post of Lieutenant-General and issued the proclamation of which Mme. de Boigne speaks.

follows. The proclamation was heard with great anxiety; it produced neither joy nor enthusiasm, but great relief. Everyone quietly returned to his business, as though he had heard a satisfactory solution to a most urgent problem and was breathing more freely. This impression seems to me to have been general, but it must be remembered that I speak only of what I saw. It is possible that in other parts of the town this effect may have been very different.

I must again delay my own story to relate another incident which I saw and which I can never remember without emotion. We were making our way with difficulty along the Rue du Roule, as we had to climb over the barricades as well as the hill. We were overtaken by a group at the head of which walked a student of the Polytechnic School, who was little more than a boy. He held his sword in his hand, and waved it, repeating in a grave and sonorous voice, "Make way for the brave!" All the barricades were lowered in an instant to permit the passing of an armed patrol, in the midst of which a wounded man was carried upon a stretcher. This procession soon passed us, but we hurried our steps in order to take advantage of the passage which opened before it and immediately closed again. When it had nearly reached the hospital of Beaujon it stopped, there was a moment's hesitation, and some words were exchanged.

The stretcher was placed upon the ground, and the young student, who was raised above the whole scene by the steep slope of the hill, stretched out his arm and his sword, and in his fine, grave, and sonorous voice, which I had already noticed, said with the deepest expressiveness, "Peace to the brave!"

Everybody in the street, including the escort which surrrounded the stretcher, fell upon their knees. After a moment's silence the stretcher was lifted, and the convoy turned back. It should be added that the uniform and the cap laid upon the stretcher clearly showed that the wounded man who had died on the way to the hospital was a grenadier of the Royal Guard. I can never recall this scene without feelings of deep emotion.

At length we reached Neuilly. Mme. de Dolomieu, lady of honour of the Duchesse d'Orléans, was waiting for me in the courtyard. I was exhausted, for the heat was suffocating. She took me to the rooms of Mme. de Montjoie for a moment's rest. But Mademoiselle came in immediately; she took me into her private room after exchanging a few politenesses with Arago. She was in a state of obvious excitement, but her bearing was calm and resolute. She showed me a letter from her brother, written in pencil, in virtually the following words:

"Undoubtedly we must not alienate Pozzo; Sébastiani will not be appointed. Try and let him know."

I readily undertook this duty.

No one at Neuilly had yet heard of the proclamation which had been read in the streets. I remembered the language fairly accurately, and repeated it to Mademoiselle. As soon as I gave the title of the proclamation as that of the Lieutenant-General, she stopped me.

"Of the Lieutenant-General? You are mistaken, my dear."

"No, Mademoiselle; I heard it three or four times, and I am certain of it."

"He only intended to take the title 'Commander of Paris.' "

"He must have been carried away by the general desires. He must be able to command outside Paris as well as within the city; everyone is agreed on that point."

This statement was precisely accurate at that time. I told Mademoiselle the names of those whom I had met the evening before and that same day. From Mme. de Rauzan and her clique to the defenders of the barricades, all demanded the interference of the Duc d'Orléans.

Mademoiselle admitted that such action was wholly necessary; but in her opinion one step was clearly indispensable. It was necessary to intervene between the combatants to prevent further bloodshed, stop the civil war, and secure a general disarmament and the reestablishment of peace and order. She was so persuaded of this fact that when her brother had been sent for the previous evening, she had given full assurances to those who wished to see him in the part of peacemaker, and when she found that his absence might produce some real delay, she had offered to go to Paris if she could be of the smallest use in reestablishing public peace. She thought, as her brother did, that upon this first step there could be no hesitation, and that he should assume the power under the most modest of all possible titles, in order to avoid frightening anyone. Then he would find himself in a position to act according to circumstances; determinations taken at leisure were always better than those made offhand at a moment of such keen excitement.

We spoke of all that was happening at Paris and at Saint-Cloud. She knew of the departure and of the retreat to Rambouillet, although the Trianon had been the place officially mentioned. She had also heard of the scene between the Dauphin and the Duc de Raguse. I cannot say whether this news had come directly to Neuilly or from Paris.

While we were talking, Mme. de Dolomieu came to take me to the Duchesse d'Orléans.

"Go to my sister at once," said Mademoiselle to me, "and try to cheer her up a little. She is in a terrible state."

I followed Mme. de Dolomieu to the Princess's room and entered alone. She was in her bedroom, in a dressing-gown and curl-papers, sitting in a great armchair with her back to the light. The Princesse Louise was on her knees before her, with her head leaning on the arm of the chair, and both were in tears. The Duchesse d'Orléans held out her hand, drew me towards her, and, leaning upon me, began to sob. The young Princess rose and went out, and I took her place. Her mother continued to cling to me, and to repeat through her tears:

"What a catastrophe! What a catastrophe! And we might have been at Eu!"

I succeeded in calming her to some degree. I spoke to her of the general desires, of the magnificent position which lay before the Duc d'Orléans, and of the universal wish for his action. I believed what I said, and moreover, I must again repeat that this was true. I also repeated to her the good effect of the proclamation. She did not pause at the title, but her attention was arrested by the expression "The Charter will be henceforward a reality." She approved of the phrase, and spoke to me of her husband and of the purity of his intentions, in all her adoration for him. I ventured to say to her:

"Well, Madame, would France be so unhappy in such hands if our Guillaume III took the title of Philippe VII?"[9]

"Heaven preserve us from that, my dear! They would call him a usurper!" And her sobs began again.

"Doubtless, Madame, they would call him a usurper, and they would be right. But if they called him a conspirator they would be wrong. Conspiracy is the only blameworthy element in usurpation, and none of his contemporaries would raise that charge against him."

"Oh yes, he most certainly has not conspired. The King knows that better than anybody. He has always spoken of him with good faith and openness! Only a month ago at Rosny they talked together more than half an hour, and at the end of the conversation he said to my husband, 'Be sure that I understand my position as you do. I am persuaded that there is no safety outside of the Charter, and I give you my word that nothing will induce me to transgress it.' And then to pass these ordinances!"

Then the poor woman began to weep again more than ever. "Oh, my dear friend, my happiness is past. I have been too happy." And clasping her hands, she exclaimed again, "O God! I hope I have not been ungrateful. I have enjoyed my happiness, but I have always been duly thankful for it." And so she continued to weep and exclaim.

I urged her to be less downcast, and pointed out that the Duc d'Orléans would need all his self-command. Nothing would be more likely to ruin him than the despair of one whom he loved more than anything in the world. She told me that she was quite aware of the fact, and that though she thus gave way before me, she would adopt a very different attitude when necessary. The glory and happiness of her husband had always been the first interests of her life, and she would not fail them now. I strongly urged her to go to Paris.

"Ride out in your carriage, Madame, with all your children. Take your state carriages and full livery, and the barricades will fall before you. People will be flattered by this confidence and will receive you

9. Allusion to William III, who shared the throne of Mary II, after her father, James II, fled the Revolution. Mme. de Boigne assumes the Duc d'Orléans would take the name Philippe VII.

with enthusiasm, and you will reach the Palais-Royal amidst cheers, without the smallest doubt."

"If my husband bade me do so, I would certainly go as you say. But, my dear, I should feel great reluctance. It would be a kind of triumph and mockery to the other side, you understand. I should very much like to reach the Palais-Royal and rejoin my husband as soon as possible, but I would rather do it quietly."

"I can understand your delicate feelings, but this is not the moment for delicacy. Anything that can confirm the popularity of the d'Orléans and show how the country desires them seems, in my opinion, valuable for its safety."

The Duchesse d'Orléans, with her accustomed kindness, was much disturbed at my fatigue and the extreme heat through which I had come to Neuilly. She had ordered a carriage to take me back to the barriers, and this carriage was now announced. She wished to keep me with her longer, but I pointed out to her that it was necessary for me to see Pozzo as soon as possible. She made me promise to return the next day, either to Neuilly, or to the Palais-Royal, where she then hoped to be. I found one of Mademoiselle's footmen waiting to take me back to her. She asked me how I had left her sister-in-law. I replied, "Somewhat calmer, but greatly moved." It was clear to me that the two Princesses, notwithstanding their close intimacy, were not in full confidence at this moment. I told Mademoiselle of the advice I had given to the Duchesse d'Orléans concerning her entry into Paris. I must admit that in her case I did not encounter the same kind of objection. But she told me that it was too important a step for her to take the initiative without her brother's orders. This was true, but if the question had been asked, an answer might have arrived in an hour, during which time the carriages could have been readied. The arrival of his family amidst the acclamations of the people, as would inevitably have happened, would have provided the Duc d'Orléans with an excellent argument against the little circle of partisans who were regarded as unduly important only because they were the ones who were seen and heard.

Fate decided otherwise. The Princesses reached the Palais-Royal at midnight and on foot, travelling unrecognised in an omnibus as far as the barricades would allow. I cannot but regret that they did not choose the course I had pointed out upon that day.

During my conversation with Mademoiselle we had not gone beyond the title of Lieutenant-General, though with her sister-in-law had ventured to pronounce the title of Philip VII. However, I went away nonetheless persuaded that Mademoiselle was keenly anxious to see the crown of France upon her brother's head, whereas the Duchesse d'Orléans regarded this prospect with horror and aversion.

This is perhaps the appropriate time to give some account of my relations with the two Princesses d'Orléans and my opinion of their characters. When the storms of the Revolution drove my parents to Naples, I had often been brought into the company of the Queen's daughters. I was nearer in age to Madame Amélie, and played most frequently with her. She preferred me over her other little playmates. Those remarks apply to the years 1794 and 1795. When she returned to France twenty years later, the Duchesse d'Orléans had not forgotten this childhood association and permitted a special degree of intimacy to exist between us. I had the opportunity to pursue this connection while my father was Ambassador in London, during which period the d'Orléans family were living in a kind of exile near London. This fact will also explain how I often knew more of the family griefs and vexations, though I was not an inmate of the Palais-Royal, than people whose intimacy might seem greater than mine.

I cannot possibly overstate the deep veneration and tender devotion which I feel for the Duchesse d'Orléans. She was adored by her husband, by her children, and by all about her, and the more often anyone came into contact with her, the deeper was the veneration and affection which she inspired. Her sympathetic tact in no way modified the loftiness of her sentiments or the strength of her character. The mother and the Princess were wonderfully conjoined in her, and though she treated everybody with that obvious kindness which was natural to her, her attitude was marked by such delicate shades of consideration that each individual knew his position in her society.

At the time of which I am speaking, the Duchesse d'Orléans had persuaded herself that she had no head for business, although her opinions enjoyed deep respect in the family councils, where the most perfect harmony prevailed. She thought that Mademoiselle had much greater capacity for dealing with affairs, because of her strong sense of right and her strength of character. She was thus ready to be taken under her sister-in-law's wing on any question of business or party politics. Possibly also this attitude was dictated by that delicate tact which directed her every action, sometimes without her awareness.

The court, especially under Louis XVIII, for Charles X treated the d'Orléans with greater respect, attempted to mark the wide difference between the position of the Duchesse d'Orléans and that of her husband and of her sister. She would willingly have been given a higher position if she had been willing to accept it. However, as all the vexations and outbreaks which troubled the existence of the happy family at the Palais-Royal were due to the animosity of the reigning branch, the Duchesse d'Orléans thought that she was doubly bound to make common cause with the members of her family and to adopt without reflection the decisions of Mademoiselle. Hence she grew accustomed to be guided by her, and never attempted to combat the influence which she was able to gain over her brother, the object of their common admiration. I do not think these scruples of the Duchesse d'Orléans were continued in the person of the Queen of France.

There has never been any coolness between the two Princesses, but they have not always been unanimous upon important questions. The Queen sometimes expressed, defended, and supported her opinions warmly, and attempted to use her influence upon the King. There was never more passionate affection than that of the Duchesse d'Orléans for her husband. She was firmly persuaded that his every decision was "Wisest, discreetest, best."[10]

This consideration was of great comfort to her amidst the troubled waters into which circumstances drove her. She entered these with extreme reluctance and prayed earnestly that the cup might be re-

10. In English, in the original text.

moved from her; but once the decision had been taken she accepted it wholeheartedly. Entirely misguided speculation has arisen concerning her reluctance. Six weeks after the morning of which I have just spoken, she said to me:

"Now that this crown of thorns is upon our head, we must wear it while life lasts, and we will lay down our lives for it if necessary."

This calm energy did not prevent her from offering the most delicate and exquisite sympathy with the griefs of others, which she could realise and understand. Kindness was the source from which she invariably drew that lustre which adorned the most real virtues that a woman and a queen can possess. It may be thought that I am writing a panegyric; if I have done so, it has been unintentional. I am drawing her picture as I see it.

My personal relations with Mademoiselle date from 1816 to 1817. I have always recognised her goodness of heart and her intellectual power, though I never felt greatly drawn to her. However, her good qualities were hers entirely, and her defects were more due to the circumstances in which she was placed. She was the frankest and most straightforward person conceivable, and these qualities made her many enemies. The first confidences of her youth were received with malevolence, and she was correspondingly embittered.

Her father, Philippe-Egalité, was kindness itself to her. Brought up by Mme. de Genlis* on the most revolutionary ideas, she had seen this unfortunate Prince gradually advance upon his fatal path and watched the sight undismayed. She was too young to judge the facts for herself at that time, and she was never afterwards willing to recognise that it was a path of crime, and that his voting for the death of Louis XVI was inexcusable. Attempts were made to make her proclaim her repugnance. After her father was executed and her mother thrown in prison, she was entrusted to the care of her great-aunt, the Princesse de Conti, who was very intelligent and appreciated and loved her but did not have the courage to protect her sufficiently and shelter her from the persecutions to which the *émigré* party subjected her. Throughout her stay with the Princesse, efforts were made to force the young girl to take a step by which she should definitely renounce her father's memory. Her remembrances of his kindness were strong, and she regarded resistance as a virtue; as a result, she spent the years of her youth in the solitude of her room.

The exiles who formed the society of the Princesse de Conti declined to associate with her, and she herself would make no concessions. Her aunt, who was a clever woman, showed her some affection, and neither scolded nor worried her, but was not sufficiently independent to take her side against the prevailing party spirit.

At a later date, she hoped to find full sympathy from her mother, who had escaped her prison and settled in Barcelona, and Mademoiselle reached Spain full of illusions on the subject of filial affection. She was coldly received, and found the Duchesse d'Orléans in so equivocal a position[11] that her stay in Barcelona soon became unendurable. She was obliged to write to her brothers that her position was unfitting for her. It is obvious that all the sentiments of youth which are usually the delight and happiness of girls were outraged. With these preliminary facts, it will be possible, I think, to understand both the good and bad qualities of Mademoiselle.

She was frank because she had never been accustomed to hide her impressions, and she was careless as to whether they were opportune or likely to please other people. At the same time, she was not expansive, having been repulsed by everyone who should have helped develop her capacities for affection during her early youth. Hence, her heart had been wholly and exclusively given to her brother, the first person who had shown her the sweetness of true intimacy, and the only person in whom she could find full sympathy for the heavy burden which she was obliged to bear. Their father's life and death will always form a stronger bond of union between them than perhaps they have ever themselves admitted. Though both of them were generally the easiest of companions, on this point they became irritable, even angry. They were never at ease with the royal family, and least of all

11. The Duchesse had a very inappropriate lover, M. de Follemont, who acted as if he were her husband.

with the wife of the Dauphin, who on her side constantly treated them with marked disdain. Mademoiselle retained all her bitterness against the nobility and the exiles who spoiled the happiness of her youth. Her goodness of heart forgave them as individuals, but her general attitude towards them was one of strong opposition and might have been seen as a kind of vengeance. This frame of mind drove her to seek support among people who felt the same aversion. She was too inclined to believe, in my opinion, that they would stop where she did, for they desired to see the power in their own hands and worked to secure it for themselves. The Liberals—Lafitte, Barrot, Dupont, and their like—had in Mademoiselle a partisan at the outset. The tenacity of her character and her fixed determination not to abandon people who seemed accused by circumstances, along with her resolution always to assume their intentions as good, induced her to lend them a support which endangered her influence on the King's mind for some considerable period. She was aware of the fact and was grieved by it, but she did not change her conduct; such was her nature.

She has been accused of parsimony with both truth and falsehood. Until the death of her mother, Mademoiselle had no means and was living at her brother's expense, so that economy at that time was a virtue. After she came into the enjoyment of a considerable revenue, she spent it generously, becoming a patroness of the arts and employing much labour upon her estates. Her private charities were enormous, but she was not accustomed to magnificence and could not spend in a royal manner, even when such expenditure was advisable. Her accounts were kept too precisely for a Princess. However, at the outset of the new reign, when the question of the Civil List[12] was under discussion, Baron Louis, the Finance Minister, came to her and asked if she would be satisfied if she were put down for a million. She objected as if he had offered her an insult, and protested that her personal income was enough and more than enough for her needs.

Mademoiselle displayed an affection for her nephews which I had

12. The Civil List is the sum given to the head of the state to pay for the expenses of his office and that of his immediate family.

thought absolutely motherly until the death of the Duc de Penthièvre, who was seven years of age and almost an idiot. The Duchesse d'Orléans was overwhelmed by grief at this loss. Mademoiselle never pretended any feelings of the kind. She was pained by her sister-in-law's sorrow, but insisted upon asserting that the death of the child was a merciful release. This was the only shade of difference that I observed in the affection of the two sisters for the children. Possibly Mademoiselle was the more inclined to indulgence of the two, although she laboured as much as anyone to give the children the excellent education which they received.

I doubt if anyone had a better head for business than Mademoiselle. She could instantly discover the critical point of a difficulty and sweep away all side issues; she refused to be led astray and pinned the interlocutor down to the single point at stake. It will readily be understood that this power could not have increased her popularity at a time when almost everyone was anxious not to speak decisively or to pledge his word. This power would have been inestimable if Mademoiselle had been at the head of affairs, but it was actually a disadvantage in her position, which should have been wholly secondary, but she was unable to appear except in the foreground. Hence she made many personal enemies, and her unpopularity was reflected to some degree upon her brother, whose interpreter she was supposed to be. She was aware of the fact, and her desire not to injure this brother, whom she deeply loved, impeded both her speech and her actions. So although her frankness reached the point of rudeness, she was considered duplicitous; and although her kindness was more than ordinary, she was considered resentful.

During the trial of the Ministers of Charles X, I remember that one evening when great anxiety prevailed, Marshal Gérard, with his usual cowardice, was explaining how dangerous it would be for the King to attempt to save M. de Polignac.[13] Mademoiselle then replied in a tone which I shall never forget:

13. Polignac was arrested as he was trying to flee to England. He was judged by the Chamber of Peers and condemned to perpetual confinement and the loss of civil rights. He was kept at the fortress of Ham until the amnesty of 1836.

"Well, Marshal, if necessary, we will all perish in the attempt."

Her usually commonplace features were for the moment transfig-ured.

I owe it to her to say that she could listen to the truth even when it displeased her, not only with patience but also with a show of grati-tude. I did not spare her feelings on many occasions, and although we may not have been precisely attracted to one another, she never showed any difference in her treatment of me.

I return to the events of July 31st. Mademoiselle asked me to bring back Mme. de Valence, the daughter of Mme. de Genlis, and her little girls. The four of us, with M. Arago, entered a carriage which was waiting. I had secured the special protection of the Princesses for the Duc de Raguse in case he should need it, and Arago had given Mme. Montjoie full details of his visit to the general staff; he had been with her during my visits to the two sisters-in-law.

When I reached the barriers, I left my friends and went immedi-ately to Pozzo. There were visitors in his reception room, and I asked for him. When he came to meet me from the anteroom, I said:

"I have just come from Neuilly, and am ordered to thank you for your good wishes, for which everyone is most grateful."

I found him a very different man from the previous evening; he was embarrassed, cold, and surly. He replied:

"Certainly they are right; you know how deeply I am attached to them, but the position is very delicate. The King is at Rambouillet; he is established there. My colleagues think that it would be advisable to rejoin the sovereign to whom we are accredited. There is a great deal to that, though we have not been summoned. However, I do not know what to do, and I am not sure what advice to give them."

I did not betray excessive astonishment at this sudden change of opinion, which I had foreseen, though I will admit that I had expected a more elaborate excuse.

"I am sure that you will do what will be most prudent and expedi-ent. By the way, I meant to tell you that Sébastiani will not enter the Ministry. I am absolutely sure of the fact."

He looked at me fixedly for a moment.

"I am theirs to the death!" he cried, and, taking me by both hands, he drew me into the middle of the drawing-room on the left. "Let us sit down. I suppose they wish to reign, do they not?"

"They say they do not."

"Then they are wrong. That is the only reasonable and only possible course. At bottom they do wish it, and if they do not wish it to-day, they will tomorrow, because it is a necessity. So we must act upon that supposition."

I will admit that though I had expected a change, this sudden reversal bewildered me. I was so struck by it that I am certain that I have reported his first words precisely as he spoke them. He then began to discuss ways and means of rejecting the foolish proposal of going to Rambouillet, which some of his colleagues had instigated. He no longer considered the question delicate or embarrassing, and had resumed his previous arguments against the older branch and in favour of the d'Orléans family. It was impossible to be clearer or more logical. After many general considerations, he gave me detailed instructions concerning the best attitude to adopt towards the diplomatic body. I asked him if he would allow me to state that this advice came from him. Not only did he give me permission, but he also begged me to do so, and also to express his entire devotion to the family. He repeated several times:

"It is their duty to reign, and loudly to proclaim their desire to do so."

We separated upon the best possible terms.

During my absence several people had called on me, including Mme. Récamier. She had waited for me a long time, and had finally left a little note on my table in which she expressed her great regret at not finding me at home, and her keen anxiety to talk with me of a person whose deep irritation she was sorry to see. I readily understood that M. de Chateaubriand was the person in question. Mademoiselle and I had spoken of him that morning, and we had agreed that it was desirable to secure his support in the interests of the country. I knew too much about him to consider him a very valuable ally, but I knew that he might be a formidable adversary. M. de Chateaubriand was a man who could be secured only by placing ourselves entirely under his wing; at the same time, he would soon grow weary of following a simple and easy path. He called that driving in a rut, and liked to create obstacles merely for the challenge of surmounting them.

I was much too tired to think of going to Mme. Récamier, as I should have had to walk. I was obliged to put off the question of her note until the next day; in any case, it was after six o'clock.

I saw a number of people in the evening. The general impression of my circle was one of sadness and gravity; we regarded what had happened as the inevitable result of earlier mistakes. This result, however, seemed to us a lamentable disaster, but we considered it our duty to prevent it from becoming an even greater calamity by throwing the country into anarchy. I must do M. Pasquier the justice to say that he was gloomier and more apprehensive than anyone else. With the same frankness I will admit that his fears seemed to me somewhat exaggerated.

On Sunday, August 1, Mme. de Montjoie came into my room at seven o'clock in the morning. She told me that Mademoiselle was anxious for a conversation with Pozzo. If he were willing to go to the Palais-Royal he might enter by a door situated at a considerable distance from the palace. If, however, he objected, Mademoiselle was ready to come and meet him at my house. Assuming that he approved the former arrangement, he would go out with me as though he were accompanying me for a walk to the Tuileries. We were to enter the Rue Saint-Honoré. Mme. de Montjoie would be waiting for us in a shop near the door at which we were to enter, and would guide us through the intricacies of the interior. Whatever Pozzo's decision might be, I promised that I myself would be at the meeting place. I immediately wrote a note to the Ambassador, asking him to come to me at once. I gave him an account of Mme. de Montjoie's visit. He replied that he would be delighted to see Mademoiselle and to have a talk with her, and was most anxious for the meeting, but he added:

"Considering the state of affairs in the Palais-Royal, the disorder of the rooms and the number of people going about, it is certain that someone would see and recognise me. The air of mystery given to this conference would give it an added importance in the eyes of the public. I am particularly afraid of such supposed indiscretions, as they might neutralise my efforts and destroy my influence. I can only retain my influence upon the diplomatic body as long as I preserve a show of impartiality upon the question and make common cause with my colleagues."

He therefore accepted Mademoiselle's second proposal, begged me to make his full excuses and to request that she would agree to a meeting at my house. We decided on a casual phrase to be sent as a message to inform him that the Princess would come.

I also sent to ask M. Pasquier to come and see me, told him the plan in progress, and asked him if he would be willing to converse with Mademoiselle, supposing that she desired a meeting. He replied that he had no objection whatever, and would be very glad of so natural an opportunity for explaining some of his ideas and for thus transmitting them directly to the Duc d'Orléans.

When these preliminaries had been settled, I set off at the appointed time, and as I have been describing what occurred in the streets, it is perhaps worthwhile to say a word of their appearance then. There were a great many people going about. A large number of patrols were seen, though they were dressed only in trousers and shirts as on the preceding days, and were almost all led by someone in uniform. Orderlies on horseback were carrying orders in great haste. Women and children were everywhere well-dressed and wandering about, or with prayer-books in hand going to church, where divine service was being celebrated and the doors were open as usual. Though everybody seemed busy, curious, and hurried, they were calm and confident. Indeed, except for the trenches across the streets and the strange costume of the troops, one might have supposed that it was an ordinary fine Sunday morning, upon which the population of the town was preparing to view some unusual spectacle which increased rapidity of movement without adding undue agitation. The town seemed as though a festivity were in progress for which the carriage traffic had been stopped.

I found Mme. de Montjoie at the meeting place, and after a long journey through the palace, which led us under the eaves, we reached Mademoiselle's rooms. She was in her little gallery: her study, which I crossed to reach her, was still strewn with glass broken from the windows during the preceding days. Bullet marks were also to be seen in the woodwork. Hardly had I arrived and given Pozzo's message when the Duchesse d'Orléans came in with great agitation.

"Sister, there is a man here, a footman from the Duchesse de Berry, whose name I have forgotten, who is waiting to take any message from me to the Duchesse de Berry. What am I to say? I cannot refuse to see him."

"Give him some ordinary message of politeness; there is no need to go into details in the case of such a messenger, but do not write."

The Duchesse d'Orléans went out, and Mademoiselle ran after her to the next room, "Above all things, sister, do not write."

"No, I will not, I promise you." Mademoiselle came back to me with a smile.

"My poor sister is so upset," she said, "that she cannot weigh her words, and it will not do to pledge ourselves in any direction."

We resumed our conversation, and Mademoiselle agreed that it would be better for her to come to my house. She was ready to come that day under my sole escort, but I should be obliged to wait for a while. Her brother was out, and she could not start until he returned.

The Duchesse d'Orléans came back a second time. "Sister, Sébastiani is here, and he is furious."

"Never mind; I will have him brought here. Whether he is furious or not, he will have to give way this time. I will undertake to talk to him."

She rang the bell to give orders that General Sébastiani should be shown into her room. I left it with the Duchesse d'Orléans. I cannot describe the confusion which then prevailed throughout the Palais-Royal. During the absence of the family at Neuilly, considerable repairs had been begun in several rooms. The floors had been taken up, and we walked over the joists amidst the plaster. In other rooms painters were at work with their tools. The furniture was out of place, and we were constantly running into upholsterers carrying ladders and footmen bringing chairs. People of all kinds were walking around in the middle of this confusion.

Meals were in progress in every room, and everybody walked in as though the palace were a street. Conversation was impossible amidst such an uproar. The Duchesse d'Orléans was able only to tell me as we withdrew through Mademoiselle's rooms that she felt easier in her mind about the Dauphine.

The latter had met the Duc de Chartres near Fontainebleau during the previous night. And as no other news of her had arrived, it was obvious that she had come to no harm and must have rejoined her family. A great weight was therefore removed from the mind of the Duchesse d'Orléans. She was deeply attached to the Dauphine, and the sad events which followed the misfortunes and the feelings of this Princess always caused the Queen[14] anxiety and despair, as I have seen for myself. Later in the morning I was shown an intercepted letter from the Dauphine to her husband. I remember one phrase which struck me greatly. After a bitterly indignant account of the scene at the theatre in Dijon as she was coming out, and of the insolent cries which were uttered, she added, "They would have liked to insult me personally, but I assumed my well-known air, and they did not venture to try it."

She was thus continuing that well-known air which we considered unfortunate. I do not, indeed, recall these words with any sense of hostility towards the Princess, whom I respect, and "whose misfortunes were in themselves a dignity," to use the expression of M. de Chateaubriand; I quote them only as further proof of the ignorance concerning the times and the mood of the country under which the elder branch

14. Mme. de Boigne is writing in 1832; thus she alludes to the Duchesse d'Orléans as the Queen.

laboured. This air, which she believed commanded respect, merely produced bitterness and ill feeling. She did not discuss the ordinances in this letter; it was as if she had already spoken of them:

"I shall not return to what I told you yesterday. What has been done is done, but I shall not breathe freely until we are united."

I return to the events at the Palais-Royal. We were supposed to spend our time in the room known as the Salon des Batailles, where a kind of *repas en ambigu*[15] had been laid. As a matter of fact, we spent the time in a room which communicated with all the other apartments, and off of which a large balcony looked onto the court. Every cry, every drum beat, every noise—and noises were frequent—echoed there. The Duchesse d'Orléans was obviously attempting to overcome her mental agitation by physical exercise for she could not sit still. After following her around for some time, I abandoned the effort, completely exhausted, and sat down in a corner where Mme. de Dolomieu, who was as tired as myself, came to keep me company. There we sat until the cheers in the square announced the approach of the Duc d'Orléans. Mademoiselle joined us then, followed by General Sébastiani. He looked very surly, and as he passed gave me a glance from which I understood that he recognised me as the intermediary in a negotiation which was so entirely against his wishes.

Everyone went out upon the great balcony to see the arrival of the Duc d'Orléans. He and his horse were literally borne along by the waves of people. I am well aware that such enthusiasm promises nothing for the next day, but, without attaching undue importance to it, it must be said that there was the utmost enthusiasm for him in that place and at that time. His poor wife was greatly touched, and it was a pleasant compensation for her previous anxieties.

At length the Duc d'Orléans emerged from the crowd, entered the palace, where the crowd was a little more select, and reached the room we were in. He stopped for a moment, embraced his youngest chil-

15. A meal which is neither lunch nor dinner, but shares the nature of both because of the time when it takes place and also of the nature of the dishes. It is a mixture of both meals with hot and cold dishes and dessert all being served at the same time.

dren, who had come from Neuilly after his departure, spoke to General Sébastiani, took my hand and said a few kind words, and went back into his private room, followed by his wife and sister. The latter did not stay there long. When she came out, she took my arm and said, "Come; I am ready to go."

We went back to her rooms, and the problem of dress began. She had a straw hat but no veil, and a veil was a necessity for our expedition. My own was deep black, for my mourning, and would not do for her. She rang for the only maid she had brought from Neuilly, but the maid had no key to the closets. At length she remembered a hat which had been left in Paris, trimmed with a large white veil, which was brought. She was afraid that it might be too conspicuous. I assured her that the streets were full of equally splendid hats, and soon she was as surprised by this as I had been during the preceding days.

We went down the little turret staircase and left the palace; no one recognised her. This was not a difficult manoeuvre in the midst of the prevailing confusion. When we reached the Rue de Chartres, she said to me in English, "We are followed." We were followed, as a matter of fact, but by my butler. I had brought him because I could rely on him as the most discreet of all my servants. I reassured her accordingly.

"Then," she said, "let us each take his arm; that will look better than the sight of two women alone."

We adopted her suggestion, and Jules Goulay was honoured with the arm of a Princess. We decided that if we should meet any of my acquaintances who might wish to speak to me, I was to stop while she went on ahead.

I told her of the note which I had received about M. de Chateaubriand; she repeated that his support was considered highly desirable, though he would not be given a place in the Cabinet. If the Ambassadorship at Rome would suit him, he might be allowed to resume it. The evening before, M. de Glandèves had begged me to say a word at the Palais-Royal concerning himself and his devotion. I had carried out this commission in the morning, and apparently Mademoiselle had spoken of the matter to her brother during her short conversation, for I was formally requested to tell M. de Glandèves to return to his rooms at the Tuileries, where his position would be formalised. I delivered the message, and he refused the offer with many kind and respect-ful words. All this shows how much people wanted at this first mo-ment to continue monarchical customs, and how necessity operating through the energy of some and the reticence of others obliged them to follow other paths. I use the word reticence because there was no hostility as yet. The party which has since been called Carlist or Le-gitimist did not exist then. As we were talking in English, the man between us was no embarrassment. I asked Mademoiselle whether she would care to see M. Pasquier, in which case I would send a message to him while she was talking with the Ambassador. She told me that she would be delighted. We had entered the garden of the Tuileries, but were obliged to turn back, as the gates leading to the Place Louis XV were still closed. We followed the Rue de Rivoli. As we approched Talleyrand's mansion on the Rue Saint-Florentin, Mademoiselle made me walk by her side in order to conceal her as much as possible.

"I do not want the old devil to notice me," she said; "He is so cun-ning, and might easily recognise me from his window. I should not care for him to see me passing, and having to speak to him would be even more unpleasant."

We reached the Rue des Champs-Elysées without meeting anyone. I stopped in order to give the agreed-upon message to the Ambassa-dor's porter. Mademoiselle went forward and I caught up with her as she was entering my house; hardly had I shown her into my room when Pozzo arrived. He told me that someone would come and ask for him to sign a paper. I brought him to the Princess and left them together; I then wrote a note to M. Pasquier to tell him that he was expected.

M. Pasquier arrived, and we waited for the conclusion of the con-ference with Pozzo, which was very long. As soon as I saw him come out, I took M. Pasquier into the room and withdrew. As will be seen, I was throughout this affair nothing more than the fly on the coach-wheel. I had observed during my morning walk that cabs were begin-ning to go about, though with difficulty. I had sent to fetch one, and when M. Pasquier had left Mademoiselle, I suggested that she should take it rather than return on foot; she agreed, and we got in. She told me that she was pleased with M. Pasquier. "It is clear," she added, "that he is a man accustomed to see a question from every point of view, and a great way of overcoming obstacles is to have foreseen them. It is also clear that he is by no means anxious to implicate himself; obviously he has been involved in many revolutions, and is afraid of them. But I am perfectly delighted with our good Pozzo. He is perfect, dear Mme. de Boigne, and entirely one of us. He has told me of the despatch which he signed, and which we could not have composed differently ourselves. I am very anxious for him to have a meeting with my brother, and shall try and arrange it for tomorrow night. In any case, the most important point is already settled: he has induced the diplomatic body to stay in Paris, and has sent off those excellent despatches."

We discussed this subject and many others during our journey, which was undisturbed except for a constant and fearful jolting. I stopped the cab in the Rue de Valois and accompanied Mademoiselle to the staircase of the turret. As soon as I had seen the door of her rooms close after her, I went down to the cab and returned home. After a pretence of dining, for the excessive heat, my fatigue, and anxiety made it almost as difficult to eat as to sleep, I took another cab and went to see Mme. Récamier. She was awaiting me impatiently to speak of M. de Chateaubriand. I soon learnt that he was angry with Charles X, who had not answered his letter; disgusted with the peers, who had not chosen him to lead the Chamber; and furious with the Lieutenant-General, who had not entrusted him with the power that events proclaimed to be his due. Moreover, he was reputed to be ill. This was his usual behaviour when his ambition received any great check, and it is possible that his disappointment was sufficiently grave to have had an effect upon his health. Mme. Récamier urged me to visit him in her company and to try to soothe him. I consented, and we entered the carriage which had brought me and reached his little house in the Rue d'Enfer.

Mme. Récamier was known to the servants, and we were shown up to his study without difficulty. We knocked at his door, and he told us to come in. We found him in a dressing-gown and slippers, with a bandana on his head, writing at a corner of the table. It was a long table, entirely disproportionate to the room, which was shaped like a gallery; it took up most of the space and gave the room a slight public-house appearance. It was covered with books and papers, remnants of food, and toilet utensils by no means elegant. M. de Chateaubriand received us very kindly. It was obvious, however, that he was ill at ease because of the disorder in the room and even more so because of the bandana. So far he was justified, for the red and green handkerchief was most unbecoming to his gloomy face.

We found him extremely bitter. Mme. Récamier induced him to read me the speech which he was preparing for the Chamber. It was extremely violent, and I can remember a passage, among others, which was afterwards inserted into one of his pamphlets, in which he depicted the Duc d'Orléans advancing towards the throne with two heads in his hands; the rest of the speech continued this tone. We listened to his reading in the profoundest silence, and when he had finished I asked him if this work, the literary excellence of which I admitted, was the work of a good citizen in his opinion.

"I do not claim to be a good citizen."

I asked whether he thought that this work was the best means of bringing the King back to the Tuileries.

"Heaven forbid! I should be very sorry to see him there."

"In that case, would it not be more prudent to join those in power, in view of the fact that they might be able to prevent the anarchical calamities which are not unreasonably to be expected and which you depict in such dire tones?"

Mme. Récamier took this opening to say that I had been at the Palais-Royal that morning. She ventured to add that great value was given to his support and cooperation. It would be understood that he might object to taking any active part in the Government, but perhaps he might consent to return to Rome.

He rose from his chair, saying, "Never!" and began to walk about at the other end of the little gallery. Mme. Récamier continued to talk with me quietly of the advantages of his position at Rome, of the service he might render religion, of the natural and valuable part which the author of the *Génie du Christianisme* might play in such a predicament, et cetera. He pretended not to listen to us. However, his temper grew milder and his steps slower; suddenly he stopped in front of a shelf full of books, and, folding his arms, he cried:

"And what shall I say to those thirty volumes which are looking me in the face? No, no! They condemn me to throw in my fortunes with the lot of those wretches. Who knows them, who despises them, and who hates them more than I?" Then he unfolded his arms and placed his hands on the end of the long table which separated us, and began a diatribe against the Princes and the court. He expressed himself in that bitter scorn which his hatred could produce, and with such violence that I was almost terrified. It was growing dark, and the attitude of this figure with the red and green handkerchief, standing before the only light that came into the room, seemed almost diabolical.

After this explosion he grew somewhat calmer, came towards us, and said in a more equable tone, "What Frenchman has not felt enthusiastic for the admirable days which have just passed? And undoubtedly the man who has done so much to bring them about cannot have remained unmoved."

He then drew a picture in the most vivid colours of the national resistance, and the brilliance of his own role through his telling of the story softened him.

"I recognise," he said in conclusion, "that it was impossible to reach the only possible result with greater nobility. I admit the fact, but I myself, a wretched serf bound to the soil, cannot free myself from this dogma of legitimacy, which I have so often praised. People will always have the right to throw my words back at me. Moreover, all the efforts of this heroic nation will be lost; no one understands it, people wish to entrust this country, so young and so beautiful, to the guidance of worn-out men, who will only work to sap its manhood, or it will be handed over to those little gentlemen"—this was his special name for M. de Broglie and M. Guizot,* the objects of his special detestation—and they will try to cut it to the model of their master.

"No, what France requires is new men, men of courage and bravery, bold and adventurous like herself, who will restore her with one stroke to the head of the nations! See how instinctively she feels the want! Whom did she choose to lead her when left to herself? School-boys and children, but they were children full of talent, vigour, and courage, able to inflame imaginations because they are themselves enthusiastic. At most some old sailor will be needed to warn of reefs and shallows, and thus not to stop progress, but to stimulate audacity."

M. de Chateaubriand's ideas of government were thus sufficiently explained by these words. He was to be the directing power, with the schoolboys and newspaper editors as his acolytes; such was the ideal he had formed for himself of the happiness and glory of France in his discontented dreams. However, it was necessary to end the encounter and to take leave of these rhapsodies. I asked him if he had any answer for the Palais-Royal, whither I should be going the next morning.

He replied in the negative. His part was already fixed by prior circumstances; he had seen this crisis long ago and had professed his faith beforehand. Personally he had a high respect for the d'Orléans family. He appreciated all the difficulties of its position, which unfortunately it would not be able to secure because it did not understand the state of affairs and would not regard them from a sufficiently revolutionary standpoint.

I left him evidently much calmer. In fact, there was a broad difference between the speech which he had read to me, with the "two heads in his hands," and that which he delivered in the Chamber, and in which "he would offer a crown to the Duc d'Orléans if he had one to give." But I rediscovered in it the same bitter sarcasm for the conquered which had formed part of his extempore speech at the end of the table, the eloquence of which had charmed him and soothed his feelings. Among others he used the expression "to drive out with a pitchfork."

Throughout this long conversation, which lasted until nightfall, I can affirm that not a word was said concerning the Duc de Bordeaux. I did not hear this subject mentioned until I returned home in the evening. I am aware that at present everyone has constantly thought of it, has always desired and wished it, but I can assert that these desires were secret. The idea of the King's abdication, and above all of that of the Dauphin, had not yet become general, and for myself I must admit it had never occurred to me independently; moreover, it seemed to me unlikely to become reality.

Yet I am certain that attempts to produce this result were made this Sunday; they had begun the previous evening and continued throughout the next day. They met with much sterner resistance at Trianon and at Rambouillet than at the Palais-Royal. I think I may positively assert that the Lieutenant-General, while rejecting responsibility for the initial request, was ready to receive the royal child alone. His wife would have received the child with delight and promised him a mother's care, but the reply from Rambouillet was harsh to the point of insult. In any case, these events were not personally known to me at the time, and therefore do not belong to what I have seen and heard, and I do not propose to relate anything else.

I should write a stout volume if I were to relate everything that I have since learnt concerning the details of these events, even if I confined myself to points upon which I am certain. Here, however, my task ends. I often served to carry messages to the Palais-Royal, but on special occasions and only when specially commissioned. Though these details might be curious, they would hardly form a story of any continued interest. In any case, if I were to continue I should be obliged to speak of the Tuesday and of the dreadful march upon Rambouillet,[16] and I do not wish to conclude with so painful a scene. That event has no connection with the noble week that had just elapsed.

At that time France rose as one man, became a giant by the unanimity of her resolve, and threw off the pigmies who attempted to enslave

16. On Tuesday, August 31, demonstrators organised by La Fayette marched on Rambouillet, where Charles X had taken refuge, and forced him to go to Cherbourg and embark for England.

her. Content with this result, her only object, she would have returned to the spiritual calm of her proud tranquillity if a handful of ambitious men and a few hundred wretches had not continued an artificial agitation which destroyed in the eyes of contemporaries the magnificence of the spectacle presented to our view. Posterity will, I believe, do more than justice to it, and I am greatly deceived if these days, now known derisively as the "Glorieuses," do not preserve their fame for centuries.

MADAME DE BOIGNE

A Life Redeemed

The French Revolution, when it swept away the Ancien Régime, did more than take away the privileges of the nobility—it also ended what could almost be called the professional status of aristocratic women. The position and ancient nobility of Mlle. d'Osmond's family would have assured her of a grand marriage and a place at court; and that, in turn, would have given her influence, a role, a job.

Women just before the Revolution were seen, often accurately, as being superior to men. They were more civilised and more practical at the same time. Because they did not have careers of their own, they could help, and indeed manage, the rise of those talented men whom they favoured. Just as important, their salons were places where reasonable discussions often provided solutions to the political problems of the day. Policy, Talleyrand commented, was made in the salons.

That should have been Mlle. d'Osmond's future—and so should have been an appointment as one of the Queen's ladies. At the very heart of the system, she would have had at least influence, and possibly real power. Instead she found herself at an early age thrown from the innermost sanctum of the court at Versailles to a life as a penniless refugee. The man she married was a commoner whose very name had been purchased: he was in reality M. Benoît, but with the money earned in the Indian kingdom of Oudh (where he is still remembered), he had purchased a title. Thus the proud, intensely aristocratic Mlle. d'Osmond lost her world all over again. It is no wonder that in the *Memoirs* she strives to make her reader see her as the quintessential *grande dame*.

One of the book's pleasures is the superior, slightly disdainful tone, which is just as much a historic reminiscence as the anecdotes she passes on to her (alas, stupid and spendthrift) nephew. As we read her, it is the tone of Versailles we hear; and for all her genuine openness of mind, the disdain of a great lady for her bourgeois acquaintances is never far away. Happily, Mme. de Boigne was also a woman of superior intelligence. Her independence of judgement, her understanding of the changes that had transformed France, all placed her in the most interesting of positions.

Between 1800 and 1850, Paris society was sharply, almost irreconcilably, divided. The returned Ancien Régime aristocrats, not as impoverished as we are often told, but resentful and embittered, excluded the rest of the world. Unfortunately for them, it was the rest of the world that governed France: the men, usually highly competent, who staffed Napoleon's Government, and the rising middle class which took over in the 1820s and 1830s.

Mme. de Boigne had access to both these worlds and was able to move freely between them. Her birth and her family ties guaranteed her place in the first; her intelligence, her thorough understanding that this was a new era, and her long liaison with Pasquier ensured that she was centrally placed in the second. She also reached out to the world of books: her vignettes of Chateaubriand are both entertaining and cruelly true.

For a few weeks in the summer of 1830, she even managed to play just as important a role as she might have in prerevolutionary Versailles. Her close friendship with the Orléans family, most particularly with the Duchess, allowed her to become a go-between when Charles X lost his throne and the Duke became Louis-Philippe, King of the French. Ironically, her liaison with the unaristocratic Pasquier also helped: he was one of the key supports of the new regime and, greatly to her pleasure, became not only Chancellor of France but also a Duke.

Here was everything Mme. de Boigne cared about: power, titles, and a place at the centre of things.

The pleasure with which she writes about her closeness to the new royal family is palpable. She had feared Napoleon, respected Louis XVIII while disliking him, and liked Charles X while understanding that his terminal stupidity would eventually be fatal. Louis-Philippe, on the other hand, had, as far as she was concerned, every quality: he was a Bourbon, descended from Louis XIII in the male line, and Louis XIV in the female; he was highly intelligent; he had adapted to the new world; and he gave Mme. de Boigne access to the inner sanctum of his court and family. As for Queen Marie-Amélie, she was the daughter of King Ferdinand IV of the Two Sicilies (another Bourbon) and the Archduchess Maria Carolina, Marie-Antoinette's sister: it was impossible to be more grandly royal.

It is thus not by chance that Mme. de Boigne tells us how like Louis XIV the new King looked when he borrowed the appropriate wig from an actor; nor can we miss the pleasure with which she describes the newly restored Versailles and the tour the King gave her. Here, we are told, is where our author belongs—right at the very top of society, right in the centre of power. Nor can we doubt, in spite of the discretion with which she refers to him, that the Chancellor listened to her. Pasquier was hardworking, reliable, thorough, but he lacked brilliance. Without Mme. de Boigne's sharp understanding of his fellow politicians, without her quick and agile intelligence, his career would no doubt have stalled; besides, who knows what, at crucial moments, she whispered in the King's ear?

So it was that, after all, Mme. de Boigne invented a life for herself, which in most respects was worthy of what it might have been before the Revolution. She had a well-attended salon and was a frequent visitor to the other salons that mattered. Pasquier provided her with the proximity to power for which she longed. Her brother, then her nephew, gave her a focus for that family pride which was so essential a part of her world; and yet it is impossible not to feel, again and again, that something is missing. Perhaps the reason why this talented woman is so fascinating is that she was a woman, not only of the past and the present, but also of the future: if she were alive today, Mme. de Boigne would surely be a high-flying politician or the head of a great corporation. This aristocratic, well-to-do friend of the great was also a woman who needed the satisfaction brought by meaningful work. It is impossible to miss the longing note with which she speaks of politics, and not to feel that she should have been the colleague of the political leaders she received.

That is where the *Memoirs* come in. For all her affected superiority, it is obvious that Mme. de Boigne was a born writer, and that she knew it. She was conscious of having something to say. She had knowledge of events and people worth preserving for posterity, and furthermore, she knew just how to do it. Today, the *Memoirs* are a mine for the historians of the period, but they are also one of its most entertaining books.

It is no wonder, after all, that Proust drew on her so heavily: he recognised in Mme. de Boigne someone who, like himself, could see through people to their essential core, someone who could describe them dispassionately, accurately, without pity, but also most of the time without malice. Because of the *Memoirs*, we have a better, deeper understanding of a slice of the eighteenth and nineteenth centuries. Mme. de Boigne did not marry a Duke; she was never one of the Queen's ladies; but when she used all that she knew, and all that she was, to write one of the most sparkling texts of her century, she redeemed her losses and fulfilled the most essential part of her being. That, at the same time, she provided us with so much entertainment is our great good luck.

Olivier Bernier

INDEX

Produced by Wilsted & Taylor Publishing Services

COPYEDITING: Caroline Roberts

DESIGN: Melissa Ehn

COMPOSITION: Sarah Lowe

PRODUCTION MANAGEMENT: Christine Taylor

Printed by Transcontinental Printing Book Group